The Collected Short Works of Thorstein Veblen

Volume I

Thorstein Veblen

VERNON PRESS

www.vernonpress.com

In the Americas:
Vernon Press
1000 N West Street,
Suite 1200, Wilmington,
Delaware 19801
United States

In the rest of the world
Vernon Press
C/ Sancti Espiritu 17,
Malaga, 29006
Spain

ISBN 978-1-62273-214-2

Contents

Publisher's Note

This three-volume collection contains Veblen's publications in academic journals and other scholarly press. The articles are organized under major chapters covering Veblen's pioneering thoughts on social organization; economic theory; social theory; institutions, social organization and economic performance; contemporary policies and social movements; social applications of evolutionary reasoning. The original outlets and years of publication are listed below.

VOLUME I

REFLECTIONS ON SOCIAL ORGANIZATION

- Some Neglected Points in the Theory of Socialism (Annals of the American Academy of Political and Social Science, 1891)
- The Socialist Economics of Karl Marx and His Followers (The Quarterly Journal of Economics)
- The Engineers and the Price System (New York, B. W. Huebsch, 1921)

REFLECTIONS ON ECONOMIC THEORY

- The Preconceptions of Economic Science (The Quarterly Journal of Economics, 1899)
- The Limitations of Marginal Utility (Journal of Political Economy, 1909)
- Fisher's Capital and Income (Political Science Quarterly, 1908)
- Fisher's Rate of Interest (Political Science Quarterly, 1909)
- Professor Clark's Economics (The Quarterly Journal of Economics, 1908)

VOLUME II

REFLECTIONS ON ECONOMIC THEORY (*continued*)

- Why is Economics not an Evolutionary Science? (The Quarterly Journal of Economics, 1898)
- Industrial and Pecuniary Employments (Publications of the American Economic Association, 1901)
- On the Nature of Capital I: The Productivity of Capital Goods (The Quarterly Journal of Economics, 1908)
- On the Nature of Capital II: Investment, Intangible Assets, and the Pecuniary Magnate (The Quarterly Journal of Economics, 1908)

- Böhm-Bawerk's Definition Of Capital And The Source Of Wages (Quarterly Journal of Economics, 1892)
- Gustav Schmoller's Economics (Quarterly Journal of Economics, 1901)
- The Use Of Loan Credit In Modern Business (The Decennial Publications Of The University Of Chicago, 1903)
- Credit and Prices (The Journal of Political Economy, 1905)
- The Overproduction Fallacy (The Quarterly Journal of Economics, 1892)

SOCIAL THEORY

- The Barbarian Status of Women (American Journal of Sociology, 1899)
- The Economic Theory of Women's Dress (Popular Science Monthly, 1894)
- The Beginnings of Ownership (American Journal of Sociology, 1898)
- The Instinct of Workmanship and the Irksomeness of Labor (American Journal of Sociology, 1898)

INSTITUTIONS, SOCIAL ORGANIZATION AND ECONOMIC PERFORMANCE

- Christian Morals and the Competitive System (International Journal of Ethics, 1910)
- The Intellectual Pre-Eminence of Jews in Modern Europe (Political Science Quarterly, 1919)
- The Opportunity of Japan (The Journal of Race Development, 1915)

VOLUME III

COMMENTARY ON CONTEMPORARY POLICIES AND SOCIAL MOVEMENTS

- The Industrial System and the Captains of Industry (DIAL. A Fortnightly, 1919)
- The Captains of Finance and the Engineers (DIAL. A Fortnightly, 1919)
- The Country Town (The Freeman, 1923)
- The Army of the Commonweal (Journal of Political Economy, 1894)
- The Price of Wheat Since 1867 (Journal of Political Economy, 1892)
- The Food Supply And The Price Of Wheat (The Journal of Political Economy, 1893)
- The Later Railway Combinations (The Journal of Political Economy, 1901)
- On the General Principles of a Policy of Reconstruction (Journal of the National Institute of Social Sciences, 1918)

PHILOSOPHY

- Kant's Critique of Judgment (The Journal of Speculative Philosophy, 1884)

SOCIAL APPLICATIONS OF EVOLUTIONARY REASONING

- The Evolution of the Scientific Point of View (The University of California Chronicle, 1908)
- The Place of Science in Modern Civilisation (American Journal of Sociology, 1906)
- The Mutation Theory and the Blond Race (The Journal of Race Development, 1913)
- The Blond Race and the Aryan Culture (University of Missouri Bulletin, 1913)
- An Early Experiment in Trusts (The Journal of Political Economy, 1904)
- As to a Proposed Inquiry into Baltic and Cretan Antiquities (The American Journal of Sociology, 1910)

REFLECTIONS ON

SOCIAL ORGANIZATION

Chapter 1

Some Neglected Points
in the Theory of Socialism

The immediate occasion for the writing of this paper was given by the publication of Mr. Spencer's essay, "From Freedom to Bondage"[1] although it is not altogether a criticism of that essay. It is not my purpose to controvert the position taken by Mr. Spencer as regards the present feasibility of any socialist scheme. The paper is mainly a suggestion, offered in the spirit of the disciple, with respect to a point not adequately covered by Mr. Spencer's discussion, and which has received but very scanty attention at the hands of any other writer on either side of the socialist controversy. This main point is as to an economic ground, as a matter of fact, for the existing unrest that finds expression in the demands of socialist agitators.

I quote from Mr. Spencer's essay a sentence which does fair justice, so far as it goes, to the position taken by agitators: "In presence of obvious improvements, joined with that increase of longevity, which even alone yields conclusive proof of general amelioration, it is proclaimed, with increasing vehemence, that things are so bad that society must be pulled to pieces and reorganised on another plan." The most obtrusive feature of the change demanded by the advocates of socialism is governmental control of the industrial activities of society - the nationalisation of industry. There is also, just at present, a distinct movement in practice, towards a more extended control of industry by the government, as Mr. Spencer has pointed out. This movement strengthens the position of the advocates of a complete nationalisation of industry, by making it appear that the logic of events is on their side. In America at least, this movement in the direction of a broader assertion of the paramount claims of the community, and an extension of corporate action on part of the community in industrial matters, has not generally been connected with or based on an adherence to socialistic dogmas. This is perhaps truer of the recent past than of the immediate present. The motive of the movement has been, in large part, the expediency of each particular step taken. Municipal supervision, and, possibly, complete municipal control, has come to be a necessity in the case of such industries - mostly of recent growth - as elementary education, street-lighting, water-supply, etc. Opinions differ widely as to how far the community should take into its own hands such industries as concern the common welfare, but the growth of sentiment may fairly be said to favor a wider scope of governmental control. But the necessity of some supervision in the interest of the public extends to industries which are not simp-

---

[1] Introductory paper of *A Plea for Liberty*, edited by Thomas Mackay.

ly of municipal importance. The modern development of industry and of the industrial organisation of society makes it increasingly necessary that certain industries often spoken of as "natural monopolies" - should be treated as being of a semi-public character. And through the action of the same forces a constantly increasing number of occupations are developing into the form of "natural monopolies".

The motive of the movement towards corporate action on the part of the community - State control of industry - has been largely that of industrial expediency. Put another motive has gone with this one, and has grown more prominent as the popular demands in this direction have gathered wider support and taken more definite form. The injustice, the inequality, of the existing system, so far as concerns these natural monopolies especially, are made much of. There is a distinct unrest abroad, a discontent with things as they are, and the cry of injustice is the expression of this more or less widely prevalent discontent. This discontent is the truly socialistic element in the situation. It is easy to make too much of this popular unrest. The clamor of the agitators might be taken to indicate a wider prevalence and a greater acuteness of popular discontent than actually exists; but after all due allowance is made for exaggeration on the part of those interested in the agitation, there can still be no doubt of the presence of a chronic feeling of dissatisfaction with the working of the existing industrial system, and a growth of popular sentiment in favor of a leveling policy. The economic ground of this popular feeling must be found, if we wish to understand the significance, for our industrial system, of the movement to which it supplies the motive. If its causes shall appear to be of a transient character, there is little reason to apprehend a permanent or radical change of our industrial system as the outcome of the agitation; while if this popular sentiment is found to be the outgrowth of any of the essential features of the existing social system, the chances of its ultimately working a radical change in the system will be much greater.

The explanation offered by Mr. Spencer, that the popular unrest is due essentially to a feeling of *ennui* - to a desire for a change of posture on part of the social body, is assuredly not to be summarily rejected; but the analogy will hardly serve to explain the sentiment away. This may be a cause, but it can hardly be accepted as a sufficient cause.

Socialist agitators urge that the existing system is necessarily wasteful and industrially inefficient. That may be granted, but it does not serve to explain the popular discontent, because the popular opinion, in which the discontent resides, does notoriously not favor that view. They further urge that the existing system is unjust, in that it gives an advantage to one man over another. That contention may also be true, but it is in itself no explanation, for it is true only if it be granted that the institutions which make this advantage of one man over another possible are unjust, and that is begging the question. This last contention is, however, not so far out of line with popular sentiment. The advantage complained of lies, under modern conditions, in the possession of property, and there is a feeling abroad that the existing order of things affords an undue advantage to property, especially to owners of property whose possessions rise much above a certain rather indefinite average. This feeling of injured justice is not always distinguishable from envy; but it is, at any rate, a factor that works towards a leveling policy. With it goes a feeling of slighted manhood, which works in the same direction. Both these elements are to a great extent of a subjective origin. They express themselves in the general, objective form, but it is safe to say that on the average they spring from a consciousness of disadvantage and slight suffered by the person expressing them, and by persons whom he classes with himself. No flippancy is intended in saying that the rich are not so generally alive to the necessity of any leveling policy as are people of slender means. Any question as to the legitimacy of the dissatisfaction, on moral grounds, or even on grounds of expediency, is not very much to the point; the question is as to its scope and its chances of persistence.

The modern industrial system is based on the institution of private property under free competition, and it cannot be claimed that these institutions have heretofore worked to the detriment of the material interests of the average member of society. The ground of discontent cannot lie in a disadvantageous comparison of the present with the past, so far as material interests are concerned. It is notorious, and, practically, none of the agitators deny, that the system of industrial competition, based on private property, has brought about, or has at least co-existed with, the most rapid advance in average wealth and industrial efficiency that the world has seen. Especially can it fairly be claimed that the result of the last few decades of our industrial development has been to increase greatly the creature comforts within the reach of the average human being. And, decidedly, the result has been an amelioration of the lot of the less favored in a relatively greater degree than that of those economically more fortunate. The claim that the system of competition has proved itself an engine for making the rich richer and the poor poorer has the fascination of epigram; but if its meaning is that the lot of the average, of the masses of humanity in civilised life, is worse to-day, as measured in the means of livelihood, than it was twenty, or fifty, or a hundred years ago, then it is farcical. The cause of discontent must be sought elsewhere than in any increased difficulty in obtaining the means of subsistence or of comfort. But there is a sense in which the aphorism is true, and in it lies at least a partial explanation of the unrest which our conservative people so greatly deprecate. The existing system has not made, and does not tend to make, the industrious poor poorer as measured absolutely in means of livelihood; but it does tend to make them relatively poorer, in their own eyes, as measured in terms of comparative economic importance, and, curious as it may seem at first sight, that is what seems to count. It is not the abjectly poor that are oftenest heard protesting; and when a protest is heard in their behalf it is through spokesmen who are from outside their own class, and who are not delegated to speak for them. They are not a negligible element in the situation, but the unrest which is ground for solicitude does not owe its importance to them. The protest comes from those who do not habitually, or of necessity, suffer physical privation. The qualification "of necessity," is to be noticed. There is a not inconsiderable amount of physical privation suffered by many people in this country, which is not physically necessary. The cause is very often that what might be the means of comfort is diverted to the purpose of maintaining a decent appearance, or even a show of luxury.

Man as we find him to-day has much regard to his good fame - to his standing in the esteem of his fellowmen. This characteristic he always has had, and no doubt always will have. This regard for reputation may take the noble form of a striving after a good name; but the existing organisation of society does not in any way preeminently foster that line of development. Regard for one's reputation means, in the average of cases, emulation. It is a striving to be, and more immediately to be thought to be, better than one's neighbor. Now, modern society, the society in which competition without prescription is predominant, is preeminently an industrial, economic society, and it is industrial - economic - excellence that most readily attracts the approving regard of that society. Integrity and personal worth will, of course, count for something, now as always; but in the case of a person of moderate pretentions and opportunities, such as the average of us are, one's reputation for excellence in this direction does not penetrate far enough into the very wide environment to which a person is exposed in modern society to satisfy even a very modest craving for respectability. To sustain one's dignity - and to sustain one's self-respect - under the eyes of people who are not socially one's immediate neighbors, it is necessary to display the token of economic worth, which practically coincides pretty closely with economic success. A person may be well-born and virtuous, but those attributes will not bring respect to the bearer from people who are not aware of his possessing them, and these are ninety-nine out of every one hundred that one meets. Conversely, by the way, knavery and vulgarity in any person are not reprobated by people who know nothing of the person's shortcomings in those respects.

In our fundamentally industrial society a person should be economically successful, if he would enjoy the esteem of his fellowmen. When we say that a man is "worth" so many dollars, the expression does not convey the idea that moral or other personal excellence is to be measured in terms of money, but it does very distinctly convey the idea that the fact of his possessing many dollars is very much to his credit. And, except in cases of extraordinary excellence, efficiency in any direction which is not immediately of industrial importance, and does not redound to a person's economic benefit, is not of great value as a means of respectability. Economic success is in our day the most widely accepted as well as the most readily ascertainable measure of esteem. All this will hold with still greater force of a generation which is born into a world already encrusted with this habit of a mind.

But there is a further, secondary stage in the development of this economic emulation. It is not enough to possess the talisman of industrial success. In order that it may mend one's good fame efficiently, it is necessary to display it. One does not "make much of a showing" in the eyes of the large majority of the people whom one meets with, except by unremitting demonstration of ability to pay. That is practically the only means which the average of us have of impressing our respectability on the many to whom we are personally unknown, but whose transient good opinion we would so gladly enjoy. So it comes about that the appearance of success is very much to be desired, and is even in many cases preferred to the substance. We all know how nearly indispensable it is to afford whatever expenditure other people with whom we class ourselves can afford, and also that it is desirable to afford a little something more than others.

This element of human nature has much to do with the "standard of living." And it is of a very elastic nature, capable of an indefinite extension. After making proper allowance for individual exceptions and for the action of prudential restraints, it may be said, in a general way, that this emulation in expenditure stands ever ready to absorb any margin of income that remains after ordinary physical wants and comforts have been provided for, and, further, that it presently becomes as bard to give up that part of one's habitual "standard of living" which is due to the struggle for respectability, as it is to give up many physical comforts. In a general way, the need of expenditure in this direction grows as fast as the means of satisfying it, and, in the long run, a large expenditure comes no nearer satisfying the desire than a smaller one. It comes about through the working of this principle that even the creature comforts, which are in themselves desirable, and, it may even be, requisite to a life on a passably satisfactory plane, acquire a value as a means of respectability quite independent of, and out of proportion to, their simple utility as a means of livelihood. As we are all aware, the chief element of value in many articles of apparel is not their efficiency for protecting the body, but for protecting the wearer's respectability; and that not only in the eyes of one's neighbors but even in one's own eyes. Indeed, it happens not very rarely that a person chooses to go ill-clad in order to be well dressed. Much more than half the value of what is worn by the American people may confidently be put down to the element of "dress," rather than to that of "clothing." And the chief motive of dress is emulation - "economic emulation." The like is true, though perhaps in a less degree, of what goes to food and shelter. This misdirection of effort through the cravings of human vanity is of course not anything new, nor is "economic emulation" a modern fact. The modern system of industry has not invented emulation, nor has even this particular form of emulation originated under that system. But the system of free competition has accentuated this form of emulation, both by exalting the industrial activity of man above the rank which it held tinder more primitive forms of social organisation, and by in great measure cutting off other forms of emulation from the chance of efficiently ministering to the craving for a good fame. Speaking generally and from the standpoint of the average man, the modern industrial organization of society has practically narrowed the scope of emulation to this one line; and at the same time it has made the means of sustenance and comfort so much easier to obtain as very materially to widen the margin of human exertion that can be devoted to purposes of emulation. Further, by increasing the freedom of movement of the individual and widening the environment to which the individual is exposed - increasing the number of persons before whose eyes each one carries on his life, and, *pari passu*, decreasing the chances which such persons have of awarding their esteem on any other basis than that of immediate appearances, it has increased the relative efficiency of the economic means of winning respect through a show of expenditure for personal comforts.

It is not probable that further advance in the same direction will lead to a different result in the immediate future; and it is the immediate future we have to deal with. A further advance in the efficiency of our industry, and a further widening of the human environment to which the individual is exposed, should logically render emulation in this direction more intense. There are, indeed, certain considerations to be set off against this tendency, but they are mostly factors of slow action, and are hardly of sufficient consequence to reverse the general rule. On the whole, other things remaining the same, it must be admitted that, within wide limits, the easier the conditions of physical life for modern civilised man become, and the wider the horizon of each and the extent of the personal contact of each with his fellowmen, and the greater the opportunity of each to compare notes with his fellows, the greater will be the preponderance of economic success as a means of emulation, and the greater the straining after economic respectability. Inasmuch as the aim of emulation is not any absolute degree of comfort or of excellence, no advance in the average well-being of the community can end the struggle or lessen the strain. A general amelioration cannot quiet the unrest whose source is the craving of everybody to compare favorably with his neighbor.

Human nature being what it is, the struggle of each to possess more than his neighbor is inseparable from the institution of private property. And also, human nature being what it is, one who possesses less will, on the average, be jealous of the one who possesses more; and "more" means not more than the average share, but more than the share of the person who makes the comparison. The criterion of complacency is, largely, the de facto possession or enjoyment; and the present growth of sentiment among the body of the people - who possess less - favors, in a vague way, a readjustment adverse to the interests of those who possess more, and adverse to the possibility of legitimately possessing or enjoying "more"; that is to say, the growth of sentiment favors a socialistic movement. The outcome of modern industrial development has been, so far as concerns the present purpose, to intensify emulation and the jealousy that goes with emulation, and to focus the emulation and the jealousy on the possession and enjoyment of material goods. The ground of the unrest with which we are concerned is, very largely, jealousy, - envy, if you choose: and the ground of this particular form of jealousy, that makes for socialism, is to be found in the institution of private property. With private property, under modern conditions, this jealousy and unrest are unavoidable. The cornerstone of the modern industrial system is the institution of private property. That institution is also the objective point of all attacks upon the existing system of competitive industry, whether open or covert, whether directed against the system as a whole or against any special feature of it. It is, moreover, the ultimate ground - and, under modern conditions, necessarily so - of the unrest and discontent whose proximate cause is the struggle for economic respectability. The inference seems to be that, human nature being what it is, there can be no peace from this - it must be admitted - ignoble form of emulation, or from the discontent that goes with it, this side of the abolition of private property. Whether a larger measure of peace is in store for us after that event shall have come to pass, is of course not a matter to be counted on, nor is the question immediately to the point.

This economic emulation is of course not the sole motive, nor the most important feature, of modern industrial life; although it is in the foreground, and it pervades the structure of modern society more thoroughly perhaps than any other equally powerful moral factor. It would be rash to predict that socialism will be the inevitable outcome of a continued development of this emulation and the discontent which it fosters, and it is by no means the purpose of this paper to insist on such an inference. The most that can be claimed is that this emulation is one of the causes, if not the chief cause, of the existing unrest and dissatisfaction with things as they are; that this unrest is inseparable from the existing system of industrial organisation; and that the growth of popular sentiment under the influence of these conditions is necessarily adverse to the institution of private property, and therefore adverse to the existing industrial system of free competition.

The emulation to which attention has been called in the preceding section of this paper is not only a fact of importance to an understanding of the unrest that is urging its towards an untried path in social development, but it has also a bearing on the question of the practicability of any scheme for the complete nationalisation of industry. Modern industry has developed to such a degree of efficiency as to make the struggle of subsistence alone, under average conditions, relatively easy, as compared with the state of the case a few generations ago. As I have labored to show, the modern competitive system has at the same time given the spirit of emulation such a direction that the attainment of subsistence and comfort no longer fixes, even approximately, the limit of the required aggregate labor on the part of the community. Under modern conditions the struggle for existence has, in a very appreciable degree, been transformed into a struggle to keep up appearances. The ultimate ground of this struggle to keep up appearance by otherwise unnecessary expenditure, is the institution of private property. Under a regime which should allow no inequality of acquisition or of income, this form of emulation, which is due to the possibility of such inequality, would also tend to become obsolete. With the abolition of private property, the characteristic of human nature which now finds its exercise in this form of emulation, should logically find exercise in other, perhaps nobler and socially more serviceable, activities; it is at any rate not easy to imagine it running into any line of action more futile or less worthy of human effort.

Supposing the standard of comfort of the community to remain approximately at its present average, the abolition of the struggle to keep up economic appearances would very considerably lessen the aggregate amount of labor required for the support of the community. How great a saving of labor might be effected is not easy to say. I believe it is within the mark to suppose that the struggle to keep up appearances is chargeable, directly and indirectly, with one-half the aggregate labor, and abstinence from labor - for the standard of respectability requires us to shun labor as well as to enjoy the fruits of it - on part of the American people. This does not mean that the same community, under a system not allowing private property, could make its way with half the labor we now put forth; but it means something more or less nearly approaching that. Any one who has not seen our modern social life from this point of view will find the claim absurdly extravagant, but the startling character of the proposition will wear off with longer and closer attention to this aspect of the facts of everyday life. But the question of the exact amount of waste due to this factor is immaterial. It will not be denied that it is a fact of considerable magnitude, and that is all that the argument requires.

It is accordingly competent for the advocates of the nationalisation of industry and property to claim that even if their scheme of organisation should prove less effective for production of goods than the present, as measured absolutely in terms of the aggregate output of our industry, yet the community might readily be maintained at the present average standard of comfort. The required aggregate output of the nation's industry would be considerably less than at present, and there would therefore be less necessity for that close and strenuous industrial organisation and discipline of the members of society under the new regime, whose evils unfriendly critics are apt to magnify. The chances of practicability for the scheme should logically be considerably increased by this lessening of the necessity for severe application. The less irksome and exacting the new regime, the less chance of a reversion to the earlier system. Under such a social order, where common labor would no longer be a mark of peculiar economic necessity and consequent low economic rank on part of the laborer, it is even conceivable that labor might practically come to assume that character of nobility in the eyes of society at large, which it now sometimes assumes in the speculations of the well-to-do, in their complacent moods. Much has sometimes been made of this possibility by socialist speculators, but the inference has something of a utopian look, and no one, certainly, is entitled to build institutions for the coming social order on this dubious ground.

What there seems to be ground for claiming is that a society which has reached our present degree of industrial efficiency would not go into the Socialist or Nationalist state with as many chances of failure as a community whose industrial development is still at the stage at which strenuous labor on the part of nearly all members is barely sufficient to make both ends meet. In Mr. Spencer's essay, in conformity with the line of argument of his "Principles of Sociology," it is pointed out that, as the result of constantly operative social forces, all social systems, as regards the form of organisation, fall into the one or the other of Sir Henry Maine's two classes - the system of status or the system of contract. In accordance with this generalisation it is concluded that whenever the modem system of contract or free competition shall be displaced, it will necessarily be replaced by the only other known system - that of status; the type of which is the military organisation, or, also, a hierarchy, or a bureaucracy. It is something after the fashion of the industrial organisation of ancient Peru that Mr. Spencer pictures as the inevitable sequel of the demise of the existing competitive system. Voluntary cooperation can be replaced only by compulsory cooperation, which is identified with the system of status and defined as the subjection of man to his fellow-man. Now, at least as a matter of speculation, this is not the only alternative. These two systems, of status, or prescription, and of contract, or competition, have divided the field of social organisation between them in some proportion or other in the past. Mr. Spencer has shown that, very generally, where human progress in its advanced stages has worked towards the amelioration of the lot of the average member of society, the movement has been away from the system of status and towards the system of contract. But there is at least one, if not more than one exception to the rule, as concerns the recent past. The latest development of the industrial organisation among civilised nations - perhaps in an especial degree in the case of the American people - has not been entirely a continuation of the approach to a regime of free contract. It is also, to say the least, very doubtful if the movement has been towards a regime of status, in the sense in which Sir Henry Maine uses the term. This is especially evident in the case of the great industries which we call "natural monopolies"; and it is to be added that the present tendency is for a continually increasing proportion of the industrial activities of the community to fall into the category of "natural monopolies." No revolution has been achieved; the system of competition has not been discarded, but the course of industrial development is not in the direction of an extension of that system at all points; nor does the principle of status always replace that of competition wherever the latter fails. The classification of methods of social organisation under the two heads of status or of contract, is not logically exhaustive. There is nothing in the meaning of the terms employed which will compel us to say that whenever man escapes from the control of his fellow man, under a system of status, he thereby falls into a system of free contract. There is a conceivable escape from the dilemma, and it is this conceivable, though perhaps impracticable, escape from both these systems that the socialist agitator wishes to effect. An acquaintance with the aims and position of the more advanced and consistent advocates of a new departure leaves no doubt but that the principles of contract and of status, both, are in substance familiar to their thoughts - though often in a vague and inadequate form - and that they distinctly repudiate both. This is perhaps less true of those who take the socialist position mainly on ethical grounds.

As bearing on this point it may be remarked that while the industrial system, in the case of all communities with whose history we are acquainted, has always in the past been organised according to a scheme of status or of contract, or of the two combined in some proportion, yet the social organisation has not in all cases developed along the same lines, so far as concerns such social functions as are not primarily industrial. Especially is this true of the later stages in the development of those communities whose institutions we are accustomed to contemplate with the most complacency, e.g., the case of the English-speaking peoples. The whole system of modern constitutional government in its latest developed forms, in theory at least, and, in a measure, in practice, does not fall under the head of either contract or status. It is the analogy of modern constitutional government through an impersonal law and impersonal institutions, that comes nearest doing justice to the vague notions of our socialist propagandists. It is true, some of the most noted among them are fond of the analogy of the military organization as a striking illustration of one feature of the system they advocate, but that must after all be taken as an *obiter dictum.*

Further, as to the manner of the evolution of existing institutions and their relation to the two systems spoken of. So far as concerns the communities which have figured largely in the civilised world, the political organisation has had its origin in a military system of government. So, also, has the industrial organisation. But while the development of industry, during its gradual escape from the military system of status, has been, at least until lately, in the direction of a system of free contract, the development of the political organisation, so far as it has escaped from the regime of status, has not been in that direction. The system of status is a system of subjection to personal authority, - of prescription and class distinctions, and privileges and immunities; the system of constitutional government, especially as seen at its best among a people of democratic traditions and habits of mind, is a system of subjection to the will of the social organism, as expressed in an impersonal law. This difference between the system of status and the "constitutional system" expresses a large part of the meaning of the boasted free institutions of the English-speaking people. Here, subjection is not to the person of the public functionary, but to the powers vested in him. This has, of course, something of the ring of latter-day popular rhetoric, but it is after all felt to be true, not only speculatively, but in some measure also in practice.

The right of eminent domain and the power to tax, as interpreted under modern constitutional forms, indicate something of the direction of development of the political functions of society at a point where they touch the province of the industrial system. It is along the line indicated by these and kindred facts that the socialists are advancing: and it is along this line that the later developments made necessary by the exigencies of industry under modern conditions are also moving. The aim of the propagandists is to sink the industrial community in the political community; or perhaps better, to identify the two organisations; but always with insistence on the necessity of making the political organisation, in some further developed form, the ruling and only one in the outcome. Distinctly, the system of contract is to be done away with; and equally distinctly, no system of status is to take its place.

All this is pretty vague, and of a negative character, but it would quickly pass the limits of legitimate inference from the accepted doctrines of the socialists if it should - attempt to be anything more. It does not have much

to say as to the practicability of any socialist scheme. As a matter of speculation, there seems to be an escape from the dilemma insisted on by Mr.
Spencer. We may conceivably have nationalism without status and without contract. In theory, both principles are entirely obnoxious to that system. The practical question, as to whether modern society affords the materials out of which an industrial structure can be erected on a system different from either of these, is a problem of constructive social engineering
which calls for a consideration of details far too comprehensive to be entered on here. Still, in view of the past course of development of character
and institutions on the part of the people to which we belong, it is perhaps
not extravagant to claim that no form of organisation which should necessarily eventuate in a thoroughgoing system of status could endure among
us. The inference from this proposition may be, either that a near approach to nationalisation of industry would involve a regime of status, a
bureaucracy, which would be unendurable, and which would therefore
drive us back to the present system before it had been entirely abandoned;
or that the nationalisation would be achieved with such a measure of success, in conformity with the requirements of our type of character, as
would make it preferable to what we had left behind. In either case the
ground for alarm does not seem so serious as is sometimes imagined. A
reversion to the system of free competition, after it had been in large part
discarded, would no doubt be a matter of great practical difficulty, and the
experiment which should demonstrate the necessity of such a step might
involve great waste and suffering, and might seriously retard the advance
of the race toward something better than our present condition; but neither a permanent deterioration of human society, nor a huge catastrophe,
is to be confidently counted on as the outcome of the movement toward
nationalisation, even if it should prove necessary for society to retrace its
steps.

It is conceivable that the application of what may be called the "constitutional method" to the organisation of industry - for that is essentially
what the advocates of Nationalisation demand - would result in a course
of development analogous to what has taken place in the case of the political organisation under modern constitutional forms. Modern constitutional government - the system of modern free institutions - is by no
means an unqualified success, in the sense of securing to each the rights
and immunities which in theory are guaranteed to him. Our modern re-
publics have hardly given us a foretaste of that political millennium
whereof they proclaim the fruition. The average human nature is as yet by
no means entirely fit for self-government according to the "constitutional
method." Shortcomings are visible at every turn. These shortcomings are
grave enough to furnish serious arguments against the practicability of
our free institutions. On the continent of Europe the belief seems to be at
present in the ascendant that man must yet, for a long time, remain under
the tutelage of absolutism before he shall be fit to organise himself into an
autonomous political body. The belief is not altogether irrational. Just how
great must be the advance of society and just what must be the character
of the advance, preliminary to its advantageously assuming the autono-

mous - republican - form of political organisation, must be admitted to be an open question. Whether we, or any people, have yet reached the required stage of the advance is also questioned by many. But the partial success which has attended the movement in this direction, among the English-speaking people for example, goes very far towards proving that the point in the development of human character at which the constitutional method may be advantageously adopted in the political field, lies far this side the point at which human nature shall have become completely adapted for that method. That is to say, it does not seem necessary, as regards the functions of society which we are accustomed to call political, to be entirely ready for nationalisation before entering upon it. How far the analogy of this will hold when applied to the industrial organisation of society is difficult to say, but some significance the analogy must be admitted to possess. Certainly, the fact that constitutional government - the nationalisation of political functions - seems to have been a move in the right direction is not to be taken as proof of the advisability of forthwith nationalising the industrial functions. At the same time this fact does afford ground for the claim that a movement in this direction may prove itself in some degree advantageous, even if it takes place at a stage in the development of human nature at which mankind is still far from being entirely fit for the duties which the new system shall impose. The question, therefore, is not whether we have reached the perfection of character which would be necessary in order to a perfect working of the scheme of nationalisation of industry, but whether we have reached such a degree of development as would make an imperfect working of the scheme possible.

Chapter 2

The Socialist Economics of Karl Marx and His Followers[1]

I. The Theories of Karl Marx

The system of doctrines worked out by Marx is characterized by a certain boldness of conception and a great logical consistency. Taken in detail, the constituent elements of the system are neither novel nor iconoclastic, nor does Marx at any point claim to have discovered previously hidden facts or to have invented recondite formulations of facts already known; but the system as a whole has an air of originality and initiative such as is rarely met with among the sciences that deal with any phase of human culture. How much of this distinctive character the Marxian system owes to the personal traits of its creator is not easy to say, but what marks it off from all other systems of economic theory is not a matter of personal idiosyncrasy. It differs characteristically from all systems of theory that had preceded it, both in its premises and in its aims. The (hostile) critics of Marx have not sufficiently appreciated the radical character of his departure in both of these respects, and have, therefore, commonly lost themselves in a tangled scrutiny of supposedly abstruse details; whereas those writers who have been in sympathy with his teachings have too commonly been disciples bent on exegesis and on confirming their fellow-disciples in the faith. Except as a whole and except in the light of its postulates and aims, the Marxian system is not only not tenable, but it is not even intelligible. A discussion of a given isolated feature of the system (such as the theory of value) from the point of view of classical economics (such as that offered by Bohm-Bawerk) is as futile as a discussion of solids in terms of two dimensions. Neither as regards his postulates and preconceptions nor as regards the aim of his inquiry is Marx's position an altogether single-minded one. In neither respect does his position come of a single line of antecedents. He is of no single school of philosophy, nor are his ideals those of any single group of speculators living before his time. For this reason he takes his place as an originator of a school of thought as well as the leader of a movement looking to a practical end.

As to the motives which drive him and the aspiration which guide him, in destructive criticism and an creative speculation alike, he is primarily a theoretician busied with the analysis of economic phenomena and their organization into a consistent and faithful system of scientific knowledge;

---

[1] The substance of lectures before students in Harvard University in April, 1906.

but he is, at the same time, consistently and tenaciously alert to the bearing which each step in the progress of his theoretical work has upon the propaganda. His work has, therefore, an air of bias, such as belongs to an advocate's argument; but it is not, therefore, to be assumed, nor indeed to be credited, that his propagandist aims have in any substantial way deflected his inquiry or his speculations from the faithful pursuit of scientific truth. His socialistic bias may color his polemics, but his logical grasp is too neat and firm to admit of a bias, other than that of his metaphysical preconceptions, affecting his theoretical work.

There is no system of economic theory more logical than that of Marx. No member of the system, no single article of doctrine, is fairly to be understood, criticised, or defended except as an articulate member of the whole and in the light of the preconceptions and postulates which afford the point of departure and the controlling norm of the whole. As regards these preconceptions and postulates, Marx draws on two distinct lines of antecedents, - the Materialistic Hegelianism and the English system of Natural Rights. By his earlier training he is an adept in the Hegelian method of speculation and inoculated with the metaphysics of development underlying the Hegelian system. By his later training he is an expert in the system of Natural Rights and Natural Liberty, ingrained in his ideals of life and held inviolate throughout. He does not take a critical attitude toward the underlying principles of Natural Rights. Even his Hegelian preconceptions of development never carry him the length of questioning the fundamental principles of that system. He is only more ruthlessly consistent in working out their content than his natural-rights antagonists in the liberal-classical school. His polemics run against the specific tenets of the liberal school, but they run wholly on the ground afforded by the premises of that school. The ideals of his propaganda are natural-rights ideals, but his theory of the working out of these ideals in the course of history rests on the Hegelian metaphysics of development, and his method of speculation and construction of theory is given by the Hegelian dialectic.

What first and most vividly centred interest on Marx and his speculations was his relation to the revolutionary socialistic movement; and it is those features of his doctrines which bear immediately on the propaganda that still continue to hold the attention of the greater number of his critics. Chief among these doctrines, in the apprehension of his critics, is the theory of value, with its corollaries: (a) the doctrines of the exploitation of labor by capital; and (b) the laborer's claim to the whole product of his labor. Avowedly, Marx traces his doctrine of labor value to Ricardo, and through him to the classical economists[2] .The laborer's claim to the whole product of labor, which is pretty constantly implied, though not frequently avowed by Marx, he has in all probability taken from English writers of the

---

[2] Cf. Critique of Political Economy, chap. i, "Notes on the History of the Theory of Commodities," pp. 56-73 (English translation, New York, 1904).

early nineteenth century[3], more particularly from William Thompson. These doctrines are, on their face, nothing but a development of the conceptions of natural rights which then pervaded English speculation and afforded the metaphysical ground of the liberal movement. The more formidable critics of the Marxian socialism have made much of these doctrinal elements that further the propaganda, and have, by laying the stress on these, diverted attention from other elements that are of more vital consequence to the system as a body of theory. Their exclusive interest in this side of "scientific socialism" has even led them to deny the Marxian system all substantial originality, and make it a (doubtfully legitimate) offshoot of English Liberalism and natural rights[4]. But this is one-sided criticism. It may hold as against certain tenets of the so-called "scientific socialism," but it is not altogether to the point as regards the Marxian system of theory. Even the Marxian theory of value, surplus value, and exploitation, is not simply the doctrine of William Thompson, transcribed and sophisticated in a forbidding terminology, however great the superficial resemblance and however large Marx's unacknowledged debt to Thompson may be on these heads. For many details and for much of his animus Marx may be indebted to the Utilitarians; but, after all, his system of theory, taken as a whole, lies within the frontiers of neo-Hegelianism, and even the details are worked out in accord with the preconceptions of that school of thought and have taken on the completion that would properly belong to them on that ground. It is, therefore, not by an itemized scrutiny of the details of doctrine and by tracing their pedigree in detail that a fair conception of Marx and his contribution to economics may be reached, but rather by following him from his own point of departure out into the ramifications of his theory, and so overlooking the whole in the perspective which the lapse of time now affords us, but which he could not himself attain, since he was too near to his own work to see why he went about it as he did.

The comprehensive system of Marxism is comprised within the scheme of the Materialistic Conception of History[5]. This materialistic conception is essentially Hegelian[6], although it belongs with the Hegelian Left, and its immediate affiliation is with Feuerbach, not with the direct line of Hegelian orthodoxy. The chief point of interest here, in identifying the materialistic conception with Hegelianism, is that this identification throws it im-

---

[3] See Menger, Right to the Whole Produce of Labor, section iii-v and viii-ix, and Foxwell's admirable Introduction to Menger.

[4] See Menger and Foxwell, as above, and Schaeffle, Quintessence of Socialism, and The Impossibility or Social Democracy.

[5] See Engels, The Development of Socialism from Utopia to Science, especially section ii. and the opening paragraphs of section iii.; also the preface of Zur Kritik der politischen Oekonomie.

[6] See Engels, as above, and also his Feuerbach: The Roots of Socialist Philosophy (translation, Chicago, Kerr & Co., 1903).

mediately and uncompromisingly into contrast with Darwinism and the post-Darwinian conceptions of evolution. Even if a plausible English pedigree should be worked out for this Materialistic Conception, or "Scientific Socialism," as has been attempted, it remains none the less true that the conception with which Marx went to his work was a transmuted framework of Hegelian dialectic.[7] .Roughly, Hegelian materialism differs from Hegelian orthodoxy by inverting the main logical sequence, not by discarding the logic or resorting to new tests of truth or finality. One might say, though perhaps with excessive crudity, that, where Hegel pronounces his dictum, 'Das Denken ist das Sein', the materialists, particularly Marx and Engels, would say 'Das Sein macht das Denken'. But in both cases some sort of a creative primacy is assigned to one or the other member of the complex, and in neither case is the relation between the two members a causal relation. In the materialistic conception man's spiritual life - what man thinks - is a reflex of what he is in the material respect, very much in the same fashion as the orthodox Hegelian would make the material world a reflex of the spirit. In both the dominant norm of speculation and formulation of theory is the conception of movement, development, evolution, progress; and in both the movement is contrived necessarily to take place by the method of conflict or struggle. The movement is of the nature of progress, - gradual advance towards a goal, toward the realization in explicit form of all that is implicit in the substantial activity involved in the movement. The movement is, further, self-conditioned and self-acting: it is an unfolding by inner necessity. The struggle which constitutes the method of movement or evolution is, in the Hegelian system proper, the struggle of the spirit for self-realization by the process of the well-known three-phase dialectic. In the materialistic conception of history this dialectical movement becomes the class struggle of the Marxian system.

The class struggle is conceived to be "material," but the term "material" is in this connection used in a metaphorical sense. It does not mean mechanical or physical, or even physiological, but economic. It is material in the sense that it is a struggle between classes for the material means of life. "The materialistic conception of history proceeds on the principle that production and, next to production, the exchange of its products is the groundwork of every social order.[8]" The social order takes its form through the class struggle, and the character of the class struggle at any given phase of the unfolding development of society is determined by "the prevailing mode of economic production and exchange." The dialectic of the movement of social progress, therefore, moves on the spiritual plane of human desire and passion, not on the (literally) material plane of mechanical and physiological stress, on which the developmental process of brute creation unfolds itself. It is a sublimated materialism; sublimated by the dominating presence of the conscious human spirit; but it is conditioned

[7] See, e.g., Seligman, The Economic Interpretation of History, Part I.
[8] Engels, Development of Socialism, beginning of section iii.

by the material facts of the production of the means of life.[9] The ultimately active forces involved in the process of unfolding social life are (apparently) the material agencies engaged in the mechanics of production; but the dialectic of the process - the class struggle - runs its course only among and in terms of the secondary (epigenetic) forces of human consciousness engaged in the valuation of the material products of industry. A consistently materialistic conception, consistently adhering to a materialistic interpretation of the process of development as well as of the facts involved in the process, could scarcely avoid making its putative dialectic struggle a mere unconscious and irrelevant conflict of the brute material forces. This would have amounted to an interpretation in terms of opaque cause and effect, without recourse to the concept of a conscious class struggle, and it might have led to a concept of evolution similar to the unteleological Darwinian concept of natural selection. It could scarcely have led to the Marxian notion of a conscious class struggle as the one necessary method of social progress, though it might conceivably, by the aid of empirical generalization, have led to a scheme of social process in which a class struggle would be included as an incidental though perhaps highly efficient factor.[10] .It would have led, as Darwinism has, to a concept of a process of cumulative change in social structure and function; but this process, being essentially a cumulative sequence of causation, opaque and unteleological, could not, without an infusion of pious fancy by the speculator be asserted to involve progress as distinct from retrogression or to tend to a "realization" or "self-realization" of the human spirit or of anything else. Neither could it conceivably be asserted to lead up to a final term, a goal to which all lines of the process should converge and beyond which the process would not go, such as the assumed goal of the Marxian process of class struggle which is conceived to cease in the classless economic structure of the socialistic final term. In Darwinism there is no such final or perfect term, and no definitive equilibrium. The disparity between Marxism and Darwinism, as well as the disparity within the Marxian system between the range of material facts that are conceived to be the fundamental forces of the process, on the one hand, and the range of spiritual facts within which the dialectic movement proceeds this disparity is shown in the character assigned the class struggle by Marx and Engels. The struggle is asserted to be a conscious one, and proceeds on a recognition by the competing classes of their mutually incompatible interests with regard to the material means of life. The class struggle proceeds on motives of interest, and a recognition of class interest can, of course, be reached only by reflection on the facts of the case. There is, therefore, not

---

[9] Cf., on this point, Max Adler, "Kausalitat und Teleologie im Streite um die Wissenschaft" (included in Marx - Studien, edited by Adler and Hilferding, vol. i), particularly section xi; cf. also Ludwig Stein, Die soziale Frage im Lichte der Philosophie, whom Adler criticizes and claims to have refuted.

[10] Cf., Alder as above.

even a direct causal connection between the material forces in the case and the choice of a given interested line of conduct. The attitude of the interested party does not result from the material forces so immediately as to place it within the relation of direct cause and effect, nor even with such a degree of intimacy as to admit of its being classed as a tropismatic, or even instinctive, response to the impact of the material force in question. The sequence of reflection, and the consequent choice of sides to a quarrel, run entirely alongside of the range of material facts concerned.

A further characteristic of the doctrine of class struggle requires mention. While the concept is not Darwinian, it is also not legitimately Hegelian, whether of the Right or the Left. It is of a utilitarian origin and of English pedigree, and it belongs to Marx by virtue of his having borrowed its elements from the system of self-interest. It is in fact a piece of hedonism, and is related to Bentham rather than to Hegel. It proceeds on the grounds of the hedonistic calculus, which is equally foreign to the Hegelian notion of an unfolding process and to the post-Darwinian notions of cumulative causation. As regards the tenability of the doctrine, apart from the question of its derivation and its compatibility with the neo-Hegelian postulates, it is to be added that it is quite out of harmony with the later results of psychological inquiry, just as is true of the use made of the hedonistic calculus by the classical (Austrian) economics.

Within the domain covered by the materialistic conception, that is to say within the domain of unfolding human culture, which is the field of Marxian speculation at large, Marx has more particularly devoted his efforts to an analysis and theoretical formulation of the present situation, - the current phase of the process, the capitalistic system. And, since the prevailing mode of the production of goods determines the institutional, intellectual, and spiritual life of the epoch, by determining the form and method of the current class struggle, the discussion necessarily begins with the theory of "capitalistic production," or production as carried on under the capitalistic system.[11] .Under the capitalistic system, that is to say under the system of modern business traffic, production is a production of commodities, merchantable goods, with a view to the price to be obtained for them in the market. The great fact on which all industry under this system hing-

---

[11] It may be noted, by way of caution to readers familiar with the terms only as employed by the classical (English and Austrian) economists, that in Marxian usage "capitalistic production" means production of goods for the market by hired labor under the direction of employers who own (or control) the means of production and are engaged in industry for the sake of profit. "Capital" is wealth (primarily funds) so employed. In these and other related points of terminological usage Marx is, of course, much more in touch with colloquial usage than those economists of the classical line who make capital signify "the products of past industry used as aids to further production." With Marx "Capitalism" implies certain relations of ownership, no less than the "productive use" which is alone insisted on by so many later economists in defining the term.

es is the price of marketable goods. Therefore it is at this point that Marx strikes into the system of capitalistic production, and therefore the theory of value becomes the dominant feature of his economics and the point of departure for the whole analysis, in all its voluminous ramifications.[12] It is scarcely worth while to question what serves as the beginning of wisdom in the current criticisms of Marx; namely, that he offers no adequate proof of his labor-value theory.[13]

It is even safe to go further, and say that he offers no proof of it. The feint which occupies the opening paragraphs of the Kapital and the corresponding passages of Zur Kritik, etc., is not to be taken seriously as an attempt to prove his position on this head by the ordinary recourse to argument. It is rather a self-satisfied superior's playful mystification of those readers (critics) whose limited powers do not enable them to see that his proposition is self-evident. Taken on the Hegelian (neo-Hegelian) ground, and seen in the light of the general materialistic conception, the proposition that value - labor-cost - is self-evident, not to say tautological. Seen in any other light, it has no particular force.

In the Hegelian scheme of things the only substantial reality is the unfolding life of the spirit. In the neo-Hegelian scheme, as embodied in the materialistic conception, this reality is translated into terms of the unfolding (material) life of man in society.[14] In so far as the goods are products of industry, they are the output of this unfolding life of man, a material residue embodying a given fraction of this forceful life process. In this life process lies all substantial reality, and all finally valid relations of quantivalence between the products of this life process must run in its terms. The life process, which, when it takes the specific form of an expenditure

---

[12] In the sense that the theory of value affords the point of departure and the fundamental concepts out of which the further theory of the workings of capitalism is constructed, - in this sense, and in this sense only, is the theory of value the central doctrine and the critical tenet of Marxism. It does not follow that Marxist doctrine of an irresistible drift towards a socialistic consummation hangs on the defensibility of the labor-value theory, nor even that the general structure of the Marxist economics would collapse if translated into other terms than those of this doctrine of labor value. Cf. B φ hm-Bawerk, Karl Marx and the Close of his System; and, on the other hand, Franz Oppenheimer, Das Grundgesetz der Marx'schen Gesellschaftslehre, and Rudolf Goldscheid, Verelendungs- oder Meliorationstheorie.

[13] Cf., e.g., B φ hm-Bawerk, as above; Georg Adler, Grundlagen der Karl Marx'schen Kritik.

[14] In much the same way, and with an analogous effect on their theoretical work, in the preconceptions of the classical (including the Austrian) economists, the balance of pleasure and pain is taken to be the ultimate reality in terms of which all economic theory must be stated and to terms of which all phenomena should finally be reduced in any definitive analysis of economic life. It is not the present purpose to inquire whether the one of these uncritical assumptions is in any degree more meritorious or more serviceable than the other.

of labor power, goes to produce goods, is a process of material forces, the spiritual or mental features of the life process and of labor being only its insubstantial reflex. It is consequently only in the material changes wrought by this expenditure of labor power that the metaphysical substance of life - labor power - can be embodied; but in these changes of material fact it cannot but be embodied, since these are the end to which it is directed.

This balance between goods in respect of their magnitude as output of human labor holds good indefeasibly, in point of the metaphysical reality of the life process, whatever superficial (phenomenal) variations from this norm may occur in men's dealings with the goods under the stress of the strategy of self-interest. Such is the value of the goods in reality; they are equivalents of one another in the proportion in which they partake of this substantial quality, although their true ratio of equivalence may never come to an adequate expression in the transactions involved in the distribution of the goods. This real or true value of the goods is a fact of production, and holds true under all systems and methods of production, whereas the exchange value (the "phenomenal form" of the real value) is a fact of distribution, and expresses the real value more or less adequately according as the scheme of distribution force at the given time conforms more or less closely to the equities given by production. If the output of industry were distributed to the productive agents strictly in proportion to their shares in production, the exchange value of the goods would be presumed to conform to their real value. But, under the current, capitalistic system, distribution is not in any sensible degree based on the equities of production, and the exchange value of goods under this system can therefore express their real value only with a very rough, and in the main fortuitous, approximation. Under a socialistic regime, where the laborer would get the full product of his labor, or where the whole system of ownership, and consequently the system of distribution, would lapse, values would reach a true expression, if any.

Under the capitalistic system the determination of exchange value is a matter of competitive profit-making, and exchange values therefore depart erratically and incontinently from the proportions that would legitimately be given them by the real values whose only expression they are. Marx's critics commonly identify the concept of "value" with that of "exchange value[15], and show that the theory of "value" does not square with the run of the facts of price under the existing system of distribution, piously hoping thereby to have refuted the Marxian doctrine; whereas, of course, they have for the most part not touched it. The misapprehension of the critics may be due to a (possibly intentional) oracular obscurity on the part of Marx. Whether by his fault or their own, their refutations have

---

[15] B ϕ hm-Bawerk, Capital and Interest, Book VI, chap. iii; also Karl Marx and the Close of his System, particularly chap. iv; Adler, Grundlagen, chaps. ii and iii.

hitherto been quite inconclusive. Marx's severest stricture on the iniquities of the capitalistic system is that contained by implication in his development of the manner in which actual exchange value of goods systematically diverges from their real (labor-cost) value. Herein, indeed, lies not only the inherent iniquity of the existing system, but also its fateful infirmity, according to Marx.

The theory of value, then, is contained in the main postulates of the Marxian system rather than derived from them. Marx identifies this doctrine, in its elements, with the labor-value theory of Ricardo,[16] but the relationship between the two is that of a superficial coincidence in their main propositions rather than a substantial identity of theoretic contents. In Ricardo's theory the source and measure of value is sought in the effort and sacrifice undergone by the producer, consistently, on the whole, with the Benthamite-utilitarian position to which Ricardo somewhat loosely and uncritically adhered. The decisive fact about labor, that quality by virtue of which it is assumed to be the final term in the theory of production, is its irksomeness. Such is of course not the case in the labor-value theory of Marx, to whom the question of the irksomeness of labor is quite irrelevant, so far as regards the relation between labor and production. The substantial diversity or incompatibility of the two theories shows itself directly when each is employed by its creator in the further analysis of economic phenomena. Since with Ricardo the crucial point is the degree of irksomeness of labor, which serves as a measure both of the labor expended and the value produced, and since in Ricardo's utilitarian philosophy there is no more vital fact underlying this irksomeness, therefore no surplus-value theory follows from the main position. The productiveness of labor is not cumulative in its own working; and the Ricardian economics goes on to seek the cumulative productiveness of industry in the functioning of the products of labor when employed in further production and in the irksomeness of the capitalist's abstinence. From which duly follows the general position of classical economics on the theory of production.

With Marx, on the other hand, the labor power expended in production being itself a product and having a substantial value corresponding to its own labor cost, the value of the labor power expended and the value of the product created by its expenditure need not be the same. They are not the same, by supposition, as they would be in any hedonistic interpretation of the facts. Hence a discrepancy arises between the value of the labor power expended in production and the value of the product created, and this discrepancy is covered by the concept of surplus value. Under the capital-

---

[16] Cf. Kapital, vol. i, chap. xv, p.486 (4th ed.). See also notes 9 and 16 to chap. i of the same volume, where Marx discusses the labor-value doctrines of Adam Smith and an earlier (anonymous) English writer and compares them with his own. Similar comparisons with the early - Classical - value theories recur from time to time in the later portions of Kapital.

istic system, wages being the value (price) of the labor power consumed in industry, it follows that the surplus product of their labor cannot go to the laborers, but becomes the profits of capital and the source of its accumulation and increase. From the fact that wages are measured by the value of labor power rather than by the (greater) value of the product of labor, it follows also that the laborers are unable to buy the whole product of their labor, and so that the capitalists are unable to sell the whole product of industry continuously at its full value, whence arise difficulties of the gravest nature in the capitalistic system, in the way of overproduction and the like.

But the gravest outcome of this systematic discrepancy between the value of labor power and the value of its product is the accumulation of capital out of unpaid labor and the effect of this accumulation on the laboring population. The law of accumulation, with its corollary, the doctrine of the industrial reserve army, is the final term and the objective point of Marx's theory of capitalist production, just as the theory of labor value is his point of departure.[17] .While the theory of value and surplus value are Marx's explanation of the possibility of existence of the capitalistic system, the law of the accumulation of capital is his exposition of the causes which must lead to the collapse of that system and of the manner in which the collapse will come. And since Marx is, always and everywhere, a socialist agitator as well as a theoretical economist, it may be said without hesitation that the law of accumulation is the climax of his great work, from whatever point of view it is looked at, whether as an economic theorem or as a tenet of socialistic doctrine. The law of capitalistic accumulation may be paraphrased as follows:[18]

Wages being the (approximately exact) value of the labor power bought in the wage contract; the price of the product being the (similarly approximate) value of the goods produced; and since the value of the product exceeds that of the labor power by a given amount (surplus value), which by force of the wage contract passes into the possession of the capitalist and is by him in part laid by as savings and added to the capital already in hand, it follows (a) that, other things equal, the larger the surplus value, the more rapid the increase of capital; and also (b), that the greater the increase of capital relatively to the labor force employed, the more productive the labor employed and the larger the surplus product available for accumulation. The process of accumulation, therefore, is evidently a cu-

---

[17] Oppenheimer (Das Grundgesetz der Marx'schen Gesellschaftslehre) is right in making the theory of accumulation the central element in the doctrines of Marxist socialism, but it does not follow, as Oppenheimer contends, that this doctrine is the keystone of Marx's economic theories. It follows logically from the theory of surplus value, as indicated above, and rests on that theory in such a way that it would fail (in the form in which it is held by Marx) with the failure of the doctrine of surplus value.

[18] See Kapital, vol. i, chap. xxiii.

mulative one; and, also evidently, the increase added to capital is an unearned increment drawn from the unpaid surplus product of labor.

But with an appreciable increase of the aggregate capital a change takes place in its technological composition, whereby the "constant" capital (equipment and raw materials) increases disproportionately as compared with the "variable" capital (wages fund). "Labor-saving devices" are used to a greater extent than before, and labor is saved. A larger proportion of the expenses of production goes for the purchase of equipment and raw materials, and a smaller proportion - though perhaps an absolutely increased amount - goes for the purchase of labor power. Less labor is needed relatively to the aggregate capital employed as well as relatively to the quantity of goods produced. Hence some portion of the increasing labor supply will not be wanted, and an "industrial reserve army," a "surplus labor population," an army of unemployed, comes into existence. This reserve grows relatively larger as the accumulation of capital proceeds and as technological improvements consequently gain ground; so that there result two divergent cumulative changes in the situation, - antagonistic, but due to the same set of forces and, therefore, inseparable: capital increases, and the number of unemployed laborers (relatively) increases also.

This divergence between the amount of capital and output, on the one hand, and the amount received by laborers as wages, on the other hand, has an incidental consequence of some importance. The purchasing power of the laborers, represented by their wages, being the largest part of the demand for consumable goods, and being at the same time, in the nature of the case, progressively less adequate for the purchase of the product, represented by the price of the goods produced, it follows that the market is progressively more subject to glut from overproduction, and hence to commercial crises and depression. It has been argued, as if it were a direct inference from Marx's position, that this maladjustment between production and markets, due to the laborer not getting the full product of his labor, leads directly to the breakdown of the capitalistic system, and so by its own force will bring on the socialistic consummation. Such is not Marx's position, however, although crises and depression play an important part in the course of development that is to lead up to socialism. In Marx's theory, socialism is to come by way of a conscious class movement on the part of the propertyless laborers, who will act advisedly on their own interest and force the revolutionary movement for their own gain. But crises and depression will have a large share in bringing the laborers to a frame of mind suitable for such a move.

Given a growing aggregate capital, as indicated above, and a concomitant reserve of unemployed laborers growing at a still higher rate, as is involved in Marx's position, this body of unemployed labor can be, and will be, used by the capitalists to depress wages, in order to increase profits. Logically, it follows that, the farther and faster capital accumulates, the larger will be the reserve of unemployed, both absolutely and relatively to the work to be done, and the more severe will be the pressure acting to reduce wages and lower the standard of living, and the deeper will be the degradation and misery of the working class and the more precipitately will their condition decline to a still lower depth. Every period of depression, with its increased body of unemployed labor seeking work, will act to hasten and accentuate the depression of wages, until there is no warrant even for holding that wages will, on an average, be kept up to the subsistence minimum.[19].

Marx, indeed, is explicit to the effect that such will be the case that wages will decline below the subsistence minimum; and he cites English conditions of child labor, misery, and degeneration to substantiate his views.[20] .When this has gone far enough, when capitalist production comes near enough to occupying the whole field of industry and has depressed the condition of its laborers sufficiently to make them an effective majority of the community with nothing to lose, then, having taken advice together, they will move, by legal or extra-legal means, by absorbing the state or by subverting it, to establish the social revolution, Socialism is to come through class antagonism due to the absence of all property interests from the laboring class, coupled with a generally prevalent misery so profound as to involve some degree of physical degeneration. This misery is to be brought about by the heightened productivity of labor due to an increased accumulation of capital and large improvements in the industrial arts; which in turn is caused by the fact that under a system of private enterprise with hired labor the laborer does not get the whole product of his labor; which, again, is only saying in other words that private ownership of capital goods enables the capitalist to appropriate and accumulate the surplus product of labor. As to what the regime is to be which the social revolution will bring in, Marx has nothing particular to say beyond the general thesis that there will be no private ownership, at least not of the means of production.

Such are the outlines of the Marxian system of socialism. In all that has been said so far no recourse is had to the second and third volumes of Kapital. Nor is it necessary to resort to these two volumes for the general theory of socialism. They add nothing essential, although many of the details of the processes concerned in the working out of the capitalist scheme are treated with greater fulness, and the analysis is carried out with great consistency and with admirable results. For economic theory at large these further two volumes are important enough, but an inquiry into their contents in that connection is not called for here.

Nothing much need be said as to the tenability of this theory. In its essentials, or at least in its characteristic elements, it has for the most part been given up by latterday socialist writers. The number of those who hold

---

[19] The "subsistence minimum" is here taken in the sense used by Marx and the classical economists, as meaning what is necessary to keep up the supply of labor at its current rate of efficiency.

[20] See Kapital, vol. i, chap. xxiii, sections 4 and 5.

to it without essential deviation is growing gradually smaller. Such is necessarily the case, and for more than one reason. The facts are not bearing it out on certain critical points, such as the doctrine of increasing misery; and the Hegelian philosophical postulates, without which the Marxism of Marx is groundless, are for the most part forgotten by the dogmatists of today. Darwinism has largely supplanted Hegelianism in their habits of thought.

The particular point at which the theory is most fragile, considered simply as a theory of social growth, is its implied doctrine of population, implied in the doctrine of a growing reserve of unemployed workmen. The doctrine of the reserve of unemployed labor involves as a postulate that population will increase anyway, without reference to current or prospective means of life. The empirical facts give at least a very persuasive apparent support to the view expressed by Marx, that misery is, or has hitherto been, no hindrance to the propagation of the race; but they afford no conclusive evidence in support of a thesis to the effect that the number of laborers must increase independently of an increase of the means of life. No one since Darwin would have the hardihood to say that the increase of the human species is not conditioned by the means of living.

But all that does not really touch Marx's position. To Marx, the neo-Hegelian history, including the economic development, is the life-history of the human species; and the main fact in this life-history, particularly in the economic aspect of it, is the growing volume of human life. This, in a manner of speaking, is the base-line of the whole analysis of the process of economic life, including the phase of capitalist production with the rest.

The growth of population is the first principle, the most substantial, most material factor in this process of economic life, so long as it is a process of growth, of unfolding, of exfoliation, and not a phase of decrepitude and decay. Had Marx found that his analysis led him to a view adverse to this position, he would logically have held that the capitalist system is the mortal agony of the race and the manner of its taking off. Such a conclusion is precluded by his Hegelian point of departure, according to which the goal of the life-history of the race in a large way controls the course of that life-history in all its phases, including the phase of capitalism. This goal or end, which controls the process of human development, is the complete realization of life in all its fullness, and the realization is to be reached by a process analogous to the three-phase dialectic, of thesis, antithesis, and synthesis, into which scheme the capitalist system, with its overflowing measure of misery and degradation, fits as the last and most dreadful phase of antithesis. Marx, as a Hegelian, - that is to say, a romantic philosopher, - is necessarily an optimist, and the evil (antithetical element) in life is to him a logically necessary evil, as the antithesis is a necessary phase of the dialectic; and it is a means to the consummation, as the antithesis is a means to the synthesis.

II. The Later Marxism

The substance of lectures before students in Harvard University in April, 1906. Marx worked out his system of theory in the main during the third quarter of the nineteenth century. He came to the work from the standpoint given him by his early training in German thought, such as the most advanced and aggressive German thinking was through the middle period of the century, and he added to this German standpoint the further premises given him by an exceptionally close contact with and alert observation of the English situation. The result is that he brings to his theoretical work a twofold line of premises, or rather of preconceptions. By early training he is a neo-Hegelian, and from this German source he derives his peculiar formulation of the Materialistic Theory of History. By later experience he acquired the point of view of that Liberal-Utilitarian school which dominated English thought through the greater part of his active life. To this experience he owes (probably) the somewhat pronounced individualistic preconceptions on which the doctrines of the Full Product of Labor and the Exploitation of Labor are based. These two not altogether compatible lines of doctrine found their way together into the tenets of scientific[21] socialism, and give its characteristic Marxian features to the body of socialist economics.

The socialism that inspires hopes and fears to-day is of the school of Marx. No one is seriously apprehensive of any other so-called socialistic movement, and no one is seriously concerned to criticise or refute the doctrines set forth by any other school of "socialists." It may be that the socialists of Marxist observance are not always or at all points in consonance with the best accepted body of Marxist doctrine. Those who make up the body of the movement may not always be familiar with the details perhaps not even with the general features - of the Marxian scheme of economics; but with such consistency as may fairly be looked for in any popular movements the socialists of all countries gravitate toward the theoretical position of the avowed Marxism. In proportion as the movement in any given community grows in mass, maturity, and conscious purpose, it unavoidably takes on a more consistently Marxian complexion. It is not the Marxism of Marx, but the materialism of Darwin, which the socialists of today have adopted. The Marxist socialists of Germany have the lead, and the socialists of other countries largely take their cue from the German leaders.

The authentic spokesmen of the current international socialism are avowed Marxists. Exceptions to that rule are very few. On the whole, substantial truth of the Marxist doctrines is not seriously questioned within the lines of the socialists, though there may be some appreciable divergence as to what the true Marxist position is on one point and another. Much and eager controversy circles about questions of that class.

---

[21] "Scientific" is here used in the half technical sense which by usage it often has in this connection, designating the theories of Marx and his followers.

The keepers of the socialist doctrines are passably agreed as to the main position and the general principles. Indeed, so secure is this current agreement on the general principles that a very lively controversy on matters of detail may go on without risk of disturbing the general position. This general position is avowedly Marxism. But it is not precisely the position held by Karl Marx. It has been modernized, adapted, tilled out, in response to exigencies of a later date than those which conditioned the original formulation of the theories. It is, of course, not admitted by the followers of Marx that any substantial change or departure from the original position has taken place. They are somewhat jealously orthodox, and are impatient of any suggested "improvements" on the Marxist position, as witness the heat engendered in the "revisionist" controversy of a few years back. But the jealous protests of the followers of Marx do not alter the fact that Marxism has undergone some substantial change since it left the hands of its creator. Now and then a more or less consistent disciple of Marx will avow a need of adapting the received doctrines to circumstances that have arisen later than the formulation of the doctrines; and amendments, qualifications, and extensions, with this need in view, have been offered from time to time. But more pervasive tho unavowed changes have come in the teachings of Marxism by way of interpretation and an unintended shifting of the point of view. Virtually, the whole of the younger generation of socialist writers shows such a growth. A citation of personal instances would be quite futile.

It is the testimony of his friends as well as of his writings that the theoretical position of Marx, both as regards his standpoint and as regards his main tenets, fell into a definitive shape relatively early, and that his later work was substantially a working out of what was contained in the position taken at the outset of his career.[22] .By the latter half of the forties, if not by the middle of the forties, Marx and Engels had found the outlook on human life which came to serve as the point of departure and the guide for their subsequent development of theory. Such is the view of the matter

---

[22] There is, indeed, a remarkable consistency, amounting substantially to an invariability of position, in Marx's writing, from the Communist Manifesto to the last volume of the Capital. The only portion of the great Manifesto which became antiquated, in the apprehension of its creators, is the polemics addressed to the "Philosophical" socialists of the forties and the illustrative material taken from contemporary politics. The main position and the more important articles of theory, the materialistic conception, the doctrine of class struggle, the theory of value and surplus value, of increasing distress, of the reserve army, of the capitalistic collapse are to be found in the Critique of Political Economy (1859), and much of them in the Misery of Philosophy (1847), together with the masterful method of analysis and construction which he employed throughout his theoretical work.

expressed by Engels during the later years of his life.[23] .The position taken by the two greater leaders, and held by them substantially intact, was a variant of neo-Hegelianism, as has been indicated in an earlier section of this paper.[24] .But neo-Hegelianism was short-lived, particularly considered as a standpoint for scientific theory. The whole romantic school of thought, comprising neo-Hegelianism with the rest, began to go to pieces very soon after it had reached an approach to maturity, and its disintegration proceeded with exceptional speed, so that the close of the third quarter of the century saw the virtual end of it as a vital factor in the development of human knowledge. In the realm of theory, primarily of course in the material sciences, the new era belongs not to romantic philosophy, but to the evolutionists of the school of Darwin. Some few great figures, of course, stood over from the earlier days, but it turns out in the sequel that they have served mainly to mark the rate and degree in which the method of scientific knowledge has left them behind. Such were Virchow and Max Möller, and such, in economic science, were the great figures of the Historical School, and such, in a degree, were also Marx and Engels. The later generation of socialists, the spokesmen and adherents of Marxism during the closing quarter of the century, belong to the new generation, and see the phenomena of human life under the new light. The materialistic conception in their handling of it takes on the color of the time in which they lived, even while they retain the phraseology of the generation that went before them.[25] The difference between the romantic school of thought, to which Marx belonged, and the school of the evolutionists into whose hands the system has fallen, - or perhaps, better, is falling, - is great and

---

[23] Cf. Engels, Feuerbach (English translation, Chicago, 1903), especially Part IV., various papers published in the Neue Zeit; also the preface to the Communist Manifesto written in 1888; also the preface to volume II of Capital, where Engels argues the question of Marx's priority in connection with the leading theoretical principles of his system.

[24] Cf. Feuerbach, as above; The Development of Socialism from Utopia to Science, especially sections II and III.

[25] Such a socialist as Anton Menger, e.g., comes into the neo-Marxian school from without, from the field of modern scientific inquiry, and shows, at least virtually, no Hegelian color, whether in the scope of his inquiry, in his method, or in the theoretical work which he puts forth. It should be added that his Neue Staatslehre and Neue Sittenlehre are the first socialistic constructive work of substantial value as a contribution to knowledge, outside of economic theory proper, that has appeared since Lassalle. The efforts of Engels (Ursprung der Familie) and Bebel (Die Frau) would scarcely be taken seriously as scientific monographs even by hot-headed socialists if it were not for the lack of anything better. Menger's work is not Marxism, whereas Engels' and Bebel's work of this class is practically without value or originality. The unfitness of the Marxian postulates and methods for the purposes of modern science shows itself in the sweeping barrenness of socialistic literature all along that line of inquiry into the evolution of institutions for the promotion of which the materialistic dialectic was invented.

pervading, though it may not show a staring superficial difference at any one point, - at least not yet. The discrepancy between the two is likely to appear more palpable and more sweeping when the new method of knowledge has been applied with fuller realization of its reach and its requirements in that domain of knowledge that once belonged to the neo-Hegelian Marxism. The supplanting of the one by the other has been taking place slowly, gently, in large measure unavowedly, by a sort of precession of the point of view from which men size up the facts and reduce them to intelligible order.

The neo-Hegelian, romantic, Marxian standpoint was wholly personal, whereas the evolutionistic - it may be called Darwinian - standpoint is wholly impersonal. The continuity sought in the facts of observation and imputed to them by the earlier school of theory was a continuity of a personal kind, - a continuity of reason and consequently of logic. The facts were construed to take such a course as could be established by an appeal to reason between intelligent and fair-minded men. They were supposed to fall into a sequence of logical consistency. The romantic (Marxian) sequence of theory is essentially an intellectual sequence, and it is therefore of a teleological character. The logical trend of it can be argued out. That is to say, it tends to a goal. It must eventuate in a consummation, a final term. On the other hand, in the Darwinian scheme of thought, the continuity sought in and imputed to the facts is a continuity of cause and effect. It is a scheme of blindly cumulative causation, in which there is no trend, no final term, no consummation. The sequence is controlled by nothing but the *vis a tergo* of brute causation, and is essentially mechanical. The neo-Hegelian (Marxian) scheme of development is drawn in the image of the struggling ambitious human spirit: that of Darwinian evolution is of the nature of a mechanical process.[26] What difference, now, does it make if the materialistic conception is translated from the romantic concepts of Marx into the mechanical concepts of Darwinism? It distorts every feature of the system in some degree, and throws a shadow of doubt on every con-

---

[26] This contrast holds between the original Marxism of Marx and the scope and method of modern science; but it does not, therefore, hold between the latterday Marxists - who are largely imbued with post-Darwinian concepts - and the non-Marxian scientists. Even Engels, in his latter-day formulation of Marxism is strongly affected with the notions of post-Darwinian science, and reads Darwinism into Hegel and Marx with a good deal of naivete. (See his Feuerbach, especially pp. 93-98 of the English translation). So, also, the serious but scarcely quite consistent qualification of the materialistic conception offered by Engels in the letters printed in the Sozialistische Akademiker, 1895.

clusion that once seemed secure.[27] The first principle of the Marxian
scheme is the concept covered by the term "Materialistic," to the effect
that the exigencies of the material means of life control the conduct of
men in society throughout, and thereby indefeasibly guide the growth of
institutions and shape every shifting trait of human culture. This control of
the life of society by the material exigencies takes effect thru men's taking
thought of material (economic) advantages and disadvantages, and
choosing that which will yield the inner material measure of life. When the
materialistic conception passes under the Darwinian norm, of cumulative
causation, it happens, first, that this initial principle itself is reduced to the
rank of a habit of thought induced in the speculator who depends on its
light by the circumstances of his life, in the way of hereditary bent, occupation, tradition, education, climate, food supply, and the like. But under
the Darwinian norm the question of whether and how far material exigencies control human conduct and cultural growth becomes a question of
the share which these material exigencies have in shaping men's habits of
thought; i.e., their ideals and aspirations, their sense of the true, the beautiful, and the good. Whether and how far these traits of human culture and
the institutional structure built out of them are the outgrowth of material
(economic) exigencies becomes a question of what kind and degree of
efficiency belongs to the economic exigencies among the complex of circumstances that conduce to the formation of habits. It is no longer a question of whether material exigencies rationally should guide men's conduct, but whether, as a matter of brute causation, they do induce such
habits of thought in men as the economic interpretation presumes, and
whether in the last analysis economic exigencies alone are, directly or indirectly, effective in shaping human habits of thought.

   Tentatively and by way of approximation some such formulation as that
outlined in the last paragraph is apparently what Bernstein and others of

---

[27] The fact that the theoretical structures of Marx collapse when their elements are
converted into the terms of modern science should of itself be sufficient proof that
those structures were not built by their maker out of such elements as modern science habitually makes use of. Marx was neither ignorant, imbecile, nor disingenuous, and his work must be construed from such a point of view and in terms of such
elements as will enable his results to stand substantially sound and convincing.

the "revisionists" have been seeking in certain of their speculations,[28] and, sitting austere and sufficient on a dry shoal up stream, Kautsky has uncomprehendingly been addressing them advice and admonition which they do not understand.[29] .

The more intelligent and enterprising among the idealist wing - where intellectual enterprise is not a particularly obvious trait have been struggling to speak for the view that the forces of the environment may effectually reach men's spiritual life thru other avenues than the calculus of the main chance, and so may give rise to habitual ideals and aspirations inde-

----

28 Cf. Voraussetzungen des Sozialismus, especially the first two (critical) chapters. Bernstein's reverent attitude toward Marx and Engels, as well as his somewhat old-fashioned conception of the scope and method of science, gives his discussion an air of much greater consonance with the orthodox Marxism than it really has. In his latter expressions this consonance and conciliatory animus show up more strongly rather than otherwise. (See Socialism and Science, including the special preface written for the French edition). That which was to Marx and Engels the point of departure and the guiding norm - the Hegelian dialectic - is to Bernstein a mistake from which scientific socialism must free itself. He says, e.g., (Voraussetzungen, end of ch. iv.), "The great things achieved by Marx and Engels they have achieved not by the help of the Hegelian dialectic, but in spite of it." The number of the "revisionists" is very considerable, and they are plainly gaining ground as against the Marxists of the older line of orthodoxy. They are by no means agreed among themselves as to details, but they belong together by virtue of their endeavor to so construe (and amend) the Marxian system as to bring it into consonance with the current scientific point of view. One should rather say points of view, since the revisionist endevors are not all directed to bringing the received views in under a single point of view. There are two main directions of movement among the revisionists: (a) those who, like Bernstein, Conrad Schmidt, Tugan-Baronowski, Labriola, Ferri, aim to bring Marxism abreast of the standpoint of modern science, essentially Darwinists; and (b) those who aim to return to some footing on the level of romantic philosophy. The best type and the strongest of the latter class are the neo-Kantians, embodying that spirit of revulsion to romantic norms of theory that makes up the philosophical side of the reactionary movement fostered by the discipline of German imperialism. (See, Die neukantische Bewegung im Sozialismus.)Except that he is not officially inscribed in the socialist calender, Sombart might be cited as a particularly effective revisionist, so far as concerns the point of modernizing Marxism and putting the modernized materialistic conception to work.

29 Cf. the files of the Neue Zeit, particularly during the controversy with Bernstein, and Bernstein und das Sozialdemokratische Programm.

pendent of, and possibly alien to, that calculus.[30] .So, again, as to the doctrine of the class struggle. In the Marxian scheme of dialectical evolution the development which is in this way held to be controlled by the material exigencies must, it is held, proceed by the method of the class struggle. This class struggle is held to be inevitable, and is held inevitably to lead at each revolutionary epoch to a more efficient adjustment of human industry to human uses, because when a large proportion of the community find themselves ill served by the current economic arrangements, they take thought, band together, and enforce a readjustment more equitable and more advantageous to them. So long as differences of economic advantage prevail, there will be a divergence of interests between those more advantageously placed and those less advantageously placed. The members of society will take sides as this line of cleavage indicated by their several economic interests may decide. Class solidarity will arise on the basis of this class interest, and a struggle between the two classes so marked off against each other will set in, - a struggle which, in the logic of the situation, can end only when the previously less fortunate class gains the ascendency, - and so must the class struggle proceed until it shall have put an end to that diversity of economic interest on which the class struggle rests. All this is logically consistent and convincing, but it proceeds on the ground of reasoned conduct, calculus of advantage, not on the ground of cause and effect. The class struggle so conceived should always and everywhere tend unremittingly toward the socialistic consummation, and should reach that consummation in the end, whatever obstructions or diversions might retard the sequence of development along the way. Such is the notion of it embodied in the system of Marx. Such, however, is not the showing of history. Not all nations or civilizations have advanced unremittingly toward a socialistic consummation, in which all divergence of economic interest has lapsed or would lapse. Those nations and civilizations which have decayed and failed, as nearly all known nations and civilizations have done, illustrate the point that, however reasonable and logical the advance by means of the class struggle may be, it is by no means inevitable. Under the Darwinian norm it must be held that men's reasoning is largely controlled by other than logical, intellectual forces; that the conclusion reached by public or class opinion is as much, or more, a matter of sentiment than of logical inference; and that the sentiment which

---

30 The "idealist" socialists are even more in evidence outside of Germany. They may fairly be said to be in the ascendant in France, and they are a very strong and free-spoken contingent of the socialist movement of America. They do not commonly speak the language either of science or of philosophy, but, so far as their contentions may be construed from the standpoint of modern science, their drift seems to be something of the kind indicated above. At the same time the spokesmen of this scattering and shifting group stand for a variety of opinions and aspirations that cannot be classified under Marxism, Darwinism, or any other system of theory. At the margin they shade off into theology and the creeds.

animates men, singly or collectively, is as much, or more, an outcome of habit and native propensity as of calculated material interest. There is, for instance, no warrant in the Darwinian scheme of things for asserting a priori that the class interest of the working class will bring them to take a stand against the propertied class. It may as well be that their training in subservience to their employers will bring them again to realize the equity and excellence of the established system of subjection and unequal distribution of wealth. Again, no one, for instance, can tell to-day what will be the outcome of the present situation in Europe and America. It may be that the working classes will go forward along the line of the socialistic ideals and enforce a new deal, in which there shall be no economic class discrepancies, no international animosity, no dynastic politics. But then it may also, so far as can be foreseen, equally well happen that the working class, with the rest of the community in Germany, England, or America, will be led by the habit of loyalty and by their sportsmanlike propensities to lend themselves enthusiastically to the game of drastic politics which alone their sportsmanlike rulers consider worthwhile. It is quite impossible on Darwinian ground to foretell whether the "proletariat" will go on to establish the socialistic revolution or turn aside again, and sink their force in the broad sands of patriotism. It is a question of habit and native propensity and of the range of stimuli to which the proletariat are exposed and are to be exposed, and what may be the outcome is not a matter of logical consistency, but of response to stimulus.

So, then, since Darwinian concepts have begun to dominate the thinking of the Marxists, doubts have now and again come to assert themselves both as to the inevitableness of the irrepressible class struggle and to its sole efficacy. Anything like a violent class struggle, a seizure of power by force, is more and more consistently deprecated. For resort to force, it is felt, brings in its train coercive control with all its apparatus of prerogative, mastery, and subservience.[31] .So, again, the Marxian doctrine of progressive proletarian distress, the so-called Verelendungstheorie, which stands pat on the romantic ground of the original Marxism, has fallen into abeyance, if not into disrepute, since the Darwinian conceptions have come to prevail. As a matter of reasoned procedure, on the ground of enlightened material interest alone, it should be a tenable position that increasing misery, increasing in degree and in volume, should be the outcome of the present system of ownership; and should at the same time result in a well-advised and well-consolidated working-class movement that would replace the present system by a scheme more advantageous to the majority. But so soon as the question is approached on the Darwinian ground of

---

[31] Throughout the revisionist literature in Germany there is visible a softening of the traits of the doctrine of the class struggle, and the like shows itself in the programs of the party. Outside of Germany the doctrinaire insistence on this tenet is weakening even more decidedly. The opportunist politicians, with strong aspirations, but with relatively few and ill-defined theoretical preconceptions, are gaining ground.

cause and effect, and is analyzed in terms of habit and of response to stimulus, the doctrine that progressive misery must effect a socialistic revolution becomes dubious, and very shortly untenable. Experience, the experience of history, teaches that abject misery carries with it deterioration and abject subjection. The theory of progressive distress fits convincingly into the scheme of the Hegelian three-phase dialectic. It stands for the antithesis that is to be merged in the ulterior synthesis; but it has no particular force on the ground of an argument from cause to effect.[32] .It fares not much better with the Marxian theory of value and its corollaries and dependent doctrines when Darwinian concepts are brought in to replace the romantic elements out of which it is built up. Its foundation is the metaphysical equality between the volume of human life force productively spent in the making of goods and the magnitude of these goods considered as human products. The question of such an equality has no meaning in terms of cause and effect, nor does it bear in any intelligible way upon the Darwinian question of the fitness of any given system of production or distribution. In any evolutionary system of economics the central question touching the efficiency and fitness of any given system of production is necessarily the question as to the excess of serviceability in the product over the cost of production.[33] .It is in such an excess of serviceability over cost that the chance of survival lies for any system of production, in so far as the question of survival is a question of production, and this matter comes into the speculation of Marx only indirectly or incidentally, and leads to nothing in his argument.

And, as bearing on the Marxian doctrines of exploitation, there is on Darwinian ground no place for a natural right to the full product of labor. What can be argued in that connection on the ground of cause and effect simply is the question as to what scheme of distribution will help or hin-

---

[32] Cf. Bernstein, Die heutige Sozialdemokratie in Theorie und Praxis, an answer to Brunhuber, Die heutige Sozialdemokratie, which should be consulted in the same connection; Goldscheid, Verelendungs- oder Meliorationstheorie; also Sombart, Sozialismus und soziale Bewegung, 5th edition, pp. 86-89.

[33] Accordingly, in later Marxian handling of the questions of exploitation and accumulation, the attention is centred on the "surplus product" rather than on the "surplus value". It is also currently held that the doctrines and practical consequences which Marx derived from the theory of surplus value would remain substantially well founded, even if the theory of surplus value were given up. These secondary doctrines could be saved - at the cost of orthodoxy - by putting a theory of surplus product in the place of the theory of surplus value, as in effect is done by Bernstein (Sozialdemokratie in Theorie und Praxis, sec. 5.

Also various essays included in Zur Geschichte und Theorie des Sozialismus.

der the survival of a given people or a given civilization.[34] .But these questions of abstruse theory need not be pursued, since they count, after all, but relatively little among the working tenets of the movement. Little need be done by the Marxists to work out or to adapt the Marxian system of value theory, since it has but slight bearing on the main question, - the question of the trend towards socialism and of its chances of success. It is conceivable that a competent theory of value dealing with the excess of serviceability over cost, on the one hand, and with the discrepancy between price and serviceability, on the other hand, would have a substantial bearing upon the advisability of the present as against the socialistic regime, and would go far to clear up the notions of both socialists and conservatives as to the nature of the points in dispute between them.

But the socialists have not moved in the direction of this problem, and they have the excuse that their critics have suggested neither a question nor a solution to a question along any such line. None of the value theorists have so far offered anything that could be called good, bad, or indifferent in this connection, and the socialists are as innocent as the rest. Economics, indeed, has not at this point yet begun to take on a modern tone, unless the current neglect of value theory by the socialists be taken as a negative symptom of advance, indicating that they at least recognize the futility of the received problems and solutions, even if they are not ready to make a positive move.

The shifting of the current point of view, from romantic philosophy to matter-of-fact, has affected the attitude of the Marxists towards the several articles of theory more than it has induced an avowed alteration or a substitution of new elements of theory for the old. It is always possible to make one's peace with a new standpoint by new interpretations and a shrewd use of figures of speech, so far as the theoretical formulation is concerned, and something of this kind has taken place in the case of Marxism; but when, as in the case of Marxism, the formulations of theory are drafted into practical use, substantial changes of appreciable magnitude are apt to show themselves in a changed attitude towards practical questions. The Marxists have had to face certain practical problems, especially problems of party tactics, and the substantial changes wrought in their theoretical outlook have come into evidence here. The real gravity of the changes that have overtaken Marxism would scarcely be seen by a scrutiny of the formal professions of the Marxists alone. But the exigencies of a changing situation have provoked readjustments of the received doc-

---

[34] The "right to the full product of labor" and the Marxian theory of exploitation associated with that principle has fallen into the background, except as a campaign designed to stir the emotions of the working class. Even as a campaign it has not the prominence, nor apparently the efficacy, which it once had. The tenet is better preserved, in fact, among the "idealists", who draw for their antecedents on the French Revolution and the English philosophy of natural rights, than among the latter-day Marxists.

trinal position, and the shifting of the philosophical standpoint and postulates has come into evidence as marking the limits of change in their professions which the socialistic doctrinaires could allow themselves.

The changes comprised in the cultural movement that lies between the middle and the close of the nineteenth century are great and grave, at least as seen from so near a standpoint as the present day, and it is safe to say that, in whatever historical perspective they may be seen, they must, in some respects, always assert themselves as unprecedented. So far as concerns the present topic, there are three main lines of change that have converged upon the Marxist system of doctrines, and have led to its latter-day modification and growth. One of these - the change in the postulates of knowledge, in the metaphysical foundations of theory - has been spoken of already, and its bearing on the growth of socialist theory has been indicated in certain of its general features. But, among the circumstances that have conditioned the growth of the system, the most obvious is the fact that since Marx's time his doctrines have come to serve as the platform of a political movement, and so have been exposed to the stress of practical party politics dealing with a new and changing situation. At the same time the industrial (economic) situation to which the doctrines are held to apply - of which they are the theoretical formulation - has also in important respects changed its character from what it was when Marx first formulated his views. These several lines of cultural change affecting the growth of Marxism cannot be held apart in so distinct a manner as to appraise the work of each separately. They belong inextricably together, as do the effects wrought by them in the system.

In practical politics the Social Democrats have had to make up their account with the labor movement, the agricultural population, and the imperialistic policy. On each of these heads the preconceived program of Marxism has come in conflict with the run of events, and on each head it has been necessary to deal shrewdly and adapt the principles to the facts of the time. The adaptation to circumstances has not been altogether of the nature of the compromise, although here and there the spirit of compromise and conciliation is visible enough. A conciliatory party policy may, of course, impose an adaptation of form and color upon the party principles, whether thereby seriously affecting the substance of the principles themselves; but the need of a conciliatory policy may, even more, provoke a substantial change of attitude toward practical questions in a case where a shifting of the theoretical point of view makes room for a substantial change.

Apart from all merely tactical expedients, the experience of the past thirty years has led the German Marxists to see the facts of the labor situation in a new light, and has induced them to attach an altered meaning to the accepted formulations of doctrine. The facts have not freely lent themselves to the scheme of the Marxist system, but the scheme has taken on such a new meaning as would be consistent with the facts. The untroubled Marxian economics, such as it finds expression in the Kapital and earlier documents of the theory, has no place and no use for a trade-union movement, or, indeed, for any similar non-political organization among the working class, and the attitude of the Social-Democratic leaders of opinion in the early days of the party's history was accordingly hostile to any such movement,[35] as much so, indeed, as the loyal adherents of the classical political economy. That was before the modern industrial era had got under way in Germany, and therefore before the German socialistic doctrinaires had learned by experience what the development of industry was to bring with it. It was also before the modern scientific postulates had begun to disintegrate the neo-Hegelian preconceptions as to the logical sequence in the development of institutions.

In Germany, as elsewhere, the growth of the capitalistic system presently brought on trade-unionism; that is to say, it brought on an organized attempt on the part of the workmen to deal with the questions of capitalistic production and distribution by business methods, to settle the problems of working-class employment and livelihood by a system of nonpolitical, businesslike bargains. But the great point of all socialist aspiration and endeavor is the abolition of all business and all bargaining, and, accordingly, the Social Democrats were heartily out of sympathy with the unions and their endeavors to make business terms with the capitalist system, and make life tolerable for the workmen under that system. But the union movement grew to be so serious a feature of the situation that the socialists found themselves obliged to deal with unions, since they could not deal with the workmen over the heads of the unions. The Social Democrats, and therefore the Marxian theorists, had to deal with a situation which included the union movement, and this movement was bent on improving the workman's conditions of life from day to day. Therefore it was necessary to figure out how the union movement could and must further the socialistic advance; to work into the body of doctrines a theory of how the unions belong in the course of economic development that leads up to socialism, and to reconcile the unionist efforts at improvement with the ends of Social Democracy. Not only were the unions seeking improvement by unsocialistic methods, but the level of comfort among the working classes was in some respects advancing, apparently as a result of these union efforts. Both the huckstering animus of the workmen in their unionist policy and the possible amelioration of working-class conditions had to be incorporated into the socialistic platform and into the Marxist theory of

---

[35] It is, of course, well known that even in the transactions and pronunciamentos of the International a good word is repeatedly said for the trade-unions, and both the Gotha and the Erfurt programs speak in favor of labor organizations, and put forth demands designed to further the trade-union endeavors. But it is equally well known that these expressions were in good part perfunctory, and that the substantial motive behind them was the politic wish of the socialists to conciliate the unionists, and make use of the unions for the propaganda. The early expressions of sympathy with the unionist cause were made for an ulterior purpose. Later on, in the nineties, there comes a change in the attitude of the socialist leaders toward the unions.

economic development. The Marxist theory of progressive misery and
degradation has, accordingly, fallen into the background, and a large proportion of the Marxists have already come to see the whole question of
working-class deterioration in some such apologetic light as is shed upon
it by Goldscheid in his Verelendungs oder Meliorationstheorie. It is now
not an unusual thing for orthodox Marxists to hold that the improvement
of the conditions of the working classes is a necessary condition to the
advance of the socialistic cause, and that the unionist efforts at amelioration must be furthered as a means toward the socialistic consummation. It
is recognized that the socialistic revolution must be carried through not by
an anaemic working class under the pressure of abject privation, but by a
body of fullblooded workingmen gradually gaining strength from improved conditions of life. Instead of the revolution being worked out by
the leverage of desperate misery, every improvement in working-class
conditions is to be counted as a gain for the revolutionary forces. This is a
good Darwinism, but it does not belong in the neo-Hegelian Marxism.

Perhaps the sorest experience of the Marxist doctrinaires has been with
the agricultural population. Notoriously, the people of the open country
have not taken kindly to socialism. No propaganda and no changes in the
economic situation have won the sympathy of the peasant farmers for the
socialistic revolution. Notoriously, too, the large-scale industry has not
invaded the agricultural field, or expropriated the small proprietors, in
anything like the degree expected by the Marxist doctrinaires of a generation ago. It is contained in the theoretical system of Marx that, as modern
industrial and business methods gain ground, the small proprietor farmers will be reduced to the ranks of the wage-proletariat, and that, as this
process of conversion goes on, in the course of time the class interest of
the agricultural population will throw them into the movement side by
side with the other wage-workmen.[36] .

But at this point the facts have hitherto not come out in consonance
with the Marxist theory. And the efforts of the Social Democrats to convert
the peasant population to socialism have been practically unrewarded. So
it has come about that the political leaders and the keepers of the doctrines have, tardily and reluctantly, come to see the facts of the agrarian
situation in a new light, and to give a new phrasing to the articles of Marxian theory that touch on the fortunes of the peasant farmer. It is no longer
held that either the small properties of the peasant farmer must be ab-
sorbed into larger properties, and then taken over by the State, or that they
must be taken over by the State directly, when the socialistic revolution is
established. On the contrary, it is now coming to be held that the peasant
proprietors will not be disturbed in their holdings by the great change. The
great change is to deal with capitalistic enterprise, and the peasant farming is not properly "capitalistic." It is a system of production in which the

---

[36] Cf. Capital, vol. i. ch. xiii., sect. 10.

producer normally gets only the product of his own labor. Indeed, under the current regime of markets and credit relations, the small agricultural producer, it is held, gets less than the product of his own labor, since the capitalistic business enterprises with which he has to deal are always able to take advantage of him. So it has become part of the overt doctrine of socialists that as regards the peasant farmer it will be the consistent aim of the movement to secure him in the untroubled enjoyment of his holding, and free him from the vexatious exactions of his creditors and the ruinous business traffic in which he is now perforce involved. According to the revised code, made possible by recourse to Darwinian concepts of evolution instead of the Hegelian three-phase dialectic, therefore, and contrary to the earlier prognostications of Marx, it is no longer held that agricultural industry must go thru the capitalistic mill, and it is hoped that under the revised code it may be possible to enlist the interest and sympathy of this obstinately conservative element for the revolutionary cause. The change in the official socialist position on the agricultural question has come about only lately, and is scarcely yet complete, and there is no knowing what degree of success it may meet with either as a matter of party tactics or as a feature of the socialistic theory of economic development. All discussions of party policy, and of theory so far as bears on policy, take up the question; and nearly all authoritative spokesmen of socialism have modified their views in the course of time on this point.

The socialism of Karl Marx is characteristically inclined to peaceable measures and disinclined to a coercive government and belligerent politics. It is, or at least it was, strongly averse to international jealousy and patriotic animosity, and has taken a stand against armaments, wars, and dynastic aggrandizement. At the time of the French-Prussian war the official organization of Marxism, the International, went so far in its advocacy of peace as to urge the soldiery on both sides to refuse to fight. After the campaign had warmed the blood of the two nations, this advocacy of peace made the International odious in the eyes of both French and Germans. War begets patriotism, and the socialists fell under the reproach of not being sufficiently patriotic. After the conclusion of the war, the Socialistic Workingmen's Party of Germany sinned against the German patriotic sentiment in a similar way and with similarly grave results. Since the foundation of the empire and of the Social-Democratic party, the socialists and their doctrines have passed thru a further experience of a similar kind, but on a larger scale and more protracted. The government has gradually strengthened its autocratic position at home, increased its warlike equipment, and enlarged its pretensions in international politics, until what would have seemed absurdly impossible a generation ago is now submitted to by the German people, not only with a good grace, but with enthusiasm. During all this time that part of the population that has adhered to the socialist ideals has also grown gradually more patriotic and more loyal, and the leaders and keepers of socialist opinion have shared in the growth of chauvinism with the rest of the German people. But at no time have the socialists been able to keep abreast of the general upward movement in this respect. They have not attained the pitch of reckless loyalty that animates the conservative German patriots, although it is probably safe to say that the Social Democrats of to-day are as good and headlong patriots as the conservative Germans were a generation ago. During all this period of the new era of German political life the socialists have been freely accused of disloyalty to the national ambition, of placing their international aspirations above the ambition of imperial aggrandizement.

The socialist spokesmen have been continually on the defensive. They set out with a round opposition to any considerable military establishment, and have more and more apologetically continued to oppose any "undue" extension of the warlike establishments and the warlike policy. But with the passage of time and the habituation to warlike politics and military discipline, the infection of jingoism has gradually permeated the body of Social Democrats, until they have now reached such a pitch of enthusiastic loyalty as they would not patiently hear a truthful characterization of. The spokesmen now are concerned to show that, while they still stand for international socialism, consonant with their ancient position, they stand for national aggrandizement first and for international comity second. The relative importance of the national and the international ideals in German socialist professions has been reversed since the seventies.[37] .The leaders are busy with interpretation of their earlier formulations. They have come to excite themselves over nebulous distinctions between patriotism and jingoism. The Social Democrats have come to be German patriots first and socialists second, which comes to saving that they are a political party working for the maintenance of the existing order, with modifications. They are no longer a party of revolution, but of reform, tho the measure of reform which they demand greatly exceeds the Hohenzollern limit of tolerance. They are now as much, if not more, in touch with the ideas of English liberalism than with those of revolutionary Marxism.

The material and tactical exigencies that have grown out of changes in the industrial system and in the political situation, then, have brought on far-reaching changes of adaptation in the position of the socialists. The change may not be extremely large at any one point, so far as regards the specific articles of the program, but, taken as a whole, the resulting modification of the socialistic position is a very substantial one. The process of change is, of course, not yet completed, - whether or not it ever will be, but it is already evident that what is taking place is not so much a change in amount or degree of conviction on certain given points as a change in kind, - a change in the current socialistic habit of mind.

The factional discrepancies of theory that have occupied the socialists of Germany for some years past are evidence that the conclusion, even a provisional conclusion, of the shifting of their standpoint has not been reached. It is even hazardous to guess which way the drift is setting. It is

---

[37] Cf. Kautsky, Erfurter Programm, ch. v., sect. 13; Bernstein, Voraussetzungen, ch. iv., sect. e.

only evident that the past standpoint, the standpoint of neo-Hegelian Marxism, cannot be regained, - it is a forgotten standpoint. For the immediate present the drift of sentiment, at least among the educated, seems to set toward a position resembling that of the National Socials and the Rev. Mr. Naumann; that is to say, imperialistic liberalism. Should the conditions, political, social, and economic, which to-day are chiefly effective in shaping the habits of thought among the German people, continue substantially unchanged and continue to be the chief determining causes, it need surprise no one to find German socialism gradually changing into a somewhat characterless imperialistic democracy. The imperial policy seems in a fair way to get the better of revolutionary socialism, not by repressing it, but by force of the discipline in imperialistic ways of thinking to which it subjects all classes of the population. How far a similar process of sterilization is under way, or is likely to overtake the socialist movement in other countries, is an obscure question to which the German object-lesson affords no certain answer.

Chapter 3

The Engineers and the Price System

I. On the Nature and Uses of Sabotage

Sabotage is a derivative of "sabot," which is French for a wooden shoe. It means going slow, with a dragging, clumsy movement, such as that manner of footgear may be expected to bring on. So it has come to describe any manoeuvre of slowing-down, inefficiency, bungling, obstruction. In American usage the word is very often taken to mean forcible obstruction, destructive tactics, industrial frightfulness, incendiarism and high explosives, although that is plainly not its first meaning nor its common meaning. Nor is that its ordinary meaning as the word is used among those who have advocated a recourse to sabotage as a means of enforcing an argument about wages or the conditions of work. The ordinary meaning of the word is better defined by an expression which has latterly come into use among the I. W.W., "conscientious withdrawal of efficiency"—although that phrase does not cover all that is rightly to be included under this technical term. The sinister meaning which is often attached to the word in American usage, as denoting violence and disorder, appears to be due to the fact that the American usage has been shaped chiefly by persons and newspapers who have aimed to discredit the use of sabotage by organized workmen, and who have therefore laid stress on its less amiable manifestations. This is unfortunate. It lessens the usefulness of the word by making it a means of denunciation rather than of understanding. No doubt violent obstruction has had its share in the strategy of sabotage as carried on by disaffected workmen, as well as in the similar tactics of rival business concerns. It comes into the case as one method of sabotage, though by no means the most usual or the most effective; but it is so spectacular and shocking a method that it has drawn undue attention to itself. Yet such deliberate violence is, no doubt, a relatively minor fact in the case, as compared with that deliberate malingering, confusion, and misdirection of work that makes up the bulk of what the expert practitioners would recognize as legitimate sabotage. The word first came into use among the organized French workmen, the members of certain syndicates, to describe their tactics of passive resistance, and it has continued to be associated with the strategy of these French workmen, who are known as syndicalists, and with their like-minded running-mates in other countries. But the tactics of these syndicalists, and their use of sabotage, do not differ, except in detail, from the tactics of other workmen elsewhere, or from the similar tactics of friction, obstruction, and delay habitually employed, from time to time, by both employees and employers to enforce an argument about wages and prices. Therefore, in the course of a quarter-century past, the word has quite unavoidably taken on a general meaning in common speech, and has been extended to cover all such peaceable or surreptitious manoeuvres of delay, obstruction, friction, and defeat, whether employed by the workmen to enforce their claims, or by the employers to defeat their employees, or by competitive business concerns to get the better of their business rivals or to secure their own advantage. Such manoeuvres of restriction, delay, and hindrance have a large share in the ordinary conduct of business; but it is only lately that this ordinary line of business strategy has come to be recognized as being substantially of the same nature as the ordinary tactics of the syndicalists.

So that it has not been usual until the last few years to speak of manoeuvres of this kind as sabotage when they are employed by employers and their business concerns. But all this strategy of delay, restriction, hindrance, and defeat is manifestly of the same character, and should conveniently be called by the same name, whether it is carried on by business men or by workmen; so that it is no longer unusual now to find workmen speaking of "capitalistic sabotage" as freely as the employers and the newspapers speak of syndicalist sabotage. As the word is now used, and as it is properly used, it describes a certain system of industrial strategy or management, whether it is employed by one or another. What it describes is a resort to peaceable or surreptitious restriction, delay, withdrawal, or obstruction.

Sabotage commonly works within the law, although it may often be within the letter rather than the spirit of the law. It is used to secure some special advantage or preference, usually of a businesslike sort. It commonly has to do with something in the nature of a vested right, which one or another of the parties in the case aims to secure or defend, or to defeat or diminish; some preferential right or special advantage in respect of income or privilege, something in the way of a vested interest. Workmen have resorted to such measures to secure improved conditions of work, or increased wages, or shorter hours, or to maintain their habitual standards, to all of which they have claimed to have some sort of a vested right. Any strike is of the nature of sabotage, of course. Indeed, a strike is a typical species of sabotage. That strikes have not been spoken of as sabotage is due to the accidental fact that strikes were in use before this word came into use. So also, of course, a lockout is another typical species of sabotage. That the lockout is employed by the employers against the employees does not change the fact that it is a means of defending a vested right by delay, withdrawal, defeat, and obstruction of the work to be done. Lockouts have not usually been spoken of as sabotage, for the same reason that holds true in the case of strikes. All the while it has been recognized that strikes and lockouts are of identically the same character. All this does not imply that there is anything discreditable or immoral about this habitual use of strikes and lockouts. They are part of the ordinary conduct of industry under the existing system, and necessarily so. So long as the system remains unchanged these measures are a necessary and legitimate part of it.

By virtue of his ownership the owner-employer has a vested right to do as he will with his own property, to deal or not to deal with any person that offers, to withhold or withdraw any part or all of his industrial equipment and natural resources from active use for the time being, to run on half time or to shut down his plant and to lockout all those persons for whom he has no present use on his own premises. There is no question that the lockout is altogether a legitimate manoeuvre. It may even be meritorious, and it is frequently considered to be meritorious when its use helps to maintain sound conditions in business - that is to say profitable conditions as frequently happens. Such is the view of the substantial citizens. So also is the strike legitimate, so long as it keeps within the law; and it may at times even be meritorious, at least in the eyes of the strikers. It is to be admitted quite broadly that both of these typical species of sabotage are altogether fair and honest in principle, although it does not therefore follow that every strike or every lockout is necessarily fair and honest in its working-out. That is in some degree a question of special circumstances. Sabotage, accordingly, is not to be condemned out of hand, simply as such.

There are many measures of policy and management both in private business and in public administration which are unmistakably of the nature of sabotage and which are not only considered to be excusable, but are deliberately sanctioned by statute and common law and by the public conscience. Many such measures are quite of the essence of the case under the established system of law and order, price and business, and are faithfully believed to be indispensable to the common good. It should not be difficult to show that the common welfare in any community which is organized on the price system cannot be maintained without a salutary use of sabotage—that it to say, such habitual recourse to delay and obstruction of industry and such restriction of output as will maintain prices at a reasonably profitable level and so guard against business depression. Indeed, it is precisely considerations of this nature that are now engaging the best attention of officials and business men in their endeavors to tide over a threatening depression in American business and a consequent season of hardship for all those persons whose main dependence is free income from investments.

Without some salutary restraint in the way of sabotage on the productive use of the available industrial plant and workmen, it is altogether unlikely that prices could be maintained at a reasonably profitable figure for any appreciable time. A businesslike control of the rate and volume of output is indispensable for keeping up a profitable market, and a profitable market is the first and unremitting condition of prosperity in any community whose industry is owned and managed by business men. And the ways and means of this necessary control of the output of industry are always and necessarily something in the nature of sabotage—something in the way of retardation, restriction, withdrawal, unemployment of plant and workmen—whereby production is kept short of productive capacity. The mechanical industry of the new order is inordinately productive. So the rate and volume of output have to be regulated with a view to what the traffic will bear—that is to say, what will yield the largest net return in terms of price to the business men who manage the country's industrial system. Otherwise there will be "overproduction," business depression, and consequent hard times all around. Overproduction means production in excess of what the market will carry off at a sufficiently profitable price. So it appears that the continued prosperity of the country from day to day hangs on a "conscientious withdrawal of efficiency" by the business men who control the country's industrial output. They control it all for their own use, of course, and their own use means always a profitable price. In any community that is organized on the price system, with investment and business enterprise, habitual unemployment of the available indus- trial plant and workmen, in whole or in part, appears to be the indispen- sable condition without which tolerable conditions of life cannot be main- tained. That is to say, in no such community can the industrial system be allowed to work at full capacity for any appreciable interval of time, on pain of business stagnation and consequent privation for all classes and conditions of men.

The requirements of profitable business will not tolerate it. So the rate and volume of output must be adjusted to the needs of the market, not to the working capacity of the available resources, equipment and man pow- er, nor to the community's need of consumable goods. Therefore there must always be a certain variable margin of unemployment of plant and man power. Rate and volume of output can, of course, not be adjusted by exceeding the productive capacity of the industrial system. So it has to be regulated by keeping short of maximum production by more or less as the condition of the market may require. It is always a question of more or less unemployment of plant and man power, and a shrewd moderation in the unemployment of these available resources, a "conscientious withdrawal of efficiency," therefore, is the beginning of wisdom in all sound workday business enterprise that has to do with industry. All this is matter of course, and notorious. But it is not a topic on which one prefers to dwell. Writers and speakers who dilate on the meritorious exploits of the nation's business men will not commonly allude to this voluminous running ad- ministration of sabotage, this conscientious withdrawal of efficiency, that goes into their ordinary day's work. One prefers to dwell on those excep- tional, sporadic, and spectacular episodes in business where business men have now and again successfully gone out of the safe and sane high- way of conservative business enterprise that is hedged about with a con- scientious withdrawal of efficiency, and have endeavored to regulate the output by increasing the productive capacity of the industrial system at one point or another.

But after all, such habitual recourse to peaceable or surreptitious measures of restraint, delay, and obstruction in the ordinary businesslike management of industry is too widely known and too well approved to call for much exposition or illustration. Yet, as one capital illustration of the scope and force of such businesslike withdrawal of efficiency, it may be in place to recall that all the civilized nations are just now undergoing an experiment in businesslike sabotage on an unexampled scale and carried out with unexampled effrontery. All these nations that have come through the war, whether as belligerents or as neutrals, have come into a state of more or less pronounced distress, due to a scarcity of the common neces- saries of life; and this distress falls, of course, chiefly on the common sort, who have at the same time borne the chief burden of the war which has brought them to this state of distress. The common man has won the war and lost his livelihood.

This need not be said by way of praise or blame. As it stands it is, broadly, an objective statement of fact, which may need some slight qualification, such as broad statements of fact will commonly need. All these nations that have come through the war, and more particularly the common run of their populations, are very much in need of all sorts of supplies for daily use, both for immediate consumption and for productive use. So much so that the prevailing state of distress rises in many places to an altogether unwholesome pitch of privation, for want of the necessary food, clothing, shelter, and fuel. Yet in all these countries the staple industries are slowing down. There is an ever increasing withdrawal of efficiency. The industrial plant is increasingly running idle or half idle, running increasingly short of its productive capacity. Workmen are being laid off and an increasing number of those workmen who have been serving in the armies are going idle for want of work, at the same time that the troops which are no longer needed in the service are being demobilized as slowly as popular sentiment will tolerate, apparently for fear that the number of unemployed workmen in the country may presently increase to such proportions as to bring on a catastrophe. And all the while all these peoples are in great need of all sorts of goods and services which these idle plants and idle workmen are fit to produce. But for reasons of business expediency it is impossible to let these idle plants and idle workmen go to work—that is to say for reasons of insufficient profit to the business men interested, or in other words, for the reasons of insufficient income to the vested interests which control the staple industries and so regulate the output of product. The traffic will not bear so large a production of goods as the community needs for current consumption, because it is considered doubtful whether so large a supply could be sold at prices that would yield a reasonable profit on the investment—or rather on the capitalization; that is to say, it is considered doubtful whether an increased production, such as to employ more workmen and supply the goods needed by the community, would result in an increased net aggregate income for the vested interests which control these industries. A reasonable profit always means, in effect, the largest obtainable profit. All this is simple and obvious, and it should scarcely need explicit statement. It is for these business men to manage the country's industry, of course, and therefore to regulate the rate and volume of output; and also of course any regulation of the output by them will be made with a view to the needs of business; that is to say, with a view to the largest obtainable net profit, not with a view to the physical needs of these peoples who have come through the war and have made the world safe for the business of the vested interests.

Should the business men in charge, by any chance aberration, stray from this straight and narrow path of business integrity, and allow the community's needs unduly to influence their management of the community's industry, they would presently find themselves discredited and would probably face insolvency. Their only salvation is a conscientious with-

drawal of efficiency. All this lies in the nature of the case. It is the working
of the price system, whose creatures and agents these business men are.
Their case is rather pathetic, as indeed they admit quite volubly. They are
not in a position to manage with a free hand, the reason being that they
have in the past, under the routine requirements of the price system as it
takes effect in corporation finance, taken on so large an overhead burden
of fixed charges that any appreciable decrease in the net earnings of the
business will bring any well-managed concern of this class face to face
with bankruptcy. At the present conjuncture, brought on by the war and
its termination, the case stands somewhat in this typical shape. In the recent past earnings have been large; these large earnings (free income)
have been capitalized; their capitalized value has been added to the corporate capital and covered with securities bearing a fixed income-charge;
this income-charge, representing free income, has thereby become a liability on the earnings of the corporation; this liability cannot be met in
case the concern's net aggregate earnings fall off in any degree; therefore
prices must be kept up to such a figure as will bring the largest net aggregate return, and the only means of keeping up prices is a conscientious
withdrawal of efficiency in these staple industries on which the community depends for a supply of the necessaries of life. The business community
has hopes of tiding things over by this means, but it is still a point in doubt
whether the present unexampled large use of sabotage in the businesslike
management of the staple industries will now suffice to bring the business
community through this grave crisis without a disastrous shrinkage of its
capitalization, and a consequent liquidation; but the point is not in doubt
that the physical salvation of these peoples who have come through the
war must in any case wait on the pecuniary salvation of these owners of
corporate securities which represent free income. It is a sufficiently difficult passage. It appears that production must be curtailed in the staple
industries, on pain of unprofitable prices. The case is not so desperate in
those industries which have immediately to do with the production of
superfluities; but even these, which depend chiefly on the custom of those
kept classes to whom the free income goes, are not feeling altogether secure. For the good of business it is necessary to curtail production of the
means of life, on pain of unprofitable prices, at the same time that the increasing need of all sorts of the necessaries of life must be met in some
passable fashion, on pain of such popular disturbances as will always
come of popular distress when it passes the limit of tolerance. Those wise
business men who are charged with administering the salutary modicum
of sabotage at this grave juncture may conceivably be faced with a dubious choice between a distasteful curtailment of the free income that goes
to the vested interests, on the one hand, and an unmanageable onset of
popular discontent on the other hand. And in either alternative lies disaster. Present indications would seem to say that their choice will fall out
according to ancient habit, that they will be likely to hold fast by an undiminished free income for the vested interests at the possible cost of any
popular discontent that may be in prospect—and then, with the help of
the courts and the military arm, presently make reasonable terms with any
popular discontent that may arise. In which event it should all occasion no

surprise or resentment, inasmuch as it would be nothing unusual or irreg-
ular and would presumably be the most expeditious way of reaching a
modus vivendi. During the past few weeks, too, quite an unusually large
number of machine guns have been sold to industrial business concerns
of the larger sort, here and there, at least so they say. Business enterprise
being the palladium of the Republic, it is right to take any necessary
measures for its safeguarding. Price is of the essence of the case, whereas
livelihood is not.

The grave emergency that has arisen out of the war and its provisional
conclusion is, after all, nothing exceptional except in magnitude and se-
verity. In substance it is the same sort of thing that goes on continually but
unobtrusively and as a matter of course in ordinary times of business as
usual. It is only that the extremity of the case is calling attention to itself.
At the same time it serves impressively to enforce the broad proposition
that a conscientious withdrawal of efficiency is the beginning of wisdom
in all established business enterprise that has to do with industrial production. But it has been found that this grave interest which the vested
interests always have in a salutary retardation of industry at one point or
another cannot well be left altogether to the haphazard and ill-
coordinated efforts of individual business concerns, each taking care of its
own particular line of sabotage within its own premises. The needed sabotage can best be administered on a comprehensive plan and by a central
authority, since the country's industry is of the nature of a comprehensive
interlocking system, whereas the business concerns which are called on to
control the motions of this industrial system will necessarily work piecemeal, in severalty and at cross-purposes. In effect, their working at cross-
purposes results in a sufficiently large aggregate retardation of industry, of
course, but the resulting retardation is necessarily somewhat blindly ap-
portioned and does not converge to a neat and perspicuous outcome.
Even a reasonable amount of collusion among the interested business
concerns will not by itself suffice to carry on that comprehensive moving
equilibrium of sabotage that is required to preserve the business community from recurrent collapse or stagnation, or to bring the nation's traffic
into line with the general needs of the vested interests.

Where the national government is charged with the general care of the
country's business interests, as is invariably the case among the civilized
nations, it follows from the nature of the case that the nation's lawgivers
and administration will have some share in administering that necessary
modicum of sabotage that must always go into the day's work of carrying
on industry by business methods and for business purposes. The government is in a position to penalize excessive or unwholesome traffic. So, it is
always considered necessary, or at least expedient, by all sound mercantilists, as by a tariff or by subsidies, to impose and maintain a certain balance
or proportion among the several branches of industry and trade that go to
make up the nation's industrial system. The purpose commonly urged for
measures of this class is the fuller utilization of the nation's industrial resources in material, equipment, and man power; the invariable effect is a
lowered efficiency and a wasteful use of these resources, together with an

increase of international jealousy. But measures of that kind are thought to be expedient by the mercantilists for these purposes—that is to say, by the statesmen of these civilized nations, for the purposes of the vested interests. The chief and nearly the sole means of maintaining such a fabricated balance and proportion among the nation's industries is to obstruct the traffic at some critical point by prohibiting or penalizing any exuberant undesirables among these branches of industry. Disallowance, in whole or in part, is the usual and standard method. The great standing illustration of sabotage administered by the government is the protective tariff, of course. It protects certain special interests by obstructing competition from beyond the frontier. This is the main use of a national boundary. The effect of the tariff is to keep the supply of goods down and thereby keep the price up, and so to bring reasonably satisfactory dividends to those special interests which deal in the protected articles of trade, at the cost of the underlying community. A protective tariff is a (typical conspiracy in restraint of trade. It brings a relatively small, though absolutely large, run or free income to the special interests which benefit by it, at a relatively, and absolutely, large cost to the underlying community, and so it gives rise to a body of vested rights and intangible assets belonging to these special interests. Of a similar character, in so far that in effect they are in the nature of sabotage—conscientious withdrawal of efficiency—are all manner of excise and revenue-stamp regulations; although they are not always designed for that purpose. Such would be, for instance, the partial or complete prohibition of alcoholic beverages, the regulation of the trade in tobacco, opium, and other deleterious narcotics, drugs, poisons, and high explosives. Of the same nature, in effect if not in intention, are such regulations as the oleomargarine law; as also the unnecessarily costly and vexatious routine of inspection imposed on the production of industrial (denatured) alcohol, which has inured to the benefit of certain business concerns that are interested in other fuels for use in internal-combustion engines; so also the singularly vexatious and elaborately imbecile specifications that limit and discourage the use of the parcel post, for the benefit of the express companies and other carriers which have a vested interest in traffic of that kind. It is worth noting in the same connection, although it comes in from the other side of the case, that ever since the express companies have been taken over by the federal administration there has visibly gone into effect a comprehensive system of vexation and delay in the detail conduct of their traffic, so contrived as to discredit federal control of this traffic and thereby provoke a popular sentiment in favor of its early return to private control.

Much the same state of things has been in evidence in the railway traffic under similar conditions. Sabotage is serviceable as a deterrent, whether in furtherance of the administration's work or in contravention of it. In what has just been said there is, of course, no intention to find fault with any of these uses of sabotage. It is not a question of morals and good intentions. It is always to be presumed as a matter of course that the guiding spirit in all such governmental moves to regularize the nation's affairs, whether by restraint or by incitement, is a wise solicitude for the nation's enduring gain and security. All that can be said here is that many of these wise measures of restraint and incitement are in the nature of sabotage, and that in effect they habitually, though not invariably, inure to the benefit of certain vested interests—ordinarily vested interests which bulk large in the ownership and control of the nation's resources. That these measures are quite legitimate and presumably salutary, therefore, goes without saying. In effect they are measures for hindering traffic and industry at one point or another, which may often be a wise business precaution.

During the period of the war administrative measures in the nature of sabotage have been greatly extended in scope and kind. Peculiar and imperative exigencies have had to be met, and the staple means of meeting many of these new and exceptional exigencies has quite reasonably been something in the way of avoidance, disallowance, penalization, hindrance, a conscientious withdrawal of efficiency from work that does not fall in with the purposes of the Administration. Very much as is true in private business when a situation of doubt and hazard presents itself, so also in the business of government at the present juncture of exacting demands and inconvenient limitations, the Administration has been driven to expedients of disallowance and obstruction with regard to some of the ordinary processes of life, as, for instance, in the non-Essential industries. It has also appeared that the ordinary equipment and agencies for gathering and distributing news and other information have in the past developed a capacity far in excess of what can safely be permitted in time of war or of returning peace. The like is true for the ordinary facilities for public discussion of all sorts of public questions. The ordinary facilities, which may have seemed scant enough in time of peace and slack interest, had after all developed a capacity far beyond what the governmental traffic will bear in these uneasy times of war and negotiations, when men are very much on the alert to know what is going on. By a moderate use of the later improvements in the technology of transport and communication, the ordinary means of disseminating information and opinions have grown so efficient that the traffic can no longer be allowed to run at full capacity during a period of stress in the business of government.

Even the mail service has proved insufferably efficient, and a selective withdrawal of efficiency has gone into effect. To speak after the analogy of private business, it has been found best to disallow such use of the mail facilities as does not inure to the benefit of the Administration in the way of good will and vested rights of usufruct. These peremptory measures of disallowance have attracted a wide and dubious attention; but they have doubtless been of a salutary nature and intention, in some way which is not to be understood by outsiders - that is to say, by citizens of the Republic. An unguarded dissemination of information and opinions or an unduly frank canvassing of the relevant facts by these outsiders, will be a handicap on the Administration's work, and may even defeat the Administration's aims. At least so they say. Something of much the same color has been observed elsewhere and in other times, so that all this nervously alert resort to sabotage on undesirable information and opinions is nothing novel, nor is it peculiarly democratic. The elder statesmen of the great monarchies, east and west, have long seen and approved the like. But these elder statesmen of the dynastic regime have gone to their work of sabotage on information because of a palpable division of sentiment between their government and the underlying population, such as does not exist in the advanced democratic commonwealths. The case of Imperial Germany during the period of the war is believed to show such a division of sentiment between the government and the underlying population, and also to show how such a divided sentiment on the part of a distrustful and distrusted population had best be dealt with. The method approved by German dynastic experience is sabotage, of a somewhat free-swung character, censorship, embargo on communication, and also, it is confidently alleged, elaborate misinformation. Such procedure on the part of the dynastic statesmen of the Empire is comprehensible even to a layman. But how it all stands with those advanced democratic nations, like America, where the government is the dispassionately faithful agent and spokesman of the body of citizens, and where there can consequently be no division of aims and sentiment between the body of officials and any underlying population—all that is a more obscure and hazardous subject of speculation. Yet there has been censorship, somewhat rigorous, and there has been selective refusal of mail facilities, somewhat arbitrary, in these democratic commonwealths also, and not least in America, freely acknowledged to be the most naively democratic of them all. And all the while one would like to believe that it all has somehow served some useful end. It is all sufficiently perplexing.

II. The Industrial System and the Captains of Industry

It has been usual, and indeed it still is not unusual, to speak of three co-ordinate "factors of production": land, labor, and capital. The reason for this threefold scheme of factors in production is that there have been three recognized classes of income: rent, wages, and profits; and it has been assumed that whatever yields an income is a productive factor. This scheme has come down from the eighteenth century. It is presumed to have been true, in a general way, under the conditions which prevailed in the eighteenth century, and it has therefore also been assumed that it should continue to be natural, or normal, true in some eminent sense, under any other conditions that have come on since that time.

Seen in the light of later events this threefold plan of coordinate factors in production is notable for what it omits. It assigns no productive effect to the industrial arts, for example, for the conclusive reason that the state of the industrial arts yields no stated or ratable income to any one class of persons; it affords no legal claim to a share in the community's yearly production of goods. The state of the industrial art is a joint stock of knowledge derived from past experience, and is held and passed on as an indivisible possession of the community at large. It is the indispensable foundation of all productive industry, of course, but except for certain minute fragments covered by patent rights or trade secrets, this joint stock is no man's individual property. For this reason it has not been counted in as a factor in production. The unexampled advance of technology during the past one hundred and fifty years has now begun to call attention to its omission from the threefold plan of productive factors handed down from that earlier time.

Another omission from the scheme of factors, as it was originally drawn, was the business man. But in the course of the nineteenth century the business man came more and more obtrusively to the front and came in for a more and more generous portion of the country's yearly income— which was taken to argue that he also contributed increasingly to the yearly production of goods. So a fourth factor of production has provisionally been added to the threefold scheme, in the person of the "entrepreneur," whose wages of management are considered to measure his creative share in the production of goods, although there still is some question as to the precise part of the entrepreneur in productive industry.

"Entrepreneur" is a technical term to designate the man who takes care of the financial end of things. It covers the same fact as the more familiar "business man," but with a vague suggestion of big business rather than small. The typical entrepreneur is the corporation financier. And since the corporation financier has habitually come in for a very substantial share of the community's yearly income he has also been conceived to render a very substantial service to the community as a creative force in that productive industry out of which the yearly income arises. Indeed, it is nearly true that in current usage "producer" has come to mean "financial manager," both in the standard economic theory and in everyday speech. There need of course be no quarrel with all this. It is a matter of usage. During the era of the machine industry—which is also the era of the commercial democracy—business men have controlled production and have managed the industry of the commonwealth for their own ends, so that the material fortunes of all the civilized peoples have continued to turn on the financial management of their business men. And during the same period not only have the conditions of life among these civilized peoples continued to be fairly tolerable on the whole, but it is also true that the industrial system which these business men have been managing for their own private gain all this time has continually been growing more efficient on the whole. Its productive capacity per unit of equipment and man power has continually grown larger.

For this very creditable outcome due credit should be, as indeed it has been, given to the business community which has had the oversight of things. The efficient enlargement of industrial capacity has, of course, been due to a continued advance in technology, to a continued increase of the available natural resources, and to a continued increase of population. But the business community have also had a part in bringing all this to pass; they have always been in a position to hinder this growth, and it is only by their consent and advice that things have been enabled to go forward so far as they have gone. This sustained advance in productive capacity, due to the continued advance in technology and in population, has also had another notable consequence. According to the Liberal principles of the eighteenth century any legally defensible receipt of income is a sure sign of productive work done. Seen in the light of this assumption, the visibly increasing productive capacity of the industrial system has enabled all men of a liberal and commercial mind not only to credit the business-like captains of industry with having created this productive capacity, but also to overlook all that the same captains of industry have been doing in the ordinary course of business to hold productive industry in check. And it happens that all this time things have been moving in such a direction and have now gone so far that it is today quite an open question whether the businesslike management of the captains is not more occupied with checking industry than with increasing its productive capacity.

This captain of industry, typified by the corporation financier, and latter-ly by the investment banker, is one of the institutions that go to make up the new order of things, which has been coming on among all the civilized peoples ever since the Industrial Revolution set in. As such, as an institu-tional growth, his life history hitherto should be worth looking into for any one who proposes to understand the recent growth and present drift of this new economic order. The beginnings of the captain of industry are to be seen at their best among those enterprising Englishmen who made it their work to carry the industrial promise of the Revolution out into tangi-ble performance, during the closing decades of the eighteenth and the early decades of the nineteenth century. These captains of the early time are likely to be rated as inventors, at least in a loose sense of the word. But it is more to the point that they were designers and builders of factory, mill, and mine equipment, of engines, processes, machines, and machine tools, as well as shop managers, at the same time that they took care, more or less effectually, of the financial end. Nowhere do these beginnings of the captain of industry stand out so convincingly as among the English tool-builders of that early time, who designed, tried out, built, and marketed that series of indispensable machine tools that has made the practical foundation of the mechanical industry. Something to much the same ef-fect is due to be said for the pioneering work of the Americans along the same general lines of mechanical design and performance at a slightly later period. To men of this class the new industrial order owes much of its early success as well as of its later growth.

These men were captains of industry, entrepreneurs, in some such sim-ple and comprehensive sense of the word as that which the economists appear to have had in mind for a hundred years after, when they have spo-ken of the wages of management that are due the entrepreneur for pro-ductive work done. They were a cross between a business man and an in-dustrial expert, and the industrial expert appears to have been the more valuable half in their composition. But factory, mine, and ship owners, as well as merchants and bankers, also made up a vital part of that business community out of whose later growth and specialization the corporation financier of the nineteenth and twentieth centuries has arisen. His origins are both technological and commercial, and in that early phase of his life history which has been taken over into the traditions of economic theory and of common sense he carried on both of these lines of interest and of work in combination. That was before the large scale, the wide sweep, and the profound specialization of the advanced mechanical industry had gathered headway. But progressively the cares of business management grew larger and more exacting, as the scale of things in business grew larger, and so the directive head of any such business concern came progressively to give his attention more and more exclusively to the financial end. At the same time and driven by the same considerations the businesslike management of industry has progressively been shifting to the footing of corporation finance. This has brought on a further division, dividing the ownership of the industrial equipment and resources from their management. But also at the same time the industrial system, on its technological side, has been progressively growing greater and going farther in scope diversity, specialization, and complexity, as well as in productive capacity per unit of equipment and man power.

The last named item of change, the progressive increase of productive capacity, is peculiarly significant in this connection. Through the earlier and pioneering decades of the machine era it appears to have been passably true that the ordinary routine of management in industrial business was taken up with reaching out for new ways and means and speeding up production to maximum capacity. That was before standardization of processes and of unit products and fabrication of parts had been carried far, and therefore before quantity production had taken on anything like its later range and reach. And, partly because of that fact—because quantity production was then still a slight matter and greatly circumscribed, as contrasted with its later growth —the ordinary volume of output in the mechanical industries was still relatively slight and manageable. Therefore those concerns that were engaged in these industries still had a fairly open market for whatever they might turn out, a market capable of taking up any reasonable increase of output. Exceptions to this general rule occurred; as, e.g., in textiles. But the general rule stands out obtrusively through the early decades of the nineteenth century so far as regards English industry, and even more obviously in the case of America.

Such an open market meant a fair chance for competitive production, without too much risk of overstocking. And running to the same effect, there was the continued increase of population and the continually increasing reach and volume of the means of transport, serving to maintain a free market for any prospective increase of output, at prices which offered a fair prospect of continued profit. In the degree in which this condition of things prevailed a reasonably free competitive production would be practicable.

The industrial situation so outlined began visibly to give way toward the middle of the nineteenth century in England, and at a correspondingly later period in America. The productive capacity of the mechanical industry was visibly overtaking the capacity of the market, so that free competition without afterthought was no longer a sound footing on which to manage production. Loosely, this critical or transitional period falls in and about the second quarter of the nineteenth century in England; elsewhere at a correspondingly later date.

Of course the critical point, when business exigencies began to dictate a policy of combination and restriction, did not come at the same date in all or in most of the mechanical industries; but it seems possible to say that, by and large, the period of transition to a general rule of restriction in industry conies on at the time and for the reason so indicated. There were also other factors engaged in that industrial situation, besides those spoken of above, less notable and less sharply defined, but enforcing limitations of the same character.

Such were, e.g., a rapidly gaining obsolescence of industrial plant, due to improvements and extensions, as also the partial exhaustion of the labor supply by persistent overwork, under-feeding, and unsanitary conditions—but this applies to the English case rather than elsewhere. In point of time this critical period in the affairs of industrial business coincides roughly with the coming in of corporation finance as the ordinary and typical method of controlling the industrial output. Of course the corporation, or company, has other uses besides the restrictive control of the output with a view to a profitable market, but it should be sufficiently obvious that the combination of ownership and centralization of control which the corporation brings about is also exceedingly convenient for that purpose. And when it appears that the general resort to corporate organization of the larger sort sets in about the time when business exigencies begin to dictate an imperative restriction of output, it is not easy to avoid the conclusion that this was one of the ends to be served by this reorganization of business enterprise. Business enterprise may fairly be said to have shifted from the footing of free-swung competitive production to that of a "conscientious withholding of efficiency," so soon and so far as corporation finance on a sufficiently large scale had come to be the controlling factor in industry.

At the same time and in the same degree the discretionary control of industry, and of other business enterprise in great part, has passed into the hands of the corporation financier. Corporate organization has continually gone forward to a larger scale and a more comprehensive coalition of forces, and at the same time, and more and more visibly, it has become the ordinary duty of the corporate management to adjust production to the requirements of the market by restricting the output to what the traffic will bear; that is to say, what will yield the largest net earnings. Under corporate management it rarely happens that production is pushed to the limit of capacity. It happens, and can happen, only rarely and intermittently. This has been true, increasingly, ever since the ordinary productive capacity of the mechanical industries seriously began to overtake and promised to exceed what the market would carry off at a reasonably profitable price. And ever since that critical turn in the affairs of industrial business—somewhere in the middle half of the nineteenth century—it has become increasingly imperative to use a wise moderation and stop down the output to such a rate and volume as the traffic will bear. The cares of business have required an increasingly undivided attention on the part of the business men, and in an ever increasing measure their day's work has come to center about a running adjustment of sabotage on production. And for this purpose, evidently, the corporate organization of this business, on an increasingly large scale, is very serviceable, since the requisite sabotage on productive industry can be effectually administered only on a large plan and with a firm hand.

"The leaders in business are men who have studied and thought all their lives. They have thus learned to decide big problems at once, basing their decisions upon their knowledge of fundamental principles." - Jeremiah W. Jenks.

That is to say, the surveillance of this financial end of industrial business, and the control of the requisite running balance of sabotage, have been reduced to a routine governed by settled principles of procedure and administered by suitably trained experts in corporation finance. But under the limitations to which all human capacity is subject it follows from this increasingly exacting discipline of business administration that the business men are increasingly out of touch with that manner of thinking and those elements of knowledge that go to make up the logic and the relevant facts of the mechanical technology. Addiction to a strict and unremitting valuation of all things in terms of price and profit leaves them, by settled habit, unfit to appreciate those technological facts and values that can be formulated only in terms of tangible mechanical performance; increasingly so with every further move into a stricter addiction to businesslike management and with every further advance of the industrial system into a still wider scope and a still more diversified and more delicately balanced give and take among its interlocking members. They are experts in prices and profits and financial manoeuvres; and yet the final discretion in all questions of industrial policy continues to rest in their hands. They are by training and interest captains of finance; and yet, with no competent grasp of the industrial arts, they continue to exercise a plenary discretion as captains of industry.

They are unremittingly engaged in a routine of acquisition, in which they habitually reach their ends by a shrewd restriction of output; and yet they continue to be entrusted with the community's industrial welfare, which calls for maximum production.

Such has been the situation in all the civilized countries since corporation finance has ruled industry, and until a recent date. Quite recently this settled scheme of business management has shown signs of giving way, and a new move in the organization of business enterprise has come in sight, whereby the discretionary control of industrial production is shifting still farther over to the side of finance and still farther out of touch with the requirements of maximum production. The new move is of a twofold character: (a) the financial captains of industry have been proving their industrial incompetence in a progressively convincing fashion, and (b) their own proper work of financial management has progressively taken on a character of standardized routine such as no longer calls for or admits any large measure of discretion or initiative. They have been losing touch with the management of industrial processes, at the same time that the management of corporate business has, in effect, been shifting into the hands of a bureaucratic clerical staff. The corporation financier of popular tradition is taking on the character of a chief of bureau. The changes which have brought the corporation financier to this somewhat inglorious position of a routine administrator set in along with the early growth of corporation finance, somewhere around the middle of the nineteenth century, and they have come to a head somewhere about the passage to the twentieth century, although it is only since the latter date that the outcome is becoming at all clearly defined. When corporate organization and the consequent control of output came into bearing there were two lines of policy open to the management: (a) to maintain profitable prices by limiting the output, and (b) to maintain profits by lowering the production cost of an increased output. To some extent both of these lines were followed, but on the whole the former proved the more attractive; it involved less risk, and it required less acquaintance with the working processes of industry. At least it appears that in effect the preference was increasingly given to the former method during this half-century of financial management. For this there were good reasons. The processes of production were continually growing more extensive, diversified, complicated, and more difficult for any layman in technology to comprehend—and the corporation financier was such a layman, necessarily and increasingly so, for reasons indicated above.

At the same time, owing to a continued increase of population and a continued extension of the industrial system, the net product of industry and its net earnings continued to increase independently of any creative effort on the part of the financial management. So the corporation financier, as a class, came in for an "unearned increment" of income, on the simple plan of "sitting tight." That plan is intelligible to any layman. All industrial innovation and all aggressive economy in the conduct of industry not only presumes an insight into the technological details of the industrial process, but to any other than the technological experts, who know the facts intimately, any move of that kind will appear hazardous. So the business men who have controlled industry, being laymen in all that concerns its management, have increasingly been content to let well enough alone and to get along with an ever increasing overhead charge of inefficiency, so long as they have lost nothing by it. The result has been an ever increasing volume of waste and misdirection in the use of equipment, resources, and man power throughout the industrial system. In time, that is to say within the last few years, the resulting lag, leak, and friction in the ordinary working of this mechanical industry under business management have reached such proportions that no ordinarily intelligent outsider can help seeing them wherever he may look into the facts of the case. But it is the industrial experts, not the business men, who have finally begun to criticize this businesslike mismanagement and neglect of the ways and means of industry. And hitherto their efforts and advice have met with no cordial response from the business men in charge, who have, on the whole, continued to let well enough alone—that is to say, what is well enough for a short-sighted business policy looking to private gain, however poorly it may serve the material needs of the community. But in the meantime two things have been happening which have deranged the regime of the corporation financier: industrial experts, engineers, chemists, mineralogists, technicians of all kinds, have been drifting into more responsible positions in the industrial system and have been growing up and multiplying within the system, because the system will no longer work at all without them; and on the other hand, the large financial interests on whose support the corporation financiers have been leaning have gradually come to realize that corporation finance can best be managed as a comprehensive bureaucratic routine, and that the two pillars of the house of corporate business enterprise of the larger sort are the industrial experts and the large financial concerns that control the necessary funds; whereas the corporation financier is little more than a dubious intermediate term between these two.

One of the greater personages in American business finance took note of this situation in the late nineties and set about turning it to account for the benefit of himself and his business associates, and from that period dates a new era in American corporation finance. It was for a time spoken of loosely as the Era of Trust-Making, but that phrase does not describe it at all adequately. It should rather be called the Era of the Investment Banker, and it has come to its present stage of maturity and stability only in the course of the past quarter-century. The characteristic features and the guiding purpose of this improved method in corporation finance are best shown by a showing of the methods and achievements of that great pioneer by whom it was inaugurated. As an illustrative case, then, the American steel business in the nineties was suffering from the continued use of out-of-date processes, equipment, and locations, from wasteful management under the control of stubbornly ignorant corporation officials, and particularly from intermittent haphazard competition and mutual sabotage between the numerous concerns which were then doing business in steel. It appears to have been the last-named difficulty that particularly claimed the attention and supplied the opportunity of the great pioneer. He can by no stretch of charity be assumed to have had even a slight acquaintance with the technological needs and shortcomings of the steel industry. But to a man of commercial vision and financial sobriety it was plain that a more comprehensive, and therefore more authoritative, organization and control of the steel business would readily obviate much of the competition which was deranging prices. The apparent purpose and the evident effect of the new and larger coalition of business interests in steel was to maintain profitable prices by a reasonable curtailment of production. A secondary and less evident effect was a more economical management of the industry, which involved some displacement of quondam corporation financiers and some introduction of industrial experts. A further, but unavowed, end to be served by the same move in each of the many enterprises in coalition undertaken by the great pioneer and by his competitors was a bonus that came to these enterprising men in the shape of an increased capitalization of the business. But the notable feature of it all as seen from the point of view of the public at large was always the stabilization of prices at a reasonably high level, such as would always assure reasonably large earnings on the increased capitalization.

Since then this manner of corporation finance has been further perfected and standardized, until it will now hold true that no large move in the field of corporation finance can be made without the advice and consent of those large funded interests that are in a position to act as investment bankers; nor does any large enterprise in corporation business ever escape from the continued control of the investment bankers in any of its larger transactions; nor can any corporate enterprise of the larger sort now continue to do business except on terms which will yield something appreciable in the way of income to the investment bankers, whose continued support is necessary to its success. The financial interest here spoken of as the investment banker is commonly something in the way of a more or less articulate syndicate of financial houses, and it is to be added that the same financial concerns are also commonly, if not invariably, engaged or interested in commercial banking of the usual kind. So that the same well-established, half-syndicated ramification of banking houses that have been taking care of the country's commercial banking, with its center of credit and of control at the country's financial metropolis, is ready from beforehand to take over and administer the country's corporation finance on a unified plan and with a view to an equitable distribution of the country's net earnings among themselves and their clients. The more inclusive this financial organization is, of course, the more able it will be to manage the country's industrial system as an inclusive whole and prevent any hazardous innovation or experiment, as well as to limit production of the necessaries to such a volume of output as will yield the largest net return to itself and its clients.

Evidently the improved plan which has thrown the discretion and responsibility into the hands of the investment banker should make for a safe and sound conduct of business, such as will avoid fluctuations of price, and more particularly avoid any unprofitable speeding-up of productive industry. Evidently, too, the initiative has hereby passed out of the hands of the corporation financier, who has fallen into the position of a financial middleman or agent, with limited discretion and with a precariously doubtful future. But all human institutions are susceptible of improvement, and the course of improvement may now and again, as in his case, result in supersession and displacement. And doubtless it is all for the best, that is to say, for the good of business, more particularly for the profit of big business. But now as always corporation finance is a traffic in credit; indeed, now more than ever before. Therefore to stabilize corporate business sufficiently in the hands of this inclusive quasi-syndicate of banking interests it is necessary that the credit system of the country should as a whole be administered on a unified plan and inclusively. All of which is taken care of by the same conjunction of circumstances; the same quasi-syndicate of banking interests that makes use of the country's credit in the way of corporation finance is also the guardian of the country's credit at large. From which it results that, as regards those large-scale credit extensions which are of substantial consequence, the credits and debits

are, in effect, pooled within the syndicate, so that no substantial derangement of the credit situation can take effect except by the free choice of this
quasi-syndicate of investment banking houses; that is to say, not except
they see an advantage to themselves in allowing the credit situation to be
deranged, and not beyond the point which will best serve their collective
purpose as against the rest of the community. With such a closed system
no extension of credit obligations or multiplication of corporate securities,
with the resulting inflation of values, need bring any risk of a liquidation,
since credits and debits are in effect pooled within the system. By way of
parenthesis it may also be remarked that under these circumstances
"credit" has no particular meaning except as a method of accounting.
Credit is also one of the timeworn institutions that are due to suffer obsolescence by improvement. This process of pooling and syndication that is
remaking the world of credit and corporation finance has been greatly
helped on in America by the establishment of the Federal Reserve system,
while somewhat similar results have been achieved elsewhere by somewhat similar devices. That system has greatly helped to extend, facilitate,
simplify, and consolidate the unified control of the country's credit arrangements, and it has very conveniently left the substantial control in the
hands of those larger financial interests into whose hands the lines of control in credit and industrial business were already being gathered by force
of circumstances and by sagacious management of the interested parties.
By this means the substantial core of the country's credit system is gathered into a self-balanced whole, closed and unbreakable, self-insured
against all risk and derangement. All of which converges to the definitive
stabilization of the country's business; but since it reduces financial traffic
to a riskless routine it also converges to the conceivable obsolescence of
corporation finance and eventually, perhaps, of the investment banker.

III. The Captains of Finance and the Engineers

In more than one respect the industrial system of today is notably different from anything that has gone before. It is eminently a system, self-
balanced and comprehensive; and it is a system of interlocking mechanical processes, rather than of skilful manipulation. It is mechanical rather
than manual. It is an organization of mechanical powers and material resources, rather than of skilled craftsmen and tools; although the skilled
workmen and tools are also an indispensable part of its comprehensive
mechanism. It is of an impersonal nature, after the fashion of the material
sciences, on which it constantly draws. It runs to "quantity production" of
specialized and standardized goods and services. For all these reasons it
lends itself to systematic control under the direction of industrial experts,
skilled technologists, who may be called "production engineers," for want
of a better term.

This industrial system runs on as an inclusive organization of many and
diverse interlocking mechanical processes, interdependent and balanced
among themselves in such a way that the due working of any part of it is

conditioned on the due working of all the rest. Therefore it will work at its best only on condition that these industrial experts, production engineers, will work together on a common understanding; and more particularly on condition that they must not work at cross purposes. These technological specialists whose constant supervision is indispensable to the due working of the industrial system constitute the general staff of industry, whose work it is to control the strategy of production at large and to keep an oversight of the tactics of production in detail. Such is the nature of this industrial system on whose due working depends the material welfare of all the civilized peoples. It is an inclusive system drawn on a plan of strict and comprehensive interdependence, such that, in point of material welfare, no nation and no community has anything to gain at the cost of any other nation or community. In point of material welfare, all the civilized peoples have been drawn together by the state of the industrial arts into a single going concern. And for the due working of this inclusive going concern it is essential that that corps of technological specialists who by training, insight, and interest make up the general staff of industry must have a free hand in the disposal of its available resources, in materials, equipment, and man power, regardless of any national pretensions or any vested interests. Any degree of obstruction, diversion, or withholding of any of the available industrial forces, with a view to the special gain of any nation or any investor, unavoidably brings on a dislocation of the system; which involves a disproportionate lowering of its working efficiency and therefore a disproportionate loss to the whole, and therefore a net loss to all its parts. And all the while the statesmen are at work to divert and obstruct the working forces of this industrial system, here and there, for the special advantage of one nation and another at the cost of the rest; and the captains of finance are working, at cross purposes and in collusion, to divert whatever they can to the special gain of one vested interest and another, at any cost to the rest. So it happens that the industrial system is deliberately handicapped with dissension, misdirection, and unemployment of material resources, equipment, and man power, at every turn where the statesmen or the captains of finance can touch its mechanism; and all the civilized peoples are suffering privation together because their general staff of industrial experts are in this way required to take orders and submit to sabotage at the hands of the statesmen and the vested interests. Politics and investment are still allowed to decide matters of industrial policy which should plainly be left to the discretion of the general staff of production engineers driven by no commercial bias. No doubt this characterization of the industrial system and its besetting tribulations will seem overdrawn.

However, it is not intended to apply to any date earlier than the twentieth century, or to any backward community that still lies outside the sweep of the mechanical industry. Only gradually during the past century, while the mechanical industry has progressively been taking over the production of goods and services, and going over to quantity production, has the industrial system taken on this character of an inclusive organization of interlocking processes and interchange of materials; and it is only in the twentieth century that this cumulative progression has come to a head with such effect that this characterization is now visibly becoming true. And even now it will hold true, visibly and securely, only as applies to the leading mechanical industries, those main lines of industry that shape the main conditions of life, and in which quantity production has become the common and indispensable rule. Such are, e.g., transport and communication; the production and industrial use of coal, oil, electricity and water power; the production of steel and other metals; of wood pulp, lumber, cement and other building materials; of textiles and rubber; as

The Captains of Finance and the Engineers also grain-milling and much of the grain-growing, together with meat-packing and a good share of the stock-raising industry. There is, of course, a large volume of industry in many lines which has not, or only in part and doubtfully, been drawn into this network of mechanical processes and quantity production, in any direct and conclusive fashion. But these other lines of industry that still stand over on another and older plan of operation are, after all, outliers and subsidiaries of the mechanically organized industrial system, dependent on or subservient to those greater underlying industries which make up the working body of the system, and which therefore set the pace for the rest. And in the main, therefore, and as regards these greater mechanical industries on whose due working the material welfare of the community depends from day to day, this characterization will apply without material abatement. But it should be added that even as regards these greater, primary and underlying, lines of production the system has not yet reached a fatal degree of close-knit interdependence, balance, and complication; it will still run along at a very tolerable efficiency in the face of a very appreciable amount of persistent derangement. That is to say, the industrial system at large has not yet become so delicately balanced a mechanical structure and process that the ordinary amount of derangement and sabotage necessary to the ordinary control of production by business methods will paralyze the whole outright. The industrial system is not yet sufficiently close-knit for that. And yet, that extent and degree of paralysis from which the civilized world's industry is suffering just now, due to legitimate businesslike sabotage, goes to argue that the date may not be far distant when the interlocking processes of the industrial system shall have become so closely interdependent and so delicately balanced that even the ordinary modicum of sabotage involved in the conduct of business as usual will bring the whole to a fatal collapse. The derangement and privation brought on by any well-organized strike of the larger sort argues to the same effect. In effect, the progressive advance of this industrial system towards an all-inclusive mechanical balance of interlocking processes appears to be approaching a critical pass, beyond which it will no longer be practicable to leave its control in the hands of business men working at cross purposes for private gain, or to entrust its continued administration to others than suitably trained technological experts, production engineers without a commercial interest. What these men may then do with it all is not so plain; the best they can do may not be good enough; but the negative proposition is becoming sufficiently plain, that this mechanical state of the industrial arts will not long tolerate the continued control of production by the vested interests under the current businesslike rule of incapacity by advisement. In the beginning, that is to say during the early growth of the machine industry, and particularly in that new growth of mechanical industries which arose directly out of the Industrial Revolution, there was no marked division between the industrial experts and the business managers. That was before the new industrial system had gone far on the road of progressive specialization and complexity, and before business had reached an exactingly large scale; so that even the business men of that time, who were without special training in technological matters, would still be able to exercise something of an intelligent oversight of the whole, and to understand something of what was required in the mechanical conduct of the work which they financed and from which they drew their income. Not unusually the designers of industrial processes and equipment would then still take care of the financial end, at the same time that they managed the shop. But from an early point in the development there set in a progressive differentiation, such as to divide those who designed and administered the industrial processes from those others who designed and managed the commercial transactions and took care of the financial end. So there also set in a corresponding division of powers between the business management and the technological experts. It became the work of the technologist to determine, on technological grounds, what could be done in the way of productive industry, and to contrive ways and means of doing it; but the business management always continued to decide, on commercial grounds, how much work should be done and what kind and quality of goods and services should be produced; and the decision of the business management has always continued to be final, and has always set the limit beyond which production must not go. With the continued growth of specialization the experts have necessarily had more and more to say in the affairs of industry; but always their findings as to what work is to be done and what ways and means are to be employed in production have had to wait on the findings of the business managers as to what will be expedient for the purpose of commercial gain. This division between business management and industrial management has continued to go forward, at a continually accelerated rate, because the special training and experience required for any passably efficient organization and direction of these industrial processes has continually grown more exacting, calling for special knowledge and abilities on the part of those who have this work to do and requiring their undivided interest and their undivided attention to the work in hand. But these specialists in technological knowledge, abilities, interest, and experience, who have increasingly come into the case in this way— inventors, designers, chemists, mineralogists, soil experts, crop specialists, production managers and engineers of many kinds and denominations —have continued to be employees of the captains of industry, that is to say, of the captains of finance, whose work it has been to commercialize the knowledge and abilities of the industrial experts and turn them to account for their own gain.

It is perhaps unnecessary to add the axiomatic corollary that the captains have always turned the technologists and their knowledge to account in this way only so far as would serve their own commercial profit, not to the extent of their ability; or to the limit set by the material circumstances; or by the needs of the community. The result has been, uniformly and as a matter of course, that the production of goods and services has advisedly been stopped short of productive capacity, by curtailment of output and by derangement of the productive system. There are two main reasons for this, and both have operated together throughout the machine era to stop industrial production increasingly short of productive capacity, (a) The commercial need of maintaining a profitable price has led to an increasingly imperative curtailment of the output, as fast as the advance of the industrial arts has enhanced the productive capacity. And (b) the continued advance of the mechanical technology has called for an ever-increasing volume and diversity of special knowledge, and so has left the businesslike captains of finance continually farther in arrears, so that they have been less and less capable of comprehending what is required in the ordinary way of industrial equipment and personnel. They have therefore, in effect, maintained prices at a profitable level by curtailment of output rather than by lowering production cost per unit of output, because they have not had such a working acquaintance with the technological facts in the case as would enable them to form a passably sound judgment of suitable ways and means for lowering production cost; and at the same time, being shrewd business men, they have been unable to rely on the hired-man's loyalty of technologists whom they do not understand. The result has been a somewhat distrustful blindfold choice of processes and personnel and a consequent enforced incompetence in the management of industry, a curtailment of output below the needs of the community, below the productive capacity of the industrial system, and below what an intelligent control of production would have made commercially profitable. Through the earlier decades of the machine era these limitations imposed on the work of the experts by the demands of profitable business and by the technical ignorance of the business men, appears not to have been a heavy handicap, whether as a hindrance to the continued development of technological knowledge or as an obstacle to its ordinary use in industry. That was before the mechanical industry had gone far in scope, complexity, and specialization; and it was also before the continued work of the technologists had pushed the industrial system to so high a productive capacity that it is forever in danger of turning out a larger product than is required for a profitable business. But gradually, with the passage of time and the advance of the industrial arts to a wider scope and a larger scale, and to an increasing specialization and standardization of processes, the technological knowledge that makes up the state of the industrial arts has called for a higher degree of that training that makes industrial specialists; and at the same time any passably efficient management of industry has of necessity drawn on them and their special abilities to an ever-increasing extent.

At the same time and by the same shift of circumstances, the captains of finance, driven by an increasingly close application to the affairs of business, have been going farther out of touch with the ordinary realities of productive industry; and, it is to be admitted, they have also continued increasingly to distrust the technological specialists, whom they do not understand, but whom they can also not get along without. The captains have per force continued to employ the technologists, to make money for them, but they have done so only reluctantly, tardily, sparingly, and with a shrewd circumspection; only because and so far as they have been persuaded that the use of these technologists was indispensable to the making of money. One outcome of this persistent and pervasive tardiness and circumspection on the part of the captains has been an incredibly and increasingly uneconomical use of material resources, and an incredibly wasteful organization of equipment and man power in those great industries where the technological advance has been most marked. In good part it was this discreditable pass, to which the leading industries had been brought by these one-eyed captains of industry, that brought the regime of the captains to an inglorious close, by shifting the initiative and discretion in this domain out of their hands into those of the investment bankers. By custom the investment bankers had occupied a position between or overlapping the duties of a broker in corporate securities and those of an underwriter of corporate flotations—such a position, in effect, as is still assigned them in the standard writings on corporation finance. The increasingly large scale of corporate enterprise, as well as the growth of a mutual understanding among these business concerns, also had its share in this new move. But about this time, too, the "consulting engineers" were coming notably into evidence in many of those lines of industry in which corporation finance has habitually been concerned.

So far as concerns the present argument the ordinary duties of these consulting engineers have been to advise the investment bankers as to the industrial and commercial soundness, past and prospective, of any enterprise that is to be underwritten. These duties have comprised a painstaking and impartial examination of the physical properties involved in any given case, as well as an equally impartial auditing of the accounts and appraisal of the commercial promise of such enterprises, for the guidance of the bankers or syndicate of bankers interested in the case as underwriters. On this ground working arrangements and a mutual understanding presently arose between the consulting engineers and those banking houses that habitually were concerned in the underwriting of corporate enterprises.

The effect of this move has been twofold: experience has brought out the fact that corporation finance, at its best and soundest, has now become a matter of comprehensive and standardized bureaucratic routine, necessarily comprising the mutual relations between various corporate concerns, and best to be taken care of by a clerical staff of trained accountants; and the same experience has put the financial houses in direct touch with the technological general staff of the industrial system, whose surveillance has become increasingly imperative to the conduct of any profitable enterprise in industry. But also, by the same token, it has appeared that the corporation financier of nineteenth-century tradition is no longer of the essence of the case in corporation finance of the larger and more responsible sort. He has, in effect, come to be no better than an idle wheel in the economic mechanism, serving only to take up some of the lubricant.

Since and so far as this shift out of the nineteenth century into the twentieth has been completed, the corporation financier has ceased to be a captain of industry and has become a lieutenant of finance; the captaincy having been taken over by the syndicated investment bankers and administered as a standardized routine of accountancy, having to do with the flotation of corporation securities and with their fluctuating values, and having also something to do with regulating the rate and volume of output in those industrial enterprises which so have passed under the hand of the investment bankers. By and large, such is the situation of the industrial system today, and of that financial business that controls the industrial system. But this state of things is not so much an accomplished fact handed on out of the recent past; it is only that such is the culmination in which it all heads up in the immediate present, and that such is the visible drift of things into the calculable future.

Only during the last few years has the state of affairs in industry been obviously falling into the shape so outlined, and it is even yet only in those larger and pace-making lines of industry which are altogether of the new technological order that the state of things has reached this finished shape. But in these larger and underlying divisions of the industrial system the present posture and drift of things is unmistakable. Meantime very much still stands over out of that regime of rule-of-thumb, competitive sabotage, and commercial logrolling, in which the businesslike captains of the old order are so altogether well at home, and which has been the best that the captains have known how to contrive for the management of that industrial system whose captains they have been. So that wherever the production experts are now taking over the management, out of the dead hand of the self? made captains, and wherever they have occasions to inquire into the established conditions of production, they find the ground cumbered with all sorts of incredible makeshifts of waste and inefficiency— such makeshifts as would perhaps pass muster with any moderately stupid elderly layman, but which look like blindfold guesswork to these men who know something of the advanced technology and its working-out. Hitherto, then, the growth and conduct of this industrial system presents this singular outcome.

The technology—the state of the industrial arts— which takes effect in this mechanical industry is in an eminent sense a joint stock of knowledge and experience held in common by the civilized peoples. It requires the use of trained and instructed workmen—born, bred, trained, and instructed at the cost of the people at large. So also it requires, with a continually more exacting insistence, a corps of highly trained and specially gifted experts, of divers and various kinds. These, too, are born, bred, and trained at the cost of the community at large, and they draw their requisite special knowledge from the community's joint stock of accumulated experience. These expert men, technologists, engineers, or whatever name may best suit them, make up the indispensable General Staff of the industrial system; and without their immediate and unremitting guidance and correction the industrial system will not work. It is a mechanically organized structure of technical processes designed, installed, and conducted by these production engineers.

Without them and their constant attention the industrial equipment, the mechanical appliances of industry, will foot up to just so much junk. The material welfare of the community is unreservedly bound up with the due working of this industrial system, and therefore with its unreserved control by the engineers, who alone are competent to manage it. To do their work as it should be done these men of the industrial general staff must have a free hand, unhampered by commercial considerations and reservations; for the production of the goods and services needed by the community they neither need nor are they in any degree benefited by any supervision or interference from the side of the owners. Yet the absentee owners, now represented, in effect, by the syndicated investment bankers, continue to control the industrial experts and limit their discretion, arbitrarily, for their own commercial gain, regardless of the needs of the community. Hitherto these men who so make up the general staff of the industrial system have not drawn together into anything like a self-directing working force; nor have they been vested with anything more than an occasional, haphazard, and tentative control of some disjointed sector of the industrial equipment, with no direct or decisive relation to that personnel of productive industry that may be called the officers of the line and the rank and file. It is still the unbroken privilege of the financial management and its financial agents to "hire and fire." The final disposition of all the industrial forces still remains in the hands of the business men, who still continue to dispose of these forces for other than industrial ends. And all the while it is an open secret that with a reasonably free hand the production experts would today readily increase the ordinary output of industry by several fold,—variously estimated at some 300 per cent, to 1200 per cent, of the current output. And what stands in the way of so increasing the ordinary output of goods and services is business as usual.

Right lately these technologists have begun to become uneasily "class-conscious" and to reflect that they together constitute the indispensable General Staff of the industrial system. Their class consciousness has taken the immediate form of a growing sense of waste and confusion in the management of industry by the financial agents of the absentee owners. They are beginning to take stock of that all-pervading mismanagement of industry that is inseparable from its control for commercial ends. All of which brings home a realization of their own shame and of damage to the common good. So the engineers are beginning to draw together and ask themselves, "What about it?"

This uneasy movement among the technologists set in, in an undefined and fortuitous way, in the closing years of the nineteenth century; when the consulting engineers, and then presently the "efficiency engineers," began to make scattered corrections in detail, which showed up the industrial incompetence of those elderly laymen who were doing a conservative business at the cost of industry. The consulting engineers of the standard type, both then and since then, are commercialized technologists, whose work it is to appraise the industrial value of any given enterprise with a view to its commercial exploitation. They are a cross between a technological specialist and a commercial agent, beset with the limitations of both and commonly not fully competent in either line. Their normal position is that of an employee of the investment bankers, on a stipend or a retainer, and it has ordinarily been their fortune to shift over in time from a technological footing to a frankly commercial one. The case of the efficiency engineers, or scientific-management experts, is somewhat similar. They too have set out to appraise, exhibit, and correct the commercial shortcomings of the ordinary management of those industrial establishments which they investigate, to persuade the business men in charge how they may reasonably come in for larger net earnings by a more closely shorn exploitation of the industrial forces at their disposal. During the opening years of the new century a lively interest centered on the views and expositions of these two groups of industrial experts; and not least was the interest aroused by their exhibits of current facts indicating an all-pervading lag, leak, and friction in the industrial system, due to its disjointed and one-eyed management by commercial adventurers bent on private gain. During these few years of the opening century the members of this informal guild of engineers at large have been taking an interest in this question of habitual mismanagement by ignorance and commercial sabotage, even apart from the commercial imbecility of it all. But it is the young rather than the old among them who see industry in any other light than its commercial value. Circumstances have decided that the older generation of the craft have become pretty well commercialized. Their habitual outlook has been shaped by a long and unbroken apprenticeship to the corporation financiers and the investment bankers; so that they still habitually see the industrial system as a contrivance for the roundabout process of making money. Accordingly, the established official Associations and Institutes of Engineers, which are officered and engineered by the elder engineers, old and young, also continue to show the commercial bias of their creators, in what they criticize and in what they propose. But the new generation which has been coming on during the present century are not similarly true to that tradition of commercial engineering that makes the technological man an awestruck lieutenant of the captain of finance. By training, and perhaps also by native bent, the technologists find it easy and convincing to size up men and things in terms of tangible performance, without commercial afterthought, except so far as their apprenticeship to the captains of finance may have made commercial afterthought a second nature to them. Many of the younger generation are beginning to understand that engineering begins and ends in the domain of tangible performance, and that commercial expediency is another matter. Indeed, they are beginning to understand that commercial expediency has nothing better to contribute to the engineer's work than so much lag, leak, and friction. The four years' experience of the war has also been highly instructive on that head.

So they are beginning to draw together on a common ground of understanding, as men who are concerned with the ways and means of tangible performance in the way of productive industry, according to the state of the industrial arts as they know them at their best; and there is a growing conviction among them that they together constitute the sufficient and indispensable general staff of the mechanical industries, on whose unhindered team-work depends the due working of the industrial system and therefore also the material welfare of the civilized peoples. So also, to these men who are trained in the stubborn logic of technology, nothing is quite real that cannot be stated in terms of tangible performance; and they are accordingly coming to understand that the whole fabric of credit and corporation finance is a tissue of make-believe.

Credit obligations and financial transactions rest on certain principles of legal formality which have been handed down from the eighteenth century, and which therefore antedate the mechanical industry and carry no secure conviction to men trained in the logic of that industry. Within this technological system of tangible performance corporation finance and all its works and gestures are completely idle; it all comes into the working scheme of the engineers only as a gratuitous intrusion which could be barred out without deranging the work at any point, provided only that men made up their mind to that effect—that is to say, provided the make-believe of absentee ownership were discontinued. Its only obvious effect on the work which the engineers have to take care of is waste of materials and retardation of the work. So the next question which the engineers are due to ask regarding this timeworn fabric of ownership, finance, sabotage, credit, and unearned income is likely to be: Why cumbers it the ground? And they are likely to find the scriptural answer ready to their hand. It would be hazardous to surmise how, how soon, on what provocation, and with what effect the guild of engineers are due to realize that they constitute a guild, and that the material fortunes of the civilized peoples already lie loose in their hands. But it is already sufficiently plain that the industrial conditions and the drift of conviction among the engineers are drawing together to some such end. Hitherto it has been usual to count on the interested negotiations continually carried on and never concluded between capital and labor, between the agents of the investors and the body of workmen, to bring about whatever readjustments are to be looked for in the control of productive industry and in the distribution and use of its product. These negotiations have necessarily been, and continue to be, in the nature of business transactions, bargaining for a price, since both parties to the negotiation continue to stand on the consecrated ground of ownership, free bargain, and self-help; such as the commercial wisdom of the eighteenth century saw, approved and certified it all, in the time before the coming of this perplexing industrial system.

In the course of these endless negotiations between the owners and their workmen there has been some loose and provisional syndication of claims and forces on both sides; so that each of these two recognized parties to the industrial controversy has come to make up a loosely knit vested inter-est, and each speaks for its own special claims as a party in interest. Each is contending for some special gain for itself and trying to drive a profita-ble bargain for itself, and hitherto no disinterested spokesman for the community at large or for the industrial system as a going concern has seriously cut into this controversy between these contending vested inter-ests. The outcome has been businesslike concession and compromise, in the nature of bargain and sale.

It is true, during the war, and for the conduct of the war, there were some half- concerted measures taken by the Administration in the interest of the nation at large, as a belligerent; but it has always been tacitly agreed that these were extraordinary war measures, not to be countenanced in time of peace. In time of peace the accepted rule is still business as usual; that is to say, investors and workmen wrangling together on a footing of business as usual. These negotiations have necessarily been inconclusive. So long as ownership of resources and industrial plant is allowed, or so long as it is allowed any degree of control or consideration in the conduct of industry, nothing more substantial can come of any readjustment than a concessive mitigation of the owners' interference with production. There is accord-ingly nothing subversive in these bouts of bargaining between the federat-ed workmen and the syndicated owners. It is a game of chance and skill played between two contending vested interests for private gain, in which the industrial system as a going concern enters only as a victim of inter-ested interference. Yet the material welfare of the community, and not least of the workmen, turns on the due working of this industrial system, without interference. Concessive mitigation of the right to interfere with production, on the part of either one of these vested interests, can evi-dently come to nothing more substantial than a concessive mitigation.

But owing to the peculiar technological character of this industrial sys-tem, with its specialized, standardized, mechanical, and highly technical interlocking processes of production, there has gradually come into being this corps of technological production specialists, into whose keeping the due functioning of the industrial system has now drifted by force of cir-cumstance. They are, by force of circumstance, the keepers of the com-munity's material welfare; although they have hitherto been acting, in effect, as keepers and providers of free income for the kept classes. They are thrown into the position of responsible directors of the industrial sys-tem, and by the same move they are in a position to become arbiters of the community's material welfare. They are becoming class-conscious, and they are no longer driven by a commercial interest, in any such degree as will make them a vested interest in that commercial sense in which the syndicated owners and the federated workmen are vested interests. They are, at the same time, numerically and by habitual outlook, no such heter-ogeneous and unwieldy body as the federated workmen, whose numbers and scattering interest has left all their endeavors substantially nugatory. In short, the engineers are in a position to make the next move. By com-parison with the population at large, including the financial powers and the kept classes, the technological specialists which come in question here are a very inconsiderable number; yet this small number is indispensable to the continued working of the productive industries. So slight are their numbers, and so sharply defined and homogeneous is their class, that a sufficiently compact and inclusive organization of their forces should arrange itself almost as a matter of course, so soon as any appreciable proportion of them shall be moved by any common purpose. And the common purpose is not far to seek, in the all-pervading industrial confusion, obstruction, waste, and retardation which business as usual continually throws in their face. At the same time they are the leaders of the industrial personnel, the workmen, of the officers of the line and the rank and file; and these are coming into a frame of mind to follow their leaders in any adventure that holds a promise of advancing the common good.

To these men, soberly trained in a spirit of tangible performance and endowed with something more than an even share of the sense of workman-ship, and endowed also with the common heritage of partiality for the rule of Live and Let Live, the disallowance of an outworn and obstructive right of absentee ownership is not likely to seem a shocking infraction of the sacred realties. That customary right of ownership by virtue of which the vested interests continue to control the industrial system for the benefit of the kept classes, belongs to an older order of things than the mechanical industry. It has come out of a past that was made up of small things and traditional make-believe. For all the purposes of that scheme of tangible performance that goes to make up the technologist's world, it is without form and void. So that, given time for due irritation, it should by no means come as a surprise if the guild of engineers are provoked to put their heads together and, quite out of hand, disallow that large absentee ownership that goes to make the vested interests and to unmake the industrial system. And there stand behind them the massed and rough-handed legions of the industrial rank and file, ill at ease and looking for new things. The older commercialized generation among them would, of course, ask themselves: Why should we worry? What do we stand to gain? But the younger generation, not so hard? Bitten by commercial experience, will be quite as likely to ask themselves: What do we stand to lose? And there is the patent fact that such a thing as a general strike of the technological specialists in industry need involve no more than a minute fraction of one per cent, of the population; yet it would swiftly bring a collapse of the old order and sweep the timeworn fabric of finance and absentee sabotage into the discard for good and all, Such a catastrophe would doubtless be deplorable. It would look something like the end of the world to all those persons who take their stand with the kept classes, but it may come to seem no more than an incident of the day's work to the engineers and to the rough-handed legions of the rank and file. It is a situation which may well be deplored. But there is no gain in losing patience with a conjunction of circumstances. And it can do no harm to take stock of the situation and recognize that, by force of circumstance, it is now open to the Council of Technological Workers' and Soldiers' Deputies to make the next move, in their own way and in their own good time.

When and what this move will be, if any, or even what it will be like, is not something on which a layman can hold a confident opinion. But so much seems clear, that the industrial dictatorship of the captain of finance is now held on sufferance of the engineers and is liable at any time to be discontinued at their discretion, as a matter of convenience.

IV. On the Danger of a Revolutionary Overturn

Bolshevism is a menace to the vested rights of property and privilege. Therefore the Guardians of the Vested Interests have been thrown into a state of Red trepidation by the continued functioning of Soviet Russia and the continual outbreaks of the same Red distemper elsewhere on the continent of Europe. It is feared, with a nerve-shattering fear, that the same Red distemper of Bolshevism must presently infect the underlying population in America and bring on an overturn of the established order, so soon as the underlying population are in a position to take stock of the situation and make up their mind to a course of action. The situation is an uneasy one, and it contains the elements of much trouble; at least such appears to be the conviction of the Guardians of the established order. Something of the kind is felt to be due, on the grounds of the accomplished facts. So it is feared, with a nerve-shattering fear, that anything like uncolored information as to the facts in the case and anything like a free popular discussion of these facts must logically result in disaster. Hence all this unseemly trepidation. The Guardians of the Vested Interests, official and quasi-official, have allowed their own knowledge of this sinister state of things to unseat their common sense. The run of the facts has jostled them out of the ruts, and they have gone in for a headlong policy of clamor and repression, to cover and suppress matters of fact and to shut off discussion and deliberation. And all the while the Guardians are also feverishly at work on a mobilization of such forces as may hopefully be counted on to "keep the situation in hand" in case the expected should happen. The one manifestly conclusive resolution to which the Guardians of the Vested Interests have come is that the underlying population is to be "kept in hand," in the face of any contingency. Their one settled principle of conduct appears to be, to stick at nothing; in all of which, doubtless, the Guardians mean well. Now, the Guardians of the Vested Interests are presumably wise in discountenancing any open discussion or any free communication of ideas and opinions. It could lead to nothing more comfortable than popular irritation and distrust. The Vested Interests are known to have been actively concerned in the prosecution of the War, and there is no lack of evidence that their spokesmen have been heard in the subsequent counsels of the Peace. And, no doubt, the less that is known and said about the doings of the Vested Interests during the War and after, the better both for the public tranquility and for the continued growth and profit of the Vested Interests. Yet it is not to be overlooked that facts of such magnitude and of such urgent public concern as the manoeuvres of the Vested Interests during the War and after can not be altogether happily covered over with a conspiracy of silence. Something like a middle course of temperate publicity should have seemed more to the point. It may be unfortunate, but it is none the less unavoidable, that something appreciable is bound to come to light; that i s to say, something sinister .It should be plain to all good citizens who have the cause of law and order at heart that in such a case a more genial policy of conciliatory promises and procrastination will be more to the purpose than any noisy recourse to the strong arm and the Star Chamber. A touch of history, and more particularly of contemporary history, would have given the Guardians a touch of sanity.

Grown wise in all the ways and means of blamelessly defeating the unblest majority, the gentlemanly government of the British manage affairs of this kind much better. They have learned that bellicose gestures provoke ill will, and that desperate remedies should be held in reserve until needed. Whereas the Guardians of the Vested Interests in America are plainly putting things in train for a capital operation, for which there is no apparent necessity. It should be evident on slight reflection that things have not reached that fateful stage where nothing short of a capital operation can be counted on to save the life of the Vested

Interests in America; not yet. And indeed, things need assuredly not reach such a stage if reasonable measures are taken to avoid undue alarm and irritation. All that is needed to keep the underlying population of America in a sweet temper is a degree of patient ambiguity and delay, something after the British pattern; and all will yet be well with the vested rights of property and privilege, for some time to come. History teaches that no effectual popular uprising can be set afoot against an outworn institutional iniquity unless the movement effectually meets the special material requirements of the situation which provokes it; nor on the other hand can an impending popular overturn be staved off without making up one's account with those material conditions which converge to bring it on. The long history of British gentlemanly compromise, collusion, conciliation, and popular defeat, is highly instructive on that head. And it should be evident to any disinterested person, on any slight survey of the pertinent facts, that the situation in America does not now offer such a combination of circumstances as would be required for any effectual overturn of the established order or any forcible dispossession of these Vested Interests that now control the material fortunes of the American people. In short, by force of circumstances, Bolshevism is not a present menace to the Vested Interests in America; provided always that the Guardians of these Vested Interests do not go out of their way to precipitate trouble by such measures as will make Bolshevism of any complexion seem the lesser evil,—which is perhaps not a safe proviso, in view of the hysterically Red state of mind of the Guardians.

No movement for the dispossession of the Vested Interests in America can hope for even a temporary success unless it is undertaken by an organization which is competent to take over the country's productive industry as a whole, and to administer it from the start on a more efficient plan than that now pursued by the Vested Interests; and there is no such organization in sight or in immediate prospect. The nearest approach to a practicable organization of industrial forces in America, just yet, is the A. F. of L.; which need only be named in order to dispel the illusion that there is anything to hope or fear in the way of a radical move at its hands. The A. F. of L. is itself one of the Vested Interests, as ready as any other to do battle for its own margin of privilege and profit. At the same time it would be a wholly chimerical fancy to believe that such an organization of workmen as the A. F. of L. could take over and manage any appreciable section of the industrial system, even if their single-minded interest in special privileges for themselves did not preclude their making a move in that direction. The Federation is not organized for production but for bargaining. It is not organized on lines that would be workable for the management of any industrial system as a whole, or of any special line of production within such a system. It is, in effect, an organization for the strategic defeat of employers and rival organizations, by recourse to enforced unemployment and obstruction; not for the production of goods and services. And it is officered by tacticians, skilled in the ways and means of bargaining with politicians and intimidating employers and employees; not by men who have any special insight into or interest in the ways and means of quantity production and traffic management. They are not, and for their purpose they need not be, technicians in any conclusive sense, and the fact should not be lost sight of that any effectual overturn, of the kind hazily contemplated by the hysterical officials, will always have to be primarily a technical affair. In effect, the Federation is officered by safe and sane politicians, and its rank and file are votaries of "the full dinner-pail." No Guardian need worry about the Federation, and there is no other organization in sight which differs materially from the Federation in those respects which would count toward a practical move in the direction of a popular overturn, - unless a doubtful exception should be claimed for the Railroad Brotherhoods.

F. of L. is a business organization with a vested interest of its own; for keeping up prices and keeping down the supply, quite after the usual fashion of management by the other Vested Interests; not for managing productive industry or even for increasing the output of goods produced under any management. At the best, its purpose and ordinary business is to gain a little something for its own members at a more than proportionate cost to the rest of the community; which does not afford either the spiritual or the material ground for a popular overturn. Nor is it the A. F. of L. or the other organizations for "collective bargaining " that come in for the comfortless attentions of the officials and of the many semi-official conspiracies in restraint of sobriety. Their nerve-shattering fears center rather on those irresponsible wayfaring men of industry who make up the I. W. W., and on the helpless and hapless alien unbelievers whose contribution to the sum total is loose talk in some foreign tongue. But if there is any assertion to be made without fear of stumbling it will be, that this flotsam of industry is not organized to take over the highly technical duties involved in the administration of the industrial system. But it is these and their like that engage the best attention of the many commissions, committees, clubs, leagues, federations, syndicates, and corporations for the chasing of wild geese under the Red flag. Wherever the mechanical industry has taken decisive effect, as in America and in the two or three industrialized regions of Europe, the community lives from hand to mouth in such a way that its livelihood depends on the effectual working of its industrial system from day to day. In such a case a serious disturbance and derangement of the balanced process of production is always easily brought on, and it always brings immediate hardship on large sections of the community. Indeed, it is this state of things—the ease with which industry can be deranged and hardship can be brought to bear on the people at large that constitutes the chief asset of such partisan organizations as the A. F. of L. It is a state of things which makes sabotage easy and effectual and gives it breadth and scope. But sabotage is not revolution. If it were, then the A. F. of L., the I. W. W., the Chicago Packers, and the U. S. Senate would be counted among the revolutionists. Far- reaching sabotage, that is to say derangement of the industrial system, such as to entail hardship on the community at large or on some particular section of it, is easily brought to bear in any country that is dominated by the mechanical industry. It is commonly resorted to by both parties in any controversy between the businesslike employers and the employees. It is, in fact, an everyday expedient of business, and no serious blame attaches to its ordinary use. Under given circumstances, as, e.g., under the circumstances just now created by the return of peace, such derangement of industry and hindrance of production is an unavoidable expedient of "business as usual." And derangement of the same nature is also commonly resorted to as a means of coercion in any attempted movement of overturn. It is the simple and obvious means of initiating any revolutionary disturbance in any industrial or commercialized country. But under the existing industrial conditions, if it is to achieve even a transient success, any such revolutionary movement of reconstruction must also be in a position from the outset to overcome any degree of initial derangement in industry, whether of its own making or not, and to do constructive work of that particular kind which is called for by the present disposition of industrial forces and by the present close dependence of the community's livelihood on the due systematic working of these industrial forces. To take effect and to hold its own even for the time being, any movement of overturn must from beforehand provide for a sufficiently productive conduct of the industrial system on which the community's material welfare depends, and for a competent distribution of goods and services throughout the community. Otherwise, under existing industrial conditions, nothing more can be accomplished than an ephemeral disturbance and a transient season of accentuated hardship. Even a transient failure to make good in the management of the industrial system must immediately defeat any movement of overturn in any of the advanced industrial countries. At this point the lessons of history fail, because the present industrial system and the manner of closely knit community life enforced by this industrial system have no example in history.

This state of things, which so conditions the possibility of any revolutionary overturn, is peculiar to the advanced industrial countries; and the limitations which this state of things imposes are binding within these countries in the same measure in which these peoples are dominated by the system of mechanical industry. In contrast with this state of things, the case of Soviet Russia may be cited to show the difference. As compared with America and much of western Europe, Russia is not an industrialized region, in any decisive sense; although Russia, too, leans on the mechanical industry in a greater degree than is commonly recognized. Indeed, so considerable is the dependence of the Russians on the mechanical industry that it may yet prove to be the decisive factor in the struggle which is now going on between Soviet Russia and the Allied Powers. Now, it is doubtless this continued success of the Soviet administration in Russia that has thrown this ecstatic scare into the Guardians of the Vested Interests in America and in the civilized countries of Europe.

There is nothing to be gained by denying that the Russian Soviet has achieved a measure of success; indeed, an astonishing measure of success, considering the extremely adverse circumstances under which the Soviet has been at work. The fact may be deplored, but there it is. The Soviet has plainly been successful, in the material respect, far beyond the reports which have been allowed to pass the scrutiny of the Seven Censors and the Associated Prevarication Bureaux of the Allied Powers. And this continued success of Bolshevism in Russia—or such measure of success as it has achieved—is doubtless good ground for a reasonable degree of apprehension among good citizens elsewhere; but it does not by any means argue that anything like the same measure of success could be achieved by a revolutionary movement on the same lines in America, even in the absence of intervention from outside. Soviet Russia has made good to the extent of maintaining itself against very great odds for some two years; and it is even yet a point in doubt whether the Allied Powers will be able to put down the Soviet by use of all the forces at their disposal and with the help of all the reactionary elements in Russia and in the neighboring countries. But the Soviet owes this measure of success to the fact that the Russian people have not yet been industrialized in anything like the same degree as their western neighbors. They have in great measure been able to fall back on an earlier, simpler, less close-knit plan of productive industry; such that any detailed part of this loose-knit Russian community is able, at a pinch, to draw its own livelihood from its own soil by its own work, without that instant and unremitting dependence on materials and wrought goods drawn from foreign ports and distant regions, that is characteristic of the advanced industrial peoples. This old-Fashioned plan of home production does not involve an "industrial system" in the same exacting sense as the mechanical industry. The Russian industrial system, it is true, also runs on something of a balanced plan of give and take; it leans on the mechanical industry in some considerable degree and draws on foreign trade for many of its necessary articles of use; but for the transient time being, and for an appreciable interval of time, such a home-bred industrious population, living close to the soil and supplying its ordinary needs by home? Bred handicraft methods, will be able to maintain itself in a fair state of efficiency if not in comfort, even in virtual isolation from the more advanced industrial centers and from the remoter sources of raw materials. To the ignorant, that is to say, to the wiseacres of commerce, this ability of the Russian people to continue alive and active under the conditions of an exemplary blockade has been a source of incredulous astonishment. It is only as a fighting power, and then only for the purposes of an aggressive war, that such a community can count for virtually nothing in a contest with the advanced industrial nations. Such a people makes an unwieldy country to conquer from the outside. Soviet Russia is self-supporting, in a loose and comfortless way, and in this sense it is a very defensible country and may yet prove extremely difficult for the Allied Powers to subdue; but in the nature of the case there need be not the slightest shadow of apprehension that Soviet Russia can successfully take the offensive against any outside people, great or small, which has the use of the advanced mechanical industry.

The statesmen of the Allied Powers, who are now carrying on a covert war against Soviet Russia, are in a position to know this state of the case; and not least those American statesmen, who have by popular sentiment been constrained reluctantly to limit and mask their cooperation with the reactionary forces in Finland, Poland, the Ukraine, Siberia, and elsewhere.

They have all been at pains diligently to inquire into the state of things in Soviet Russia; although, it is true, they have also been at pains to give out surprisingly little information, that being much of the reason for the Seven Censors. The well- published official and semi-official apprehension of a Bolshevist offensive to be carried on beyond the Soviet frontiers may quite safely be set down as an article of statesmanlike subterfuge. The statesmen know better. What is feared in fact is infection of the Bolshevist spirit beyond the Soviet frontiers, to the detriment of those Vested Interests whose guardians these statesmen are.

And on this head the apprehensions of these Elder Statesmen are not altogether groundless; for the Elder Statesmen are also in a position to know, without much inquiry, that there is no single spot or corner in civilized Europe or America where the underlying population would have anything to lose by such an overturn of the established order as would cancel the vested rights of privilege and property, whose guardians they are. But commercialized America is not the same thing as Soviet Russia. By and large, America is an advanced industrial country, bound in the web of a fairly close-knit and inclusive industrial system. The industrial situation, and therefore the conditions of success, are radically different in the two countries in those respects that would make the outcome in any effectual revolt. So that, for better or worse, the main lines that would necessarily have to be followed in working out any practicable revolutionary movement in this country are already laid down by the material conditions of its productive industry. On provocation there might come a flare of riotous disorder; but it would come to nothing, however substantial the provocation might be, so long as the movement does not fall in with those main lines of management which the state of the industrial system requires in order to insure any sustained success. These main lines of revolutionary strategy are lines of technical organization and industrial management; essentially lines of industrial engineering; such as will fit the organization to take care of the highly technical industrial system that constitutes the indispensable material foundation of any modern civilized community. They will accordingly not only be of a profoundly different order from what may do well enough in the case of such a loose-knit and backward industrial region as Russia, but they will necessarily also be of a kind which has no close parallel in the past history of revolutionary movements. Revolutions in the eighteenth century were military and political; and the Elder Statesmen who now believe themselves to be making history still believe that revolutions can be made and unmade by the same ways and means in the twentieth century. But any substantial or effectual overturn in the twentieth century will necessarily be an industrial overturn; and by the same token, any twentieth-century revolution can be combated or neutralized only by industrial ways and means. The case of America, therefore, considered as a candidate for Bolshevism, will have to be argued on its own merits, and the argument will necessarily turn on the ways and means of productive industry as conditioned by the later growth of technology. It has been argued, and it seems not unreasonable to believe, that the established order of business enterprise, vested rights, and commercialized nationalism, is due presently to go under in a muddle of shame and confusion, because it is no longer a practicable system of industrial management under the conditions created by the later state of the industrial arts. Twentieth-century technology has outgrown the eighteenth-century system of vested rights. The experience of the past few years teaches that the usual management of industry by business methods has become highly inefficient and wasteful, and the indications are many and obvious that any business-like control of production and distribution is bound to run more and more consistently at cross purposes with the community's livelihood, the farther the industrial arts advance and the wider the industrial system extends. So that it is perhaps not reasonably to be questioned that Vested Interests in business are riding for a fall. But the end is not yet; although it is to be admitted, regretfully perhaps, that with every further advance in technological knowledge and practice and with every further increase in the volume and complexity of the industrial system, any businesslike control is bound to grow still more incompetent, irrelevant, and impertinent.

It would be quite hazardous to guess, just yet, how far off that consummation of commercial imbecility may be. There are those who argue that the existing system of business management is plainly due to go under within two years' time; and there are others who are ready, with equal confidence, to allow it a probable duration of several times that interval; although, it is true, these latter appear, on the whole, to be persons who are less intimately acquainted with the facts in the case. Many men experienced in the larger affairs of industrial business are in doubt as to how long things will hold together. But, one with another, these men who so are looking into the doubtful future are, somewhat apprehensively, willing to admit that there is yet something of a margin to go on; so much so that, barring accident, there should seem to be no warrant for counting at all confidently on a disastrous breakdown of the business system within anything like a two-year period. And, for the reassurance of the apprehensive Guardian of the Vested Interests, it is to be added that should such a break in the situation come while things are standing in their present shape, the outcome could assuredly not be an effectual overturn of the established order; so long as no practicable plan has been provided for taking over the management from the dead hand of the Vested Interests.

Should such a self-made breakdown come at the present juncture, the outcome could, in fact, scarcely be anything more serious than an interval, essentially transient though more or less protracted, of turmoil and famine among the underlying population, together with something of a setback to the industrial system as a whole. There seems no reason to apprehend any substantial disallowance of the vested rights of property to follow from such an essentially ephemeral interlude of dissension. In fact, the tenure of the Vested Interests in America should seem to be reasonably secure, just yet.

Something in the nature of riotous discontent and factional disorder is perhaps to be looked for in the near future in this country, and there may even be some rash gesture of revolt on the part of ill? Advised malcontents. Circumstances would seem to favor something of the kind. It is conservatively estimated that there is already a season of privation and uncertainty in prospect for the underlying population, which could be averted only at the cost of some substantial interference with the vested rights of the country's business men,—which should seem a highly improbable alternative, in view of that spirit of filial piety with which the public officials guard the prerogatives of business as usual. So, e.g., it is now (September, 1919) confidently expected, or rather computed, that a fuel famine is due in America during the approaching winter, for reasons of sound business management; and it is likewise to be expected that for the like reason the American transportation system is also due to go into a tangle of congestion and idleness about the same time—barring providential intervention in the way of unexampled weather conditions. But a season of famine and disorderly conduct does not constitute a revolutionary overturn of the established order; and the Vested Interests are secure in their continued usufruct of the country's industry, just yet. This hopeful posture of things may be shown convincingly enough and with no great expenditure of argument. To this end it is proposed to pursue the argument somewhat further presently; by describing in

outline what are the infirmities of the regime of the Vested Interests, which the more sanguine malcontents count on to bring that regime to an inglorious finish in the immediate future; and also to set down, likewise in outline, what would have to be the character of any organization of industrial forces which could be counted on effectually to wind up the regime of the Vested Interests and take over the management of the industrial system on a deliberate plan.

V. On the Circumstances Which Make for a Change

The state of industry, in America and in the other advanced industrial countries, will impose certain exacting conditions on any movement that aims to displace the Vested Interests. These conditions lie in the nature of things; that is to say, in the nature of the existing industrial system; and until they are met in some passable fashion, this industrial system can not be taken over in any effectual or enduring manner. And it is plain that whatever is found to be true in these respects for America will also hold true in much the same degree for the other countries that are dominated by the mechanical industry and the system of absentee ownership. It may also confidently be set down at the outset that such an impartial review of the evidence as is here aimed at will make it appear that there need be no present apprehension of the Vested Interests' being unseated by any popular uprising in America, even if the popular irritation should rise very appreciably above its present pitch, and even if certain advocates of "direct action," here and there, should be so ill-advised as to make some rash gesture of revolt.

The only present danger is that a boisterous campaign of repression and inquisition on the part of the Guardians of the Vested Interests may stir up some transient flutter of seditious disturbance. To this end, then, it will be necessary to recall, in a summary way, those main facts of the industrial system and of the present businesslike control of this system which come immediately into the case. By way of general premise it is to be noted that the established order of business rests on absentee ownership and is managed with an eye single to the largest obtainable net return in terms of price; that is to say, it is a system of businesslike management on a commercial footing. The underlying population is dependent on the working of this industrial system for its livelihood; and their material interest therefore centers in the output and distribution of consumable goods, not in an increasing volume of earnings for the absentee owners. Hence there is a division of interest between the business community, who do business for the absentee owners, and the underlying population, who work for a living; and in the nature of the case this division of interest between the absentee owners and the underlying population is growing wider and more evident from day to day; which engenders a certain division of sentiment and a degree of mutual distrust.

With it all the underlying population are still in a sufficiently deferential frame of mind toward their absentee owners, and are quite conscientiously delicate about any abatement of the free income which their owners come in for, according to the rules of the game as it is played. The business concerns which so have the management of industry on this plan of absentee ownership are capitalized on their business capacity, not on their industrial capacity; that is to say, they are capitalized on their capacity to produce earnings, not on their capacity to produce goods. Their capitalization has, in effect, been calculated and fixed on the highest ordinary rate of earnings previously obtained; and on pain of insolvency their businesslike managers are now required to meet fixed income charges on this capitalization.

Therefore, as a proposition of safe and sane business management, prices have to be maintained or advanced. From this businesslike requirement of meeting these fixed overhead charges on the capitalization there result certain customary lines of waste and obstruction, which are unavoidable so long as industry is managed by businesslike methods and for businesslike ends. These ordinary lines of waste and obstruction are necessarily (and blamelessly) included in the businesslike conduct of production. They are many and various in detail, but they may for convenience be classed under four heads: (a) Unemployment of material resources, equipment and manpower, in whole or in part, deliberately or through ignorance; (b) Salesmanship (includes, e.g., needless multiplication of merchants and shops, wholesale and retail, newspaper advertising and bill-boards, sales-exhibits, sales-agents, fancy packages and labels, adulteration, multiplication of brands and proprietary articles); (c) Production (and sales? cost) of superfluities and spurious goods; (d) Systematic dislocation, sabotage and duplication, due in part to businesslike strategy, in part to businesslike ignorance of industrial requirements (includes, e.g., such things as cross-freights, monopolization of resources, withholding of facilities and information from business rivals whom it is thought wise to hinder or defeat).There is, of course, no blame, and no sense of blame or shame attaching to all this everyday waste and confusion that goes to make up the workday total of businesslike management. All of it is a legitimate and necessary part of the established order of business enterprise, within the law and within the ethics of the trade. Salesmanship is the most conspicuous, and perhaps the gravest, of these wasteful and industrially futile practices that are involved in the businesslike conduct of industry; it bulks large both in its immediate cost and in its meretricious consequences.

It also is altogether legitimate and indispensable in any industrial business that deals with customers, in buying or selling; which comes near saying, in all business that has to do with the production or distribution of goods or services. Indeed, salesmanship is, in a way, the whole end and substance of business enterprise; and except so far as it is managed with a constant view to profitable bargains, the production of goods is not a business proposition. It is the elimination of profitable transactions of purchase and sale that is hoped for by any current movement looking to an overturn; and it is the same elimination of profitable bargaining that is feared, with a nerve-shattering fear, by the Guardians of the established order. Salesmanship is also the most indispensable and most meritorious of those qualities that go to make a safe and sane business man It is doubtless within the mark to say that, at an average, one-half the price paid for goods and services by consumers is to be set down to the account of salesmanship—that is, to sales cost and to the net gains of salesmanship. But in many notable lines of merchandise the sales-cost will ordinarily foot up to some ten or twenty times the production cost proper, and to not less than one hundred times the necessary cost of distribution.

All this is not a matter for shame or distaste. In fact, just now more than ever, there is a clamorous and visibly growing insistence on the paramount merit and importance of salesmanship as the main stay of commerce and industry, and a strenuous demand for more extensive and more thorough training in salesmanship of a larger number of young men—at the public expense— to enable a shrewdly limited output of goods to be sold at more profitable prices—at the public cost. So also there is a visibly increasing expenditure on all manner of advertising; and the spokesmen of this enterprise in conspicuous waste are "pointing with pride" to the fact that the American business community have already spent upward of $600,000,000 on bill-boards alone within the past year, not to speak of much larger sums spent on newspapers and other printed matter for the same purpose and the common man pays the cost.

At the same time advertising and manoeuvres of salesmanlike spellbinding appear to be the only resource to which the country's business men know how to turn for relief from that tangle of difficulties into which the outbreak of a businesslike peace has precipitated the commercialized world. Increased sales cost is to remedy the evils of under-production. In this connection it may be worth while to recall, without heat or faultfinding, that all the costly publicity that goes into sales costs is in the nature of prevarication, when it is not good broad mendacity; and quite necessarily so. And all the while the proportion of sales costs to production costs goes on increasing, and the cost of living grows continually greater for the underlying population, and business necessities continue to enlarge the necessary expenditure on ways and means of salesmanship. It is reasonable to believe that this state of things, which has been coming on gradually for some time past, will in time come to be understood and appreciated by the underlying population, at least in some degree. And it is likewise reasonable to believe that so soon as the underlying population come to realize that all this wasteful traffic of salesmanship is using up their productive forces, with nothing better to show for it than an increased cost of living, they will be driven to make some move to abate the nuisance. And just so far as this state of things is now beginning to be understood, its logical outcome is a growing distrust of the business men and all their works and words. But the underlying population is still very credulous about anything that is said or done in the name of Business, and there need be no apprehension of a mutinous outbreak, just yet. But at the same time it is evident that any plan of management which could contrive to dispense with all this expenditure on salesmanship, or that could materially reduce sales costs, would have that much of a free margin to go on, and therefore that much of an added chance of success; and so also it is evident that any other than a businesslike management could so contrive, inasmuch as sales costs are incurred solely for purposes of business, not for purposes of industry; they are incurred for the sake of private gain, not for the sake of productive work.

But there is in fact no present promise of a breakdown of business, due to the continued increase of sales costs; although sales costs are bound to go on increasing so long as the country's industry continues to be managed on anything like the present plan. In fact, salesmanship is the chief factor in that ever increasing cost of living, which is in its turn the chief ground of prosperity among the business community and the chief source of perennial hardship and discontent among the underlying population. Still it is worth noting that the eventual elimination of salesmanship and sales cost would lighten the burden of workday production for the underlying population by some fifty per cent. There is that much of a visible inducement to disallow that system of absentee ownership on which modern business enterprise rests; and—for what it may be worth—it is to be admitted that there is therefore that much of a drift in the existing state of things toward a revolutionary overturn looking to the unseating of the Vested Interests.

But at the same time the elimination of salesmanship and all its voluminous apparatus and traffic would also cut down the capitalized income of the business community by something like one-half; and that contingency is not to be contemplated, not to say with equanimity, by the Guardians; and it is after all in the hands of these Guardians that the fortunes of the community rest. Such a move is a moral impossibility, just yet. Closely related to the wasteful practices of salesmanship as commonly understood, if it should not rather be counted in as an extension of salesmanship, is that persistent unemployment of men, equipment, and material resources, by which the output of goods and services is kept down to the "requirements of the market," with a view to maintaining prices at a "reasonably profitable level." Such unemployment, deliberate and habitual, is one of the ordinary expedients employed in the businesslike management of industry. There is always more or less of it in ordinary times. "Reasonable earnings" could not be assured without it; because "what the traffic will bear" in the way of an output of goods is by no means the same as the productive capacity of the industrial system; still less is it the same as the total consumptive needs of the community; in fact, it does not visibly tend to coincide with either. It is more particularly in times of popular distress, such as the present year, when the current output of goods is not nearly sufficient to cover the consumptive needs of the community, that considerations of business strategy call for a wise unemployment of the country's productive forces. At the same time, such businesslike unemployment of equipment and man power is the most obvious cause of popular distress.

All this is well known to the Guardians of the Vested Interests, and their knowledge of it is, quite reasonably, a source of uneasiness to them. But they see no help for it; and indeed there is no help for it within the framework of "business as usual," since it is the essence of business as usual. So also, the Guardians are aware that this businesslike sabotage on productive industry is a fruitful source of discontent and distrust among the underlying population who suffer the inconvenience of it all; and they are beset with the abiding fear that the underlying population may shortly be provoked into disallowing those Vested Interests for whose benefit this deliberate and habitual sabotage on production is carried on. It is felt that here again is a sufficient reason why the businesslike management of industry should be discontinued; which is the same as saying that here again is a visibly sufficient reason for such a revolutionary overturn as will close out the Old Order of absentee ownership and capitalized income. It is also evident that any plan which shall contrive to dispense with, this deliberate and habitual unemployment of men and equipment will have that much more of a margin to go on, both in respect of practical efficiency and in respect of popular tolerance; and evidently, too, any other than a business-like management of industry can so contrive, as a matter of course; inasmuch as any such unbusinesslike administration—as, e.g., the Soviet—will be relieved of the businesslike manager's blackest bug-bear, "a reasonably profitable level of prices." But for all that, those shudderingly sanguine persons who are looking for a dissolution of the system of absentee ownership within two years' time are not counting on salesmanlike waste and businesslike sabotage to bring on the collapse, so much as they count on the item listed under (d) above— the systematic dislocation and all-round defeat of productive industry which is due in part to shrewd manoeuvres of businesslike strategy, in part to the habitual ignorance of business men touching the systematic requirements of the industrial system as a whole.

The shrewd worldly wisdom of the businesslike managers, looking consistently to the main chance, works in harmoniously with their trained ignorance on matters of technology, to bring about what amounts to effectual team-work for the defeat of the country's industrial system as a going concern. Yet doubtless this sinister hope of a collapse within two years is too sanguine. Doubtless the underlying population can be counted on stolidly to put up with what they are so well used to, just yet; more particularly so long as they are not in the habit of thinking about these things at all. Nor does it seem reasonable to believe that this all- pervading waste and confusion of industrial forces will of itself bring the business organization to a collapse within so short a time. It is true, the industrial system is continually growing, in volume and complication; and with every new extension of its scope and range, and with every added increment of technological practice that goes into effect, there comes a new and urgent opportunity for the business men in control to extend and speed up their strategy of mutual obstruction and defeat; it is all in the day's work.

As the industrial system grows larger and more closely interwoven it offers continually larger and more enticing opportunities for such businesslike manoeuvres as will effectually derange the system at the same time that they bring the desired tactical defeat on some business rival; whereby the successful business strategist is enabled to get a little something for nothing at a constantly increasing cost to the community at large. With every increment of growth and maturity the country's industrial system becomes more delicately balanced, more intricately bound in a web of industrial give and take, more sensitive to far- reaching derangement by any local dislocation, more widely and instantly responsive to any failure of the due correlation at any point; and by the same move the captains of industry, to whose care the interests of absentee ownership are entrusted, are enabled, or rather they are driven by the necessities of competitive business, to plan their strategy of mutual defeat and derangement on larger and more intricate lines, with an ever wider reach and a more massive mobilization of forces.

From which follows an ever increasing insecurity of work and output from day to day and an increased assurance of general loss and disability in the long run; incidentally coupled with increased hardship for the underlying population, which comes in all along as a subsidiary matter of course, unfortunate but unavoidable. It is this visibly growing failure of the present businesslike management to come up to the industrial necessities of the case; its unfitness to take anything like reasonable care of the needed correlation of industrial forces within the system; its continual working at cross purposes in the allocation of energy resources, materials, and man power—it is this fact, that any businesslike management of necessity runs at cross purposes with the larger technical realities of the industrial system, that chiefly goes to persuade apprehensive persons that the regime of business enterprise is fast approaching the limit of tolerance. So it is held by many that this existing system of absentee ownership must presently break down and precipitate the abdication of the Vested Interests, under conviction of total imbecility.

The theory on which these apprehensive persons proceed appears to be substantially sound, so far as it goes, but they reach an unguardedly desperate conclusion because they overlook one of the main facts of the case. There is no reasonable exception to be taken to the statement that the country's industrial system is forever growing more extensive and more complex; that it is continually taking on more of the character of a close-knit, interwoven, systematic whole; a delicately balanced moving equilibrium of working parts, no one of which can do its work by itself at all, and none of which can do its share of the work well except in close correlation with all the rest. At the same time it is also true that, in the commercialized nature of things, the businesslike management of industry is forever playing fast and loose with this delicately balanced moving equilibrium of forces, on which the livelihood of the underlying population depends from day to day; more particularly is this true for that large-scale business enterprise that rests on absentee ownership and makes up the country's greater Vested Interests. But to all this it is to be added, as a corrective and a main factor in the case, that this system of mechanical industry is an extremely efficient contrivance for the production of goods and services, even when, as usual, the business men, for business reasons, will allow it to work only under a large handicap of unemployment and obstructive tactics. Hitherto the margin for error, that is to say for wasteful strategy and obstructive ignorance, has been very wide; so wide that it has saved the life of the Vested Interests; and it is accordingly by no means confidently to be believed that all these ampler opportunities for swift and wide- reaching derangement will enable the strategy of business enterprise to bring on a disastrous collapse, just yet.

It is true, if the country's productive industry were competently organized as a systematic whole, and were then managed by competent technicians with an eye single to maximum production of goods and services; instead of, as now, being manhandled by ignorant business men with an eye single to maximum profits; the resulting output of goods and services would doubtless exceed the current output by several hundred per cent.

But then, none of all that is necessary to save the established order of things. All that is required is a decent modicum of efficiency, very far short of the theoretical maximum production. In effect, the community is in the habit of getting along contentedly on something appreciably less than one-half the output which its industrial equipment would turn out if it were working uninterruptedly at full capacity; even when, as usual, something like one-half of the actual output is consumed in wasteful superfluities. The margin for waste and error is very wide, fortunately; and, in effect, a more patient and more inclusive survey of the facts in the case would suffice to show that the tenure of the Vested Interests is reasonably secure just yet; at least in so far as it turns on considerations of this nature. There is, of course, the chance, and it is by no means a remote chance, that the rapidly increasing volume and complexity of the industrial system may presently bring the country's industry into such a ticklish state of unstable equilibrium that even a reasonable modicum of willful derangement can no longer be tolerated, even for the most urgent and most legitimate reasons of businesslike strategy and vested rights. In time, such an outcome is presumably due to be looked for.

There is, indeed, no lack of evidence that the advanced industrial countries are approaching such a state of things, America among the rest. The margin for error and wasteful strategy is, in effect, being continually narrowed by the further advance of the industrial arts. With every further advance in the way of specialization and standardization, in point of kind, quantity, quality, and time, the tolerance of the system as a whole under any strategic maladjustment grows continually narrower. How soon the limit of tolerance for willful derangement is due to be reached, would be a hazardous topic of speculation. There is now a fair prospect that the coming winter may throw some light on that dark question; but this is not saying that the end is in sight. What is here insisted on is that that sinister eventuality lies yet in the future, although it may be in the calculable future. So also it is well to keep in mind that even a fairly disastrous collapse of the existing system of businesslike management need by no means prove fatal to the Vested Interests, just yet; not so long as there is no competent organization ready to take their place and administer the country's industry on a more reasonable plan.

It is necessarily a question of alternatives. In all this argument that runs on perennial dislocation and cross purposes, it is assumed that the existing businesslike management of industry is of a competitive nature and necessarily moves on lines of competitive strategy.

As a subsidiary premise it is, of course, also assumed that the captains of industry who have the direction of this competitive strategy are ordinarily sufficiently ill informed on technological matters to go wrong, industrially speaking, even with the most pacific and benevolent intentions. They are laymen in all that concerns the technical demands of industrial production. This latter, and minor, assumption therefore need not be argued; it is sufficiently notorious. On the other hand, the first assumption spoken of above, that current business enterprise is of a competitive nature, is likely to be questioned by many who believe themselves to be familiar with the facts in the case.

It is argued, by one and another, that the country's business concerns have entered into consolidations, coalitions, understandings and working arrangements among themselves—syndicates, trusts, pools, combinations, interlocking directorates, gentlemen's agreements, employers' unions— to such an extent as virtually to cover the field of that large-scale business that sets the pace and governs the movements of the rest; and that where combination takes effect in this way, competition ceases. So also it will be argued that where there has been no formal coalition of interests the business men in charge will still commonly act in collusion, with much the same result. The suggestion is also ready to hand that in so far as business-like sabotage of this competitive order is still to be met with, it can all be corrected by such a further consolidation of interests as will do away with all occasion for competitive cross purposes within the industrial system.

It is not easy to see just how far that line of argument would lead; but to make it effective and to cover the case it would plainly have to result in so wide a coalition of interests and pooling of management as would, in effect, eliminate all occasion for businesslike management within the system, and leave the underlying population quite unreservedly at the disposal of the resulting coalition of interests—an outcome which is presumably not contemplated. And even so, the argument takes account of only one strand in that three-ply rope that goes to fashion the fatal noose. The remaining two are stout enough, and they have not been touched. It is true, economists and others who have canvassed this matter of competition have commonly given their attention to this one line of competition alone—between rival commercial interests—because this competition is conceived to be natural and normal and to serve the common good. But there remains (a) the competition between those business men who buy cheap and sell dear and the underlying population from and to whom they buy cheap and sell dear, and (b) the competition between the captains of industry and those absentee owners in whose name and with whose funds the captains do business. In the typical case, modern business enterprise takes the corporate form, is organized on credit, and therefore rests on absentee ownership; from which it follows that in all large-scale business the owners are not the same persons as the managers, nor does the interest of the manager commonly coincide with that of his absentee owners, particularly in the modern "big business." So it follows that even a coalition of Vested Interests which should be virtually all-inclusive, would still have to make up its account with "what the traffic will bear," that is to say what will bring the largest net income in terms of price; that is to say, the coalition would still be under the competitive necessity of buying cheap and selling dear, to the best of its ability and with the use of all the facilities which its dominant position in the market would give.

The coalition, therefore, would still be under the necessity of shrewdly limiting the output of goods and services to such a rate and volume as will maintain or advance prices; and also to vary its manipulation of prices and supply from place to place and from time to time, to turn an honest penny; which leaves the case very near the point of beginning. But then, such a remedy for these infelicities of the competitive system will probably be admitted to be chimerical, without argument.

But what is more to the point is the fact, known even when it is not avowed, that the consolidations which have been effected hitherto have not eliminated competition, nor have they changed the character of the competitive strategy employed, although they have altered its scale and methods. What can be said is that the underlying corporations of the holding companies, e.g., are no longer competitors among themselves on the ancient footing. But strategic dislocation and cross purposes continue to be the order of the day in the businesslike management of industry; and the volume of habitual unemployment, whether of equipment or of man power, continues undiminished and unashamed—which is after all a major count in the case It is well to recognize what the business men among themselves always recognize as a matter of course, that business is in the last analysis always carried on for the private advantage of the individual business men who carry it on. And these enterprising persons, being business men, will always be competitors for gain among themselves, however much and well they may combine for a common purpose as against the rest of the community.

The end and aim of any gainful enterprise carried through in common is always the division of the joint gains, and in this division the joint participants always figure as competitors. The syndicates, coalitions, corporations, consolidations of interests, so entered into in the pursuit of gain are, in effect, in the nature of conspiracies between business men each seeking his own advantage at the cost of any whom it may concern.

There is no ulterior solidarity of interests among the participants in such a joint enterprise. By way of illustration, what is set forth in the voluminous testimony taken in the Colton case, before the California courts, having to do with the affairs of the Southern Pacific and its subsidiaries, will show in what fashion the businesslike incentives of associated individuals may be expected to work out in the partition of benefits within a given coalition. And not only is there no abiding solidarity of interests between the several participants in such a joint enterprise, so far as regards the final division of the spoils, but it is also true that the business interest of the manager in charge of such a syndicate of absentee ownership will not coincide with the collective interest of the coalition as a going concern. As an illustrative instance may be cited the testimony of the great president of the two Great Northern railways, taken before a Congressional commission, wherein it is explained somewhat fully that for something like a quarter-century the two great roads under his management had never come in for reasonable earnings on their invested capital. And it is a matter of common notoriety, although it was charitably not brought out in the hearings of the commission, that during his incumbency as manager of the two great railway systems this enterprising railway president had by thrift and management increased his own private possessions from $20 to something variously estimated at \$150,000,000 to \$200,000,000; while his two chief associates in this adventure had retired from the management on a similarly comfortable footing; so notably comfortable, indeed, as to have merited a couple of very decent peerages under the British crown.

In effect, there still is an open call for shrewd personal strategy at the cost of any whom it may concern; all the while that there is also a very appreciable measure of collusion among the Vested Interests, at the cost of any whom it may concern. Business is still competitive business, competitive pursuit of private gain; as how should it not be seeing that the incentive to all business is after all private gain at the cost of any whom it may concern. By reason of doctrinal consistency and loyalty to tradition, the certified economists have habitually described business enterprise as a rational arrangement for administering the country's industrial system and assuring a full and equitable distribution of consumable goods to the consumers. There need be no quarrel with that view. But it is only fair to enter the reservation that, considered as an arrangement for administering the country's industrial system, business enterprise based on absentee ownership has the defects of its qualities; and these defects of this good old plan are now calling attention to themselves. Hitherto, and ever since the mechanical industry first came into the dominant place in this industrial system, the defects of this businesslike management of industry have continually been encroaching more and more on its qualities. It took its rise as a system of management by the owners of the industrial equipment, and it has in its riper years grown into a system of absentee ownership managed by quasi-responsible financial agents.

Having begun as an industrial community which centered about an open market, it has matured into a community of Vested Interests whose vested right it is to keep up prices by a short supply in a closed market. There is no extravagance in saying that, by and large, this arrangement for controlling the production and distribution of goods and services through the agency of absentee ownership has now come to be, in the main, a blundering muddle of defects. For the purpose in hand, that is to say with a view to the probable chance of any revolutionary overturn, this may serve as a fair characterization of the regime of the Vested Interests; whose continued rule is now believed by their Guardians to be threatened by a popular uprising in the nature of Bolshevism. Now, as to the country's industrial system which is manhandled on this businesslike plan; it is a comprehensive and balanced scheme of technological administration.

Industry of this modern sort—mechanical, specialized, standardized, running to quantity production, drawn on a large scale— is highly productive; provided always that the necessary conditions of its working are met in some passable fashion. These necessary conditions of productive industry are of a well-defined technical character, and they are growing more and more exacting with every farther advance in the industrial arts.

This mechanical industry draws always more and more largely and urgently on the natural sources of mechanical power, and it necessarily makes use of an ever increasingly wide and varied range of materials, drawn from all latitudes and all geographical regions, in spite of obstruc-

tive national frontiers and patriotic animosities; for the mechanical technology is impersonal and dispassionate, and its end is very simply to serve
human needs, without fear or favor or respect of persons, prerogatives, or
politics. It makes up an industrial system of an unexampled character—a
mechanically balanced and interlocking system of work to be done, the
prime requisite of whose working is a painstaking and intelligent coordination of the processes at work, and an equally painstaking allocation
of mechanical power and materials. The foundation and driving force of it
all is a massive body by technological knowledge, of a highly impersonal
and altogether unbusinesslike nature, running in close contact with the
material sciences, on which it draws freely at every turn—exactingly specialized, endlessly detailed, reaching out into all domains of empirical fact.
Such is the system of productive work which has grown out of the Industrial Revolution, and on the full and free run of which the material welfare
of all the civilized peoples now depends from day to day. Any defect or
hindrance in its technical administration, any intrusion of nontechnical
considerations, any failure or obstruction at any point, unavoidably results in a disproportionate set-back to the balanced whole and brings a
disproportionate burden of privation on all these peoples whose productive industry has come within the sweep of the system. It follows that
those gifted, trained, and experienced technicians who now are in possession of the requisite technological information and experience are the first
and instantly indispensable factor in the everyday work of carrying on the
country's productive industry. They now constitute the General Staff of the
industrial system, in fact; whatever law and custom may formally say in
protest. The "captains of industry" may still vaingloriously claim that distinction, and law and custom still countenance their claim; but the captains have no technological value, in fact.

   Therefore any question of a revolutionary overturn, in America or in any
other of the advanced industrial countries, resolves itself in practical fact
into a question of what the guild of technicians will do. In effect it is a
question whether the discretion and responsibility in the management of
the country's industry shall pass from the financiers, who speak for the
Vested Interests, to the technicians, who speak for the industrial system as
a going concern.

   There is no third party qualified to make a colorable bid, or able to make
good its pretensions if it should make a bid. So long as the vested rights of
absentee ownership remain intact, the financial powers—that is to say the
Vested Interests will continue to dispose of the country's industrial forces
for their own profit; and so soon, or so far, as these vested rights give way,
the control of the people's material welfare will pass into the hands of the
technicians. There is no third party. The chances of anything like a Soviet
in America, therefore, are the chances of a Soviet of technicians. And, to
the due comfort of the Guardians of the Vested Interests and the good citizens who make up their background, it can be shown that anything like a
Soviet of Technicians is at the most a remote contingency in America. It is
true, so long as no such change of base is made, what is confidently to be
looked for is a regime of continued and increasing shame and confusion,

hardship and dissension, unemployment and privation, waste and insecurity of person and property—such as the rule of the Vested Interests in business has already made increasingly familiar to all the civilized peoples. But the vested rights of absentee ownership are still embedded in the sentiments of the underlying population, and still continue to be the Palladium of the Republic; and the assertion is still quite safe that anything like a Soviet of Technicians is not a present menace to the Vested Interests in America. By settled habit the technicians, the engineers and industrial experts, are a harmless and docile sort, well fed on the whole, and somewhat placidly content with the "full dinner pail" which the lieutenants of the Vested Interests habitually allow them. It is true, they constitute the indispensable General Staff of that industrial system which feeds the Vested Interests; but hitherto at least, they have had nothing to say in the planning and direction of this industrial system, except as employees in the pay of the financiers.

They have, hitherto, been quite unreflectingly content to work piecemeal, without much of an understanding among themselves, unreservedly doing job work for the Vested Interests; and they have without much reflection lent themselves and their technical powers freely to the obstructive tactics of the captains of industry; all the while that the training which makes them technicians is but a specialized extension of that joint stock of technological knowledge that has been carried forward out of the past by the community at large. But it remains true that they and their dear-bought knowledge of ways and means—dear-bought on the part of the underlying community— are the pillars of that house of industry in which the Vested Interests continue to live. Without their continued and unremitting supervision and direction the industrial system would cease to be a working system at all; whereas it is not easy to see how the elimination of the existing businesslike control could bring anything but relief and heightened efficiency to this working system, The technicians are indispensable to productive industry of this mechanical sort; the Vested Interests and their absentee owners are not. The technicians are indispensable to the Vested Interests and their absentee owners, as a working force without which there would be no industrial output to control or divide; whereas the Vested Interests and their absentee owners are of no material consequence to the technicians and their work, except as an extraneous interference and obstruction. It follows that the material welfare of all the advanced industrial peoples rests in the hands of these technicians, if they will only see it that way, take counsel together, constitute themselves the self-directing

General Staff of the country's industry, and dispense with the interference of the lieutenants of the absentee owners. Already they are strategically in a position to take the lead and impose their own terms of leadership, so soon as they, or a decisive number of them, shall reach a common understanding to that effect and agree on a plan of action. But there is assuredly no present promise of the technicians' turning their insight and common sense to such a use. There need be no present apprehension. The technicians are a "safe and sane" lot, on the whole; and they are pretty well commercialized, particularly the older generation, who speak with authority and conviction, and to whom the younger generation of engineers defer, on the whole, with such a degree of filial piety as should go far to reassure all good citizens. And herein lies the present security of the Vested Interests, as well as the fatuity of any present alarm about

Bolshevism and the like; for the whole-hearted cooperation of the technicians would be as indispensable to any effectual movement of overturn as their unwavering service in the employ of the Vested Interests is indispensable to the maintenance of the established order. VI. A Memorandum on a Practicable Soviet of Technicians It is the purpose of this memorandum to show, in an objective way, that under existing circumstances there need be no fear, and no hope, of an effectual revolutionary overturn in America, such as would unsettle the established order and unseat those Vested Interests that now control the country's industrial system.

In an earlier paper (Chapter IV,) it has been argued that no effectual move in the direction of such an overturn can be made except on the initiative and under the direction of the country's technicians, taking action in common and on a concerted plan. Notoriously, no move of this nature has been made hitherto, nor is there evidence that anything of the kind has been contemplated by the technicians. They still are consistently loyal, with something more than a hired-man's loyalty, to the established order of commercial profit and absentee ownership. And any adequate plan of concerted action, such as would be required for the enterprise in question, is not a small matter that can be arranged between two days. Any plan of action that shall hope to meet the requirements of the case in any passable fashion must necessarily have the benefit of mature deliberation among the technicians who are competent to initiate such an enterprise; it must engage the intelligent co-operation of several thousand technically trained men scattered over the face of the country, in one industry and another; must carry out a passably complete cadastration of the country's industrial forces; must set up practicable organization tables covering the country's industry in some detail, energy-resources, materials, and man power; and it must also engage the aggressive support of the trained men at work in transportation, mining, and the greater mechanical industries. These are initial requirements, indispensable to the initiation of any enterprise of the kind in such an industrial country as America; and so soon as this is called to mind it will be realised that any fear of an effectual move in this direction at present is quite chimerical. So that, in fact, it may be set down without a touch of ambiguity that absentee ownership is secure, just yet.

Therefore, to show conclusively and in an objective way how remote any contingency of this nature still is, it is here proposed to set out in a summary fashion the main lines which any such concerted plan of action would have to follow, and what will of necessity be the manner of organization which alone can hope to take over the industrial system, following the eventual abdication or dispossession of the Vested Interests and their absentee owners. And, by way of parenthesis, it is always the self-made though reluctant abdication of the Vested Interests and their absentee owners, rather than their forcible dispossession, that is to be looked for as a reasonably probable event in the calculable future. It should, in effect, cause no surprise to find that they will, in a sense, eliminate themselves, by letting go quite involuntarily after the industrial situation gets quite beyond their control. In fact, they have, in the present difficult juncture, already sufficiently shown their unfitness to take care of the country's material welfare, which is after all the only ground on which they can set up a colorable claim to their vested rights. At the same time something like an opening bid for a bargain of abdication has already come in from more than one quarter.

So that a discontinuance of the existing system of absentee ownership, on one plan or another, is no longer to be considered a purely speculative novelty; and an objective canvass of the manner of organization that is to be looked to take the place of the control now exercised by the Vested Interests—in the event of their prospective abdication— should accordingly have some present interest, even apart from its bearing on the moot question of any forcible disruption of the established system of absentee ownership. As a matter of course, the powers and duties of the incoming directorate will be of a technological nature, in the main if not altogether; inasmuch as the purpose of its coming into control is the care of the community's material welfare by a more competent management of the country's industrial system.

It may be added that even in the unexpected event that the contemplated, overturn should, in the beginning, meet with armed opposition from the partisans of the old order, it will still be true that the duties of the incoming directorate will be of a technological character, in the main; inasmuch as warlike operations are also now substantially a matter of technology, both in the immediate conduct of hostilities and in the still more urgent work of material support and supply. The incoming industrial order is designed to correct the shortcomings of the old. The duties and powers of the incoming directorate will accordingly converge on those points in the administration of industry where the old order has most signally fallen short; that is to say, on the due allocation of resources and a consequent full and reasonably proportioned employment of the available equipment and man power; on the avoidance of waste and duplication of work; and on an equitable and sufficient supply of goods and services to consumers.

Evidently the most immediate and most urgent work to be taken over by the incoming directorate is that for want of which under the old order the industrial system has been working slack and at cross purposes; that is to say the due allocation of available resources, in power, equipment, and materials, among the greater primary industries. For this necessary work of allocation there has been substantially no provision under the old order. To carry on this allocation, the country's transportation system must be placed at the disposal of the same staff that has the work of allocation to do; since, under modern conditions, any such allocation will take effect only by use of the transportation system. But, by the same token, the effectual control of the distribution of goods to consumers will also necessarily fall into the same hands; since the traffic in consumable goods is also a matter of transportation, in the main. On these considerations, which would only be reinforced by a more detailed inquiry into the work to be done, the central directorate will apparently take the shape of a loosely tripartite executive council, with power to act in matters of industrial administration; the council to include technicians whose qualifications enable them to be called

Resource Engineers, together with similarly competent spokesmen of the transportation system and of the distributive traffic in finished products and services. With a view to efficiency and expedition, the executive council will presumably not be a numerous body; although its staff of intelligence and advice may be expected to be fairly large, and it will be guided by current consultation with the accredited spokesmen (deputies, commissioners, executives, or whatever they may be called) of the several main subdivisions of productive industry, transportation, and distributive traffic. Armed with these powers and working in due consultation with a sufficient ramification of sub-centers and local councils, this industrial directorate should be in a position to avoid virtually all unemployment of serviceable equipment and man power on the one hand, and all local or seasonal scarcity on the other hand.

The main line of duties indicated by the character of the work incumbent on the directorate, as well as the main line of qualifications in its personnel, both executive and advisory, is such as will call for the services of Production Engineers, to use a term which is coming into use. But it is also evident that in its continued work of planning and advisement the directorate will require the services of an appreciable number of consulting economists; men who are qualified to be called Production Economists. The profession now includes men with the requisite qualifications, although it cannot be said that the gild of economists is made up of such men in the main. Quite blamelessly, the economists have, by tradition and by force of commercial pressure, habitually gone in for a theoretical inquiry into the ways and means of salesmanship, financial traffic, and the distribution of income and property, rather than a study of the industrial system considered as a ways and means of producing goods and services. Yet there now are, after all, especially among the younger generation, an appreciable number, perhaps an adequate number, of economists who have learned that "business" is not "industry" and that investment is not production.

And, here as always, the best is good enough, perforce. "Consulting economists" of this order are a necessary adjunct to the personnel of the central directorate, because the technical training that goes to make a resource engineer, or a production engineer, or indeed a competent industrial expert in any line of specialization, is not of a kind to give him the requisite sure and facile insight into the play of economic forces at large; and as a matter of notorious fact, very few of the technicians have gone at all far afield to acquaint themselves with anything more to the point in this connection than the half-forgotten commonplaces of the old order. The "consulting economist" is accordingly necessary to cover an otherwise uncovered joint in the new articulation of things.

His place in the scheme is analogous to the part which legal counsel now plays in the manoeuvres of diplomatists and statesmen; and the discretionary personnel of the incoming directorate are to be, in effect, something in the way of industrial statesmen under the new order.

There is also a certain general reservation to be made with regard to personnel, which may conveniently be spoken of at this point. To avoid persistent confusion and prospective defeat, it will be necessary to exclude from all positions of trust and executive responsibility all persons who have been trained for business or who have had experience in business undertakings of the larger sort. This will apply generally, throughout the administrative scheme, although it will apply more imperatively as regards the responsible personnel of the directorate, central and subordinate, together with their staff of intelligence and advice, wherever judgment and insight are essential. What is wanted is training in the ways and means of productive industry, not in the ways and means of salesmanship and profitable investment. By force of habit, men trained to a businesslike view of what is right and real will be irretrievably biased against any plan of production and distribution that is not drawn in terms of commercial profit and loss and does not provide a margin of free income to go to absentee owners. The personal exceptions to the rule are apparently very few. But this one point is after all of relatively minor consequence.

What is more to the point in the same connection is that the commercial bias induced by their training in businesslike ways of thinking leaves them incapable of anything like an effectual insight into the use of resources or the needs and aims of productive industry, in any other terms than those of commercial profit and loss. Their units and standards of valuation and accountancy are units and standards of price, and of private gain in terms of price; whereas for any scheme of productive industry which runs, not on salesmanship and earnings, but on tangible performances and tangible benefit to the community at large, the valuations and accountancy of salesmanship and earnings are misleading. With the best and most benevolent intentions, men so trained will unavoidably make their appraisals of production and their disposition of productive forces in the only practical terms with which they are familiar, the terms of commercial accountancy ; which is the same as saying, the accountancy of absentee ownership and free income; all of which it is the abiding purpose of the projected plan to displace. For the purposes of this projected new order of production, therefore, the experienced and capable business men are at the best to be rated as well-intentioned deaf mute blind men. Their wisest judgment and sincerest endeavors become meaningless and misguided so soon as the controlling purpose of industry shifts from the footing of profits on absentee investment to that of a serviceable output of goods. All this abjuration of business principles and businesslike sagacity may appear to be a taking of precautions about a vacant formality; but it is as well to recall that by trained propensity and tradition the business men, great and small, are after all, each in their degree, lieutenants of those Vested Interests which the projected organization of industry is designed to displace, schooled in their tactics and marching under their banners. The experience of the war administration and its management of industry by help of the business men during the past few years goes to show what manner of industrial wisdom is to be looked for where capable and well-intentioned business men are called in to direct industry with a view to maximum production and economy. For its responsible personnel the administration has uniformly drawn on experienced business men, preferably men of successful experience in Big Business; that is to say, trained men with a shrewd eye to the main chance. And the tale of its adventures, so far as a businesslike reticence has allowed them to become known, is an amazing comedy of errors; which runs to substantially the same issue whether it is told of one or another of the many departments, boards, councils, commissions, and administrations, that have had this work to do.

Notoriously, this choice of personnel has with singular uniformity proved to be of doubtful availability, not to choose a harsher epithet. The policies pursued, doubtless with the best and most sagacious intentions of which this businesslike personnel have been capable, have uniformly resulted in the safeguarding of investments and the allocation of commercial profits; all the while that the avowed aim of it all, and doubtless the conscientious purpose of the businesslike administrators, has been quantity production of essential goods. The more that comes to light, the more visible becomes the difference between the avowed purpose and the tangible performance. Tangible performance in the way of productive industry is precisely what the business men do not know how to propose, but it is also that on which the possible success of any projected plan of overturn will always rest. Yet it is also to be remarked that even the reluctant and blindfold endeavors of these business-like administrators to break away from their life-long rule of reasonable earnings, appear to have resulted in a very appreciably increased industrial output per unit of man power and equipment employed. That such was the outcome under the war administration is presumably due in great part to the fact that the business men in charge were unable to exercise so strict a control over the working force of technicians and skilled operatives during that period of stress. And here the argument comes in touch with one of the substantial reasons why there need be no present fear of a revolutionary overturn. By settled habit, the American population are quite unable to see their way to entrust any appreciable responsibility to any other than business men; at the same time that such a move of overturn can hope to succeed only if it excludes the business men from all positions of responsibility. This sentimental deference of the American people to the sagacity of its business men is massive, profound, and alert. So much so that it will take harsh and protracted experience to remove it, or to divert it sufficiently for the purpose of any revolutionary diversion. And more particularly, popular sentiment in this country will not tolerate the assumption of responsibility by the technicians, who are in the popular apprehension conceived to be a somewhat fantastic brotherhood of over-specialized cranks, not to be trusted out of sight except under the restraining hand of safe and sane business men. Nor are the technicians themselves in the habit of taking a greatly different view of their own case. They still feel themselves, in the nature of things, to fall into place as employees of those enterprising business men who are, in the nature of things, elected to get something for nothing. Absentee ownership is secure, just yet. In time, with sufficient provocation, this popular frame of mind may change, of course; but it is in any case a matter of an appreciable lapse of time. Even such a scant and bare outline of generalities as has been hastily sketched above will serve to show that any effectual overturn of the established order is not a matter to be undertaken out of hand, or to be manoeuvred into shape by makeshifts after the initial move has been made.

There is no chance without deliberate preparations from beforehand. There are two main lines of preparations that will have to be taken care of by any body of men who may contemplate such a move: (a) An inquiry into existing conditions and into the available ways and means; and (b) the setting up of practicable organization tables and a survey of the available personnel. And bound up with this work of preparation, and conditioning it, provision must also be made for the growth of such a spirit of teamwork as will be ready to undertake and undergo this critical adventure. All of which will take time. It will be necessary to investigate and to set out in a convincing way what are the various kinds and lines of waste that are necessarily involved in the present businesslike control of industry; what are the abiding causes of these wasteful and obstructive practices; and what economies of management and production will become practicable on the elimination of the present businesslike control. This will call for diligent teamwork on the part of a suitable group of economists and engineers, who will have to be drawn together by self-selection on the basis of a common interest in productive efficiency, economical use of resources, and an equitable distribution of the consumable output. Hitherto no such self-selection of competent persons has visibly taken place, and the beginnings of a plan for team-work in carrying on such an inquiry are yet to be made. In the course of this contemplated inquiry and on the basis afforded by its findings there is no less serious work to be done in the way of deliberation and advisement, among the members of the group in question and in consultation with outside technological men who know what can best be done with the means in hand, and whose interest in things drives them to dip into the same gainless adventure. This will involve the setting up of organization tables to cover the efficient use of the available resources and equipment, as well as to reorganize the traffic involved in the distribution of the output.

By way of an illustrative instance, to show by an example something of what the scope and method of this inquiry and advisement will presumably be like, it may be remarked that under the new order the existing competitive commercial traffic engaged in the distribution of goods to consumers will presumably fall away, in the main, for want of a commercial incentive. It is well known, in a general way, that the present organization of this traffic, by wholesale and retail merchandising, involves a very large and very costly duplication of Work, equipment, stock, and personnel, several hundred per cent, more than would be required by an economically efficient management of the traffic on a reasonable plan. In looking for a way out of the present extremely wasteful merchandising traffic, and in working out organization tables for an equitable and efficient distribution of goods to consumers, the experts in the case will, it is believed, be greatly helped out by detailed information on such existing organizations as, e.g., the distributing system of the Chicago Packers, the chain stores, and the mail- order houses. These are commercial organizations, of course, and as such they are managed with a view to the commercial gain of their owners and managers; but they are at the same time designed to avoid the ordinary wastes of the ordinary retail distribution, for the benefit of their absentee owners. There are not a few object-lessons of economy of this practical character to be found among the Vested Interests; so much so that the economies which result from them are among the valuable capitalized assets of these business concerns.

This contemplated inquiry will, of course, also be useful in the way of publicity; to show, concretely and convincingly, what are the inherent defects of the present businesslike control of industry, why these defects are inseparable from a businesslike control under existing circumstances, and what may fairly be expected of an industrial management which takes no account of absentee ownership. The ways and means of publicity to be employed is a question that plainly cannot profitably be discussed beforehand, so long as the whole question of the contemplated inquiry itself has little more than a speculative interest; and much the same will have to be said as to the scope and detail of the inquiry, which will have to be determined in great part by the interest and qualifications of the men who are to carry it on. Nothing but provisional generalities could at all confidently be sketched into its program until the work is in hand.

The contemplated eventual shift to a new and more practicable system of industrial production and distribution has been here spoken of as a "revolutionary overturn" of the established order. This flagitious form of words is here used chiefly because the Guardians of the established order are plainly apprehensive of something sinister that can be called by no gentler name, rather than with the intention of suggesting that extreme and subversive measures alone can now save the life of the underlying population from the increasingly disserviceable rule of the Vested Interests.

The move which is here discussed in a speculative way under this sinister form of words, as a contingency to be guarded against by fair means and foul, need, in effect, be nothing spectacular; assuredly it need involve no clash of arms or fluttering of banners, unless, as is beginning to seem likely, the Guardians of the old order should find that sort of thing expedient. In its elements, the move will be of the simplest and most matter-of-fact character; although there will doubtless be many intricate adjustments to be made in detail. In principle, all that is necessarily involved is a disallowance of absentee ownership; that is to say, the disestablishment of an institution which has, in the course of time and change, proved to be noxious to the common good. The rest will follow quite simply from the cancelment of this outworn and footless vested right. By absentee ownership, as the term applies in this connection, is here to be understood the ownership of an industrially useful article by any person or persons who are not habitually employed in the industrial use of it.

In this connection, office work of a commercial nature is not rated as industrial employment. A corollary of some breadth follows immediately, although it is so obvious an implication of the main proposition that it should scarcely need explicit statement: An owner who is employed in the industrial use of a given parcel of property owned by him, will still be an "absentee owner," within the meaning of the term, in case he is not the only person habitually employed in its use.

A further corollary follows, perhaps less obvious at first sight, but no less convincing on closer attention to the sense of the terms employed: Collective ownership, of the corporate form, that is to say ownership by a collectivity instituted ad hoc, also falls away as being unavoidably absentee ownership, within the meaning of the term. It will be noted that all this does not touch joint ownership of property held in undivided interest by a household group and made use of by the members of the household conjointly. It is only in so far as the household is possessed of useful property not made use of by its members, or not made use of without hired help, that its ownership of such property falls within the meaning of the term, absentee ownership. To be sufficiently explicit, it may be added that the cancelment of absentee ownership as here understood will apply indiscriminately to all industrially useful objects, whether realty or personality, whether natural resources, equipment, banking capital, or wrought goods in stock.

As an immediate consequence of this cancelment of absentee ownership it should seem to be altogether probable that industrially useful articles will presently cease to be used for purposes of ownership, that is to say for purposes of private gain; although there might be no administrative interference with such use. Under the existing state of the industrial arts, neither the natural resources drawn on for power and materials nor the equipment employed in the great and controlling industries are of a nature to lend themselves to any other than absentee ownership; and these industries control the situation, so that private enterprise for gain on a small scale would scarcely find a suitable market. At the same time the inducement to private accumulation of wealth at the cost of the community would virtually fall away, inasmuch as the inducement to such accumulation now is in nearly all cases an ambition to come in for something in the way of absentee ownership. In effect, other incentives are a negligible quantity.

Evidently, the secondary effects of such cancelment will go far, in more than one direction, but evidently, too, there could be little profit in endeavoring to follow up these ulterior contingencies in extended speculations here. As to the formalities, of a legal complexion, that would be involved in such a disallowance of absentee ownership, they need also be neither large nor intricate; at least not in their main incidence. It will in all probability take the shape of a cancelment of all corporation securities, as an initial move. Articles of partnership, evidences of debt, and other legal instruments which now give title to property not in hand or not in use by the owner, will be voided by the same act. In all probability this will be sufficient for the purpose.

This act of disallowance may be called subversive and revolutionary; but while there is no intention here to offer anything in the way of exculpation, it is necessary to an objective appraisal of the contemplated move to note that the effect of such disallowance would be subversive or revolutionary only in a figurative sense of the words. It would all of it neither subvert nor derange any substantial mechanical contrivance or relation, nor need it materially disturb the relations, either as workman or as consumer of goods and services, of any appreciable number of persons now engaged in productive industry. In fact, the disallowance will touch nothing more substantial than a legal make-believe. This would, of course, be serious enough in its consequences to those classes—called the kept classes—whose livelihood hangs on the maintenance of this legal make-believe. So, likewise, it would vacate the occupation of the "middleman," which likewise turns on the maintenance of this legal make-believe; which gives "title" to that to which one stands in no material relation.

Doubtless, hardship will follow thick and fast, among those classes who are least inured to privation; and doubtless all men will agree that it is a great pity. But this evil is, after all, a side issue, as regards the present argument, which has to do with nothing else than the practicability of the scheme. So it is necessary to note that, however detrimental to the special interests of the absentee owners this move may be, yet it will not in any degree derange or diminish those material facts that constitute the ways and means of productive industry; nor will it in any degree enfeeble or mutilate that joint stock of technical knowledge and practice that constitutes the intellectual working force of the industrial system.

It does not directly touch the material facts of industry, for better or worse. In this sense it is a completely idle matter, in its immediate incidence, whatever its secondary consequences may be believed to be. But there is no doubt that a proposal to disallow absentee ownership will shock the moral sensibilities of many persons; more particularly the sensibilities of the absentee owners. To avoid the appearance of willful neglect, therefore, it is necessary to speak also of the "moral aspect." There is no intention here to argue the moral merits of this contemplated disallowance of absentee ownership; or to argue for or against such a move, on moral or other grounds.

Absentee ownership is legally sound today. Indeed, as is well known, the Constitution includes a clause which specially safeguards its security. If, and when, the law is changed, in this respect, what is so legal today will of course cease to be legal. There is, in fact, not much more to be said about it; except that, in the last resort, the economic moralities wait on the economic necessities. The economic-moral sense of the American community today runs unequivocally to the effect that absentee ownership is fundamentally and eternally right and good; and it should seem reasonable to believe that it will continue to run to that effect for some time yet. There has lately been some irritation and faultfinding with what is called "profiteering" and there may be more or less uneasy discontent with what is felt to be an unduly disproportionate inequality in the present distribution of income; but apprehensive persons should not lose sight of the main fact that absentee ownership after all is the idol of every true American heart. It is the substance of things hoped for and the reality of things not seen. To achieve (or to inherit) a competency, that is to say to accumulate such wealth as will assure a "decent" livelihood in industrial absentia, is the universal, and universally laudable, ambition of all who have reached years of discretion; but it all means the same thing—to get something for nothing, at any cost.

Similarly universal is the awestruck deference with which the larger absentee owners are looked up to for guidance and example. These substantial citizens are the ones who have "made good," in the popular apprehension. They are the great and good men whose lives "all remind us we can make our lives sublime, etc." This commercialized frame of mind is a sturdy outgrowth of many generations of consistent training in the pursuit of the main chance; it is second nature, and there need be no fear that it will allow the Americans to see workday facts in any other than its own perspective, just yet. The most tenacious factor in any civilization is a settled popular frame of mind, and to this abiding American frame of mind absentee ownership is the controlling center of all the economic realities. So, having made plain that all this argument on a practicable overturn of the established order has none but a speculative interest, the argument can go on to consider what will be the nature of the initial move of overturn which is to break with the old order of absentee ownership and set up a regime of workmanship governed by the country's technicians.

As has already been called to mind, repeatedly, the effective management of the industrial system at large is already in the hands of the technicians, so far as regards the work actually done; but it is all under the control of the Vested Interests, representing absentee owners, so far as regards its failure to work. And the failure is, quite reasonably, attracting much attention lately. In this two-cleft, or bi-cameral, administration of industry, the technicians may be said to represent the community at large in its industrial capacity, or in other words the industrial system as a going concern; whereas the business men speak for the commercial interest of the absentee owners, as a body which holds the industrial community in usufruct. It is the part of the technicians, between them, to know the country's available resources, in mechanical power and equipment; to know and put in practice the joint stock of technological knowledge which is indispensable to industrial production; as well as to know and take care of the community's habitual need and use of consumable goods. They are, in effect, the general staff of production engineers, under whose surveillance the required output of goods and services is produced and distributed to the consumers. Whereas it is the part of the business men to know what rate and volume of production and distribution will best serve the commercial interest of the absentee owners, and to put this commercial knowledge in practice by nicely limiting production and distribution of the output to such a rate and volume as their commercial traffic will bear—that is to say, what will yield the largest net income to the absentee owners in terms of price. In this work of sagaciously retarding industry the captains of industry necessarily work at cross purposes, among themselves, since the traffic is of a competitive nature.

Accordingly, in this two-cleft arrangement of administrative functions, it is the duty of the technicians to plan the work and to carry it on; and it is the duty of the captains of industry to see that the work will benefit none but the captains and their associated absentee owners, and that it is not pushed beyond the salutary minimum which their commercial traffic will bear. In all that concerns the planning and execution of the work done, the technicians necessarily take the initiative and exercise the necessary creative surveillance and direction; that being what they, and they alone, are good for; whereas the businesslike deputies of the absentee owners sagaciously exercise a running veto power over the technicians and their productive industry. They are able effectually to exercise this commercially sagacious veto power by the fact that the technicians are, in effect, their employees, hired to do their bidding and fired if they do not; and perhaps no less by this other fact, that the technicians have hitherto been working piecemeal, as scattered individuals under their master's eye; they have hitherto not drawn together on their own ground and taken counsel together as a general staff of industry, to determine what had best be done and what not. So that they have hitherto figured in the conduct of the country's industrial enterprise only as a technological extension of the business men's grasp on the commercial main chance.

Yet, immediately and unremittingly, the technicians and their advice and surveillance are essential to any work whatever in those great primary industries on which the country's productive systems turn, and which set the pace for all the rest. And it is obvious that so soon as they shall draw together, in a reasonably inclusive way, and take common counsel as to what had best be done, they are in a position to say what work shall be done and to fix the terms on which it is to be done. In short, so far as regards the technical requirements of the case, the situation is ready for a self-selected, but inclusive, Soviet of technicians to take over the economic affairs of the country and to allow and disallow what they may agree on; provided always that they live within the requirements of that state of the industrial arts whose keepers they are, and provided that their pretensions continue to have the support of the industrial rank and file; which comes near saying that their Soviet must consistently and effectually take care of the material welfare of the underlying population. Now, this revolutionary posture of the present state of the industrial arts may be undesirable, in some respects, but there is nothing to be gained by denying the fact. So soon—but only so soon— as the engineers draw together, take common counsel, work out a plan of action, and decide to disallow absentee ownership out of hand, that move will have been made. The obvious and simple means of doing it is a conscientious withdrawal of efficiency; that is to say the general strike, to include so much of the country's staff of technicians as will suffice to incapacitate the industrial system at large by their withdrawal, for such time as may be required to enforce their argument.

In its elements, the project is simple and obvious, but its working out will require much painstaking preparation, much more than appears on the face of this bald statement; for it also follows from the present state of the industrial arts and from the character of the industrial system in which modern technology works out, that even a transient failure to make good in the conduct of productive industry will result in a precipitate collapse of the enterprise.

By themselves alone, the technicians can, in a few weeks, effectually incapacitate the country's productive industry sufficiently for the purpose. No one who will dispassionately consider the technical character of this industrial system will fail to recognize that fact. But so long as they have not, at least, the tolerant consent of the population at large, backed by the aggressive support of the trained working force engaged in transportation and in the greater primary industries, they will be substantially helpless to set up a practicable working organization on the new footing; which is the same as saying that they will in that case accomplish nothing more to the purpose than a transient period of hardship and dissension. Accordingly, if it be presumed that the production engineers are of a mind to play their part, there will be at least two main lines of subsidiary preparation to be taken care of before any overt move can reasonably be undertaken: (a) An extensive campaign of inquiry and publicity, such as will bring the underlying population to a reasonable understanding of what it is all about; and (b) the working-out of a common understanding and a solidarity of sentiment between the technicians and the working force engaged in transportation and in the greater underlying industries of the system: to which is to be added as being nearly indispensable from the outset, an active adherence to this plan on the part of the trained workmen in the great generality of the mechanical industries.

Until these prerequisites are taken care of, any project for the overturn of the established order of absentee ownership will be nugatory. By way of conclusion it may be recalled again that, just yet, the production engineers are a scattering lot of fairly contented subalterns, working piecemeal under orders from the deputies of the absentee owners; the working force of the great mechanical industries, including transportation, are still nearly out of touch and out of sympathy with the technical men, and are bound in rival trade organizations whose sole and self-seeking interest converges on the full dinner-pail; while the underlying population are as nearly uninformed on the state of things as the Guardians of the Vested Interests, including the commercialized newspapers, can manage to keep them, and they are consequently still in a frame of mind to tolerate no substantial abatement of absentee ownership; and the constituted authorities are competently occupied with maintaining the status quo. There is nothing in the situation that should reasonably flutter the sensibilities of the Guardians or of that massive body of well-to-do citizens who make up the rank and file of absentee owners, just yet.

REFLECTIONS ON

ECONOMIC THEORY

Chapter 1

The Preconceptions
of Economic Science

Part I. In an earlier paper[1] the view has been expressed that the economics handed down by the great writers of a past generation is substantially a taxonomic science. A view of much the same purport, so far as concerns the point here immediately in question, is presented in an admirably lucid and cogent way by Professor Clark in a recent number of this journal.[2] .There is no wish hereby to burden Professor Clark with a putative sponsorship of any ungraceful or questionable generalisations reached in working outward from this main position, but expression may not be denied the comfort which his unintended authentication of the main position affords. It is true, Professor Clark does not speak of taxonomy, but employs the term "statics" which is this connection, through its use by Professor Clark and by other writers eminent in the science, it is fairly to be questioned whether the term can legitimately be used to characterize the received economic theories.

The word is borrowed from the jargon of physics, where it is used to designate the theory of bodies at rest or of forces in equilibrium. But there is much in the received economic theories to which the analogy of bodies at rest or of forces in equilibrium will not apply. It is perhaps not too much to say that those articles of economic theory that do not lend themselves to this analogy make up the major portion of the received doctrines. So, for instance, it seems scarcely to the point to speak of the statics of production, exchange, consumption, circulation. There are, no doubt, appreciable elements in the theory of these several processes that may fairly be characterized as statical features of the theory; but the doctrines handed down are after all, in the main, theories of the process discussed under each head, and the theory of a process does not belong in statics. The epithet "statical" would, for instance, have to be wrenched somewhat ungently to make it apply to Quesnay's classic *Tableau Economique* or to the great body of Physiocratic speculations that take their rise from it. The like is true for Adam Smith's *Wealth of Nations,* as also for considerable portions generation, for much of Marshall's *Principles,* and for such a modern discussion as Smart's Studies in Economics, as well as for the fruitful activity of the Austrians and of the later representatives of the Historical School. But to return from this terminological digression.

---

[1] "Why is Economics not an Evolutionary Science?" Quarterly Journal of Economics, July, 1898.

[2] ""The Future of Economic Theory," ibid., October, 1898.

While economic science in the remoter past of its history has been mainly of a taxonomic character, later writers of all schools show something of
a divergence from the taxonomic line and an inclination to make the science a genetic account of the economic life process, sometimes even
without an ulterior view to the taxonomic value of the results obtained.
The divergence from the ancient canons of theoretical formulation is to be
taken as an episode of the movement that is going forward in latter-day
science generally; and the progressive change which thus affects the ideals
and the objective point of the modern sciences seems in its turn to be an
expression of that matter-of-fact habit of mind which the prosy but exacting exigencies of life in a modern industrial community breed in men exposed to their unmitigated impact. In speaking of this matter-of-fact character of the modern sciences it has been broadly characterized as "evolutionary"; and the evolutionary method and the evolutionary ideals have
been placed in antithesis to the taxonomic methods and ideals of pre-
evolutionary days.

But the characteristic attitude, aims, and ideals which are so designated
here are by no means peculiar to the group of sciences that are professedly
occupied with a process of development, taking that term in its most
widely accepted meaning. The latter-day inorganic sciences are in this
respect like the organic. They occupy themselves with "dynamic" relations
and sequences. The question which they ask is always, What takes place
next, and why? Given a situation wrought out by the forces under inquiry,
what follows as the consequence of the situation so wrought out? or what
follows upon the accession of further element of force? Even in so non-
evolutionary a science as inorganic chemistry the inquiry consistently
runs on a process, an active sequence, and the value of the resulting situation as a point of departure for the next step in an interminable cumulative sequence. The last step in the chemist's experimental inquiry into any
substance is, What comes of the substance determined? What will it do?
What will it lead to, when it is made the point of departure in further
chemical action? There is no ultimate term, and no definite solution except in terms of further action.

The theory worked out is always a theory of a genetic succession of phenomena, and the relations determined and elaborated into a body of doctrine are always genetic relations. In modern chemistry no cognisance is
taken of the honorific bearing of reactions or molecular formulae. The
modern chemist, as contrasted with this ancient congener, knows nothing
of the worth, elegance, or cogency of the relations that may subsist between the particles of matter with which he busies himself, for any other
than the genetic purpose. The spiritual element and the elements of worth
and propensity no longer count. Alchemic symbolism and the hierarchical
glamour and virtue that once hedged about the nobler and more potent
elements and reagents are almost altogether a departed glory of the science.

Even the modest imputation of propensity involved in the construction
of a scheme of coercive normality, for the putative guidance of reactions,
finds little countenance with the later adepts of chemical science. The

science has outlived that phase of its development at which the taxonomic feature was the dominantone. In the modern sciences, of which chemistry is one, there has been a gradual shifting of the point of view from which the phenomena which the science treats of are apprehended and passed upon; and to the historian of chemical science this shifting of the point of view must be a factor of great weight in the development of chemical knowledge.

Something of a like nature is true for economic science; and it is the aim here to present, in outline, some of the successive phases that have passed over the spiritual attitude of the adepts of the science, and to point out the manner in which the transition from one point of view to the next has been made. As has been suggested in the paper already referred to, the characteristic spiritual attitude or point of view of a given generation or group of economists is shown not so much in their detail work as in their higher syntheses - the terms of their definite formulations - the grounds of their final valuation of the facts handled for purpose of theory. This line of recondite inquiry into the spiritual past and antecedents of the science has not often been pursued seriously or with singleness of purpose, perhaps because it is, after all, of but slight consequence to the practical efficiency of the present-day science.

Still, not a little substantial work has been done towards this end by such writers as Hasbach, Oncken, Bonar, Cannan, and Marshall. And much that is to the purpose is also due to writers outside of economics, for the aims of economic speculation have never been insulated from the work going forward in other lines of inquiry. As would necessarily be the case, the point of view of the enlightened common sense of their time. The spiritual attitude of a given generation of economists is therefore in good part a special outgrowth of the ideals and preconceptions current in the world about them. So, for instance, it is quite the conventional thing to say that the speculations of the Physiocrats were dominated and shaped by the preconception of Natural Rights. Account has been taken of the effect of natural-rights preconceptions upon the Physiocratic schemes of policy and economic reform, as well as upon the details of their doctrines.[3] .

But little has been said of the significance of these preconceptions for the lower courses of the Physiocrats' theoretical structure. And yet that habit of mind to which the natural-rights view is wholesome and adequate is answerable both for the point of departure and for the objective point of the Physiocratic theories, both for the range of facts to which they turned and for the terms in which they were content to formulate their knowledge of the facts which they handled. The failure of their critics to place themselves at the Physiocratic point of view has led to much destructive criticism of their work; whereas, when seen through Physiocratic eyes, such

---

[3]See, for instance, Hasbuch, Allgemeine philosophische Grundlagen der von Francois Quesnay und Adam Smith begróndeten politischen Oekonomie.

doctrines as those of the net product and of the barrenness of the artisan class appear to be substantially true.

The speculations of the Physiocrats are commonly accounted the first articulate and comprehensive presentation of economic theory that is in line with later theoretical work. The Physiocratic point of view may, therefore, well be taken as the point of departure in an attempt to trace that shifting of aims and norms of procedure that comes into view in the work of later economists when compared with earlier writers.Physiocratic economics is a theory of the working-out of the Law of Nature (loi naturelle) in its economic bearing, and this Law of Nature is a very simple matter.

Les lois naturelles sont on physiques ou morales. On entend ici, par loi physique, le cours regie de tout evenement physique de l'ordre naturel, evidemment le plus avatageux au genre humain.On entend ici, par loi morale, the regle de toute action humaine de l'ordre morale, conforme a l'ordre physique evidemment le plus advantageux au genre humain.Ces lois forment ensemble ce qu'on appelle la loi naturelle. Tous les hommes et toutes les puissances humaines doivent etre soumis a ces lois souveraines, instituees par l' Etre-Supreme: elles sont immuables et irrefragables, et les meilleures lois possible.[4] .

The settled course of material facts tending beneficently to the highest welfare of the human race, - this is the final term in the Physiocratic speculations. This is the touchstone of substantiality. Conformity to these "immutable and unerring" laws of nature is the test of economic truth. The laws are immutable and unerring, but that does not mean that they rule the course of events with a blind fatality that admits of no exception and no divergence from the direct line. Human nature may, through infirmity or perversity, willfully break over the beneficent trend of the laws of nature; but to the Physiocrat's sense of the matter the laws are none the less immutable and irrefragable on that account. They are not empirical generalisations on the course of phenomena, like the law of falling bodies or of the angle of reflection; although many of the details of their action are to be determined only by observation and experience, helped out, of course, by interpretation of the facts of observation under the light of reason. So, for instance, Turgot, in his Reflections, empirically works out a doctrine of the reasonable course of development through which wealth is accumulated and reaches the existing state of unequal distribution; so also his doctrines of interest and of money.

The immutable natural laws are rather of the nature of canons of conduct governing nature than generalisations of mechanical sequence, although in a general way the phenomena of mechanical sequence are details of the conduct of nature working according to these canons of conduct. The great law of the order of nature is of the character of a propensity

---

[4] Quesnay, Droit Naturel, ch. v. (Ed. Daire, Physiocrates, pp. 52-53).

working to an end, to the accomplishment of a purpose. The processes of nature working under the quasi-spiritual stress of this immanent propensity may be characterised as nature's habits of life. Not that nature is conscious of its travail, and knows and desires the worthy end of its endeavors; but for all that there is a quasi-spiritual nexus between antecedent and consequent in the scheme of operation in which nature is engaged. Nature is not uneasy about interruptions of its course or occasional deflections from the direct line through an untoward conjunction of mechanical causes, nor does the validity of the great overruling law suffer through such an episode. The introduction of a mere mechanically effective causal factor cannot thwart the course of Nature from reaching the goal to which she animistically tends. Nothing can thwart this teleological propensity of nature except counter-activity or divergent activity of a similarly teleological kind. Men can break over the law, and have short-sightly and willfully done so; for men are also agents who guide their actions by an end to be achieved. Human conduct is activity of the same kind - on the same plane of spiritual reality or competency - as the course of Nature, and it may therefore traverse the latter. The remedy for this short-sighted traffic of misguided human nature is enlightenment, - *"instruction publique et prive des lois de l'ordre naturel"*.[5] .

The nature in terms of which all knowledge of phenomena - for the present purpose economic phenomena - is to be finally synthesised is, therefore, substantially of a quasi-spiritual or animistic character. The laws of nature are in the last resort teleological; they are of the nature of a propensity. The substantial fact in all the sequences of nature is the end to which the sequence naturally tends, not the brute fact of mechanical compulsion or causally effective forces. Economic theory is accordingly the theory

(1) of how the efficient causes of the *ordre naturel* work in an orderly unfolding sequence, guided by the underlying natural law - the propensity immanent in nature to establish the highest well-being of mankind, and

(2) of the conditions imposed upon human conduct by these natural laws in order to reach the ordained goal of supreme human welfare. The conditions so imposed on human conduct are as definitive as the laws and the order by force of which they are imposed; and the theoretical conclusions reached, when these laws and this order are known, are therefore expressions of absolute economic truth. Such conclusions are an expression of reality, but not necessarily of fact. Now, the objective end of this propensity that determines the course of nature is human well-being. But economic speculation has to do with the workings of nature only so far as regards the *ordre physique*. And the laws of nature in the *ordre physique*, working through mechanical sequence, can only work out the physical well-being of man, not necessarily the spiritual.

---

[5] Quesnay, Droit Naturel, ch. v. (Ed. Daire, Physiocrates, p. 53).

This propensity to the physical well-being of man is therefore the law of nature to which economic science must bring its generalisations, and this law of physical beneficence is the substantial ground of economic truth. Wanting this, all our speculations are vain; but having its authentication they are definitive. The great, typical function, to which all the other functioning of nature is incidental if not subsidiary, is accordingly that of the alimentation, nutrition of mankind. In so far, and only in so far as the physical processes contribute to human sustenance and fullness of life, can they, therefore, further the great work of nature. Whatever processes contribute to human sustenance by adding to the material available for human assimilation and nutrition, by increasing the substantial disposable for human comfort, therefore count towards the substantial end.

All other processes, however serviceable in other than this physiological respect, lack the substance of economic reality. Accordingly, human industry is productive, economically speaking, if it heightens the effectiveness of the natural processes out of which the material of human sustenance emerges; otherwise not. The test of productivity, or economic reality in material facts, is the increase of nutritive material. Whatever employment of time or effort does not afford an increase of such material is unproductive, however profitable it may be to the person employed, and however useful or indispensable it may be to the community. The type of such productive industry is the husbandman's employment, which yields a substantial (nutritive) gain. The artisan's work may be useful to the community and profitable to himself, but its economic effect does not extend beyond an alteration of the form in which the material afforded by nature already lies at hand. It is formally productive only, not really productive. It bears no part in the creative or generative work of nature; and therefore it lacks the character of economic substantiality. It does not enhance nature's output of vital force. The artisan's labors, therefore, yield no net product, whereas the husbandman's labors do.

Whatever constitutes a material increment of this output of vital force is wealth, and nothing else is. The theory of value contained in this position has not to do with value according to men's appraisement of the valuable article. Given items of wealth may have assigned to them certain relative values at which they exchange, and these conventional values may differ more or less widely from the natural or intrinsic value of the goods in question; but all that is beside the substantial point. The point in question is not the degree of predilection shown by certain individuals or bodies of men for certain goods. That is a matter of caprice and convention, and it does not directly touch the substantial ground of the economic life. The question of value is a question of the extent to which the given item of wealth forwards the end of nature's unfolding process. It is valuable, intrinsically and really, in so far as it avails the great work which nature has in hand.

Nature, then, is the final term in the Physiocratic speculations. Nature works by impulse and in an unfolding process, under the stress of a propensity to the accomplishment of a given end. The propensity, taken as the final cause that is operative in any situation, furnishes the basis on which to coordinate all our knowledge of those efficient causes through which Nature works to her ends. For the purpose of economic theory proper, this is the ultimate ground of reality to which our quest of economic truth must penetrate. But back of Nature and her works there is, in the Physiocratic scheme of the universe, the Creator, by whose all-wise and benevolent power the order of nature has been established in all the strength and beauty of its inviolate and immutable perfection. But the Physiocratic conception of the Creator is essentially a deistic one: he stands apart from the course of nature which he has established, and keeps his hands off. In the last resort, of course, "*Dieu seul est producteur. Les hommes travaillent, receuillent, economisent, conservent; mais economiser n'est par produire*".[6].

But this last resort does not bring the Creator into economic theory as a fact to be counted with in formulating economic laws. He serves a homiletical purpose in the Physiocratic speculations rather than fills an office essential to the theory. He comes within the purview of the theory by way of authentication rather than as a subject of inquiry or a term in the formulation of economic knowledge. The Physiocratic God can scarcely be said to be an economic fact, but it is otherwise with that Nature whose ways and means constitute the subject-matter of the Physiocratic inquiry. When this natural system of the Physiocratic speculation is looked at from the side of the psychology of the investigators, or from that of the logical premises employed, it is immediately recognised as essentially animistic. It runs consistently on animistic ground; but it is animism of a high grade, - highly integrated and enlightened, but, after all, retaining very much of that primitive force and naivete which characterise the animistic explanations of phenomena in vogue among the untroubled barbarians. It is not the disjected animism of the vulgar, who see a willful propensity - often a willful perversity - in given objects or situations to work towards a given outcome, good or bad. It is not the gambler's haphazard sense of fortuitous necessity or the housewife's belief in lucky days, numbers or phases of the moon.

The Physiocrats' animism rests on a broader outlook, and does not proceed by such an immediately impulsive imputation of propensity. The teleological element - the element of propensity - is conceived in a large way, unified and harmonised, as a comprehensive order of nature as a whole. But it vindicates its standing as a true animism by never becoming fatalistic and never being confused or confounded with the sequence of cause and effect. It has reached the last stage of integration and definition, beyond which the way lies downward from the high, quasi-spiritual ground of animism to the tamer levels of normality and causal uniformities.

---

[6] Dupont de Nemours, Correspondence avec J.-B. Say (Ed. Daire, Physiocrates, premiere partie, p. 399).

There is already discernible a tone of dispassionate and colorless "tendency" about the Physiocratic animism, such as to suggest a wavering towards the side of normality. This is especially visible in such writers as the half-protestant Turgot. In his discussion of the development of farming, for instance, Turgot speaks almost entirely of human motives and the material conditions under which the growth takes place. There is little metaphysics in it, and that little does not express the law of nature in an adequate form. But, after all has been said, it remains true that the Physiocrats' sense of substantiality is not satisfied until he reaches the animistic ground; and it remains true also that the arguments of their opponents made little impression on the Physiocrats so long as they were directed to other than this animistic ground of their doctrine. This is true in great measure even of Turgot, as witness his controversy with Hume. Whatever criticism is directed against them on other grounds is met with impatience, as being inconsequential, if not disingenuous.[7] .

To an historian of economic theory the source and the line of derivation whereby this precise form of the order-of-nature preconception reached the Physiocrats are of first-rate importance; but it is scarcely a question to be taken up here, - in part because it is too large a question to be handled here, in part because it has met with adequate treatment at more competent hands,(8*) and in part because it is somewhat beside the immediate point under discussion. This point is the logical, or perhaps better the psychological, value of the Physiocrats' preconception, as a factor in shaping their point of view and the terms of their definitive formulation of economic knowledge. For this purpose it may be sufficient to point out that the preconception in question belongs to the generation in which the Physiocrats lived, and that it is the guiding norm of all serious thought that found ready assimilation into the common-sense views of that time. It is the characteristic and controlling feature of what may be called the common-sense metaphysics of the eighteenth century, especially so far as concerns the enlightened French community. It is to be noted as a point bearing more immediately on the question in hand that this imputation of final causes to the course of phenomena expresses a spiritual attitude which has prevailed, one might almost say, always and everywhere, but which reached its finest, most effective development, and found its most finished expression, in the eighteenth-century metaphysics.

It is nothing recondite; for it meets us at every turn, as a matter of course, in the vulgar thinking of to-day, - in the pulpit and in the market place, - although it is not so ingenuous, nor does it so unquestionedly hold the primacy in the thinking of any class to-day as it once did. It meets us likewise, with but little change of features, at all past stages of culture, late

---

[7]See, for instance, the concluding chapters of La Riviere's Ordre Naturel des Societies Politiques.

or early. Indeed, it is the most generic feature of human thinking, so far as regards a theoretical or speculative formulation of knowledge.

Accordingly, it seems scarcely necessary to trace the lineage of this characteristic preconception of the era of enlightenment, through specific channels, back to the ancient philosophers or jurists of the empire. Some of the specific forms of its expression - as, for instance, the doctrine of Natural Rights - are no doubt traceable through medieval channels to the teachings of the ancients; but there is no need of going over the brook for water, and tracing back to specific teachings the main features of that habit of mind or spiritual attitude of which the doctrines of Natural Rights and the Order of Nature are specific elaborations only. This dominant habit of mind came to the generation of the Physiocrats on the broad ground of group inheritance, not by lineal devolution from any one of the great thinkers of past ages who had thrown its deliverances into a similarly competent form for the use of his own generation. In leaving the Physiocratic discipline and the immediate sphere of Physiocratic influence for British ground, we are met by the figure of Hume.

Here, also, it will be impracticable to go into details as to the remoter line of derivation of the specific point of view that we come upon on making the transition, for reasons similar to those already given as excuse for passing over the similar question with regard to the Physiocratic point of view. Hume is, of course, not primarily an economist; but that placid unbeliever is none the less a large item in any inventory of eighteenth-century economic thought. Hume was not gifted with a facile acceptance of the group inheritance that made the habit of mind of his generation. Indeed, he was gifted with an alert, though somewhat histrionic, skepticism touching everything that was well received. It is his office to prove all things, though not necessarily to hold fast that which is good. Aside from the strain of affectation discernible in Hume's scepticism, he may be taken as an accentuated expression of that characteristic bent which distinguishes British thinking in his time from the thinking of the Continent, and more particularly of the French.

There is in Hume, and in the British community, an insistence on the prosy, not to say the seamy, side of human affairs. He is not content with formulating his knowledge of things in terms of what ought to be or in terms of the objective point of the course of things. He is not even content with adding to the teleological account of phenomena a chain of empirical, narrative generalisations as to the usual course of things. He insists, in season and out of season, on an exhibition of the efficient causes engaged in any sequence of phenomena; and he is sceptical - irreverently sceptical - as to the need or the use of any formulation of knowledge that outruns the reach of his own matter-of-fact, step-by-step argument from cause to effect.

In short, he is too modern to be wholly intelligible to those of his contemporaries who are most neatly abreast of their time. He out-Britishes the British; and, in his footsore quest for a perfectly tame explanation of things, he finds little comfort, and indeed scant courtesy, at the hands of his own generation. He is not in sufficiently naive accord with the range of preconceptions then in vogue.

But, while Hume may be an accentuated expression of a national characteristic, he is not therefore an untrue expression of this phase of British eighteenth-century thinking. The peculiarity of point of view and of method for which he stands has sometimes been called the critical attitude, sometimes the inductive method, sometimes the materialistic or mechanical, and again, though less aptly, the historical method. Its characteristic is an insistence on matter-of-fact. This matter-of-fact animus that meets any historian of economic doctrine on his introduction to British economics is a large, but not the largest, feature of the British scheme of early economic thought. It strikes the attention because it stands in contrast with the relative absence of this feature in the contemporary speculations of the Continent. The most potent, most formative habit of thought concerned in the early development of economic teaching on British ground is best seen in the broader generalisations of Adam Smith, and this more potent factor in Smith is a bent that is substantially identical with that which gives consistency to the speculations of the Physiocrats. In Adam Smith the two are happily combined, not to say blended; but the animistic habit still holds the primacy, with the matter-of-fact as a subsidiary though powerful factor. He is said to have combined deduction with induction. The relatively great prominence given the latter marks the line of divergence of British from French economics, not the line of coincidence; and on this account it may not be out of place to look more narrowly into the circumstances to which the emergence of this relatively greater penchant for a matter-of-fact explanation of things in the British community is due.

To explain the characteristic animus for which Hume stands, on grounds that might appeal to Hume, we should have to inquire into the peculiar circumstances - ultimately material circumstances - that have gone to shape the habitual view of things within the British community, and that so have acted to differentiate the British preconceptions from the French, or from the general range of preconceptions prevalent on the Continent. These peculiar formative circumstances are no doubt to some extent racial peculiarities; but the racial complexion of the British community is not widely different from the French, and especially not widely different from certain other Continental communities which are for the present purpose roughly classed with the French. Race difference can therefore not wholly, nor indeed for the greater part, account for the cultural difference of which this difference in preconceptions is an outcome.

Through its cumulative effect on institutions the race difference must be held to have had a considerable effect on the habit of mind of the community, but, if the race difference is in this way taken as the remoter ground of an institutional peculiarity, which in its turn has shaped prevalent habits of thought, then the attention may be directed to the proximate causes, the concrete circumstances, through which this race difference has acted, in conjunction with other ulterior circumstances, to work out the psychological phenomena observed. Race differences, it may be remarked, do not so nearly coincide with national lines of demarcation as differences in the point of view from which things are habitually apprehended or differences in the standards according to which facts are rated.

If the element of race difference be not allowed definitive weight in discussing national peculiarities that underlie the deliverances of common sense, neither can these national peculiarities be confidently traced to a national difference in the transmitted learning that enters into the common-sense view of things. So far as concerns the concrete facts embodied in the learning of the various nations within the European culture, these nations make up but a single community. What divergence is visible does not touch the character of the positive information with which the learning of the various nations is occupied.

Divergence is visible in the higher syntheses, the methods of handling the material of knowledge, the basis of valuation of the facts taken up, rather than in the material of knowledge. But this divergence must be set down to a cultural difference, a difference of point of view, not to a difference in inherited information. When a given body of information passes the national frontiers it acquires a new complexion, a new national, cultural physiognomy. It is this cultural physiognomy of learning that is here under inquiry, and a comparison of early French economics (the Physiocrats) with early British economics (Adam Smith) is here entered upon merely with a view to making out what significance this cultural physiognomy of the science has for the past progress of economic speculation.

The broad features of economic speculation, as it stood at the period under consideration, may be briefly summed up, disregarding the element of policy, or expediency, which is common to both groups of economists, and attending to their theoretical work alone. With the Physiocrats, as with Adam Smith, there are two main points of view from which economic phenomena are treated: (a) the matter-of-fact point of view or preconception, which yields a discussion of causal sequences and correlations; and (b) what, for want of a more expressive word, is here called the animistic point of view or preconception, which yields a discussion of teleological sequences and correlations, a discussion of the function of this and that "organ," of the legitimacy of this or the other range of facts.

The former preconception is allowed a larger scope in the British than in the French economics: there is more of "induction" in the British. The latter preconception is present in both, and is the definitive element in both but the animistic element is more colorless in the British, it is less constantly in evidence, and less able to stand alone without the support of arguments from cause to effect. Still, the animistic element is the controlling factor in the higher syntheses of both; and for both alike it affords the definitive ground on which the argument finally comes to rest. In neither group of thinkers is the sense of substantiality appeased until this quasi-spiritual ground, given by the natural propensity of the course of events, is reached. But the propensity in events, the natural or normal course of things, as appealed to by the British speculators, suggests less of an imputation of will-power, or personal force, to the propensity in question. It may be added, as has already been said in another place, that the tacit imputation of will-power or spiritual consistency to the natural or normal course of events has progressively weakened in the later course of economic speculation, so that in this respect, the British economists of the eighteenth century may be said to represent a later phase of economic inquiry than the Physiocrats.

Unfortunately, but unavoidably, if this question as to the cultural shifting of the point of view in economic science is taken up from the side of the causes to which the shifting is traceable, it will take the discussion back to ground on which an economist must at best feel himself to be but a raw layman, with all a layman's limitations and ineptitude, and with the certainty of doing badly what might be done well by more competent hands. But, with a reliance on charity where charity is most needed, it is necessary to recite summarily what seems to be the psychological bearing of certain cultural facts. A cursory acquaintance with any of the more archaic phases of human culture enforces the recognition of this fact, - that the habit of construing the phenomena of the inanimate world in animistic terms prevails pretty much universally on these lower levels. Inanimate phenomena are apprehended to work out a propensity to an end; the movements of the elements are construed in terms of quasi-personal force. So much is well authenticated by the observations on which anthropologists and ethnologists draw for their materials. This animistic habit, it may be said, seems to be more effectual and far-reaching among those primitive communities that lead a predatory life.

But along with this feature of archaic methods of thought or of knowledge, the picturesqueness of which has drawn the attention of all observers, there goes a second feature, no less important for the purpose in hand, though less obtrusive. The latter is of less interest to the men who have to do with the theory of cultural development, because it is a matter of course. This second feature of archaic thought is the habit of also apprehending facts in non-animistic, or impersonal, terms. The imputation of propensity in no case extends to all the mechanical facts in the case.

There is always a substratum of matter of fact, which is the outcome of an habitual imputation of causal sequence, or, perhaps better, an imputation of mechanical continuity, if a new term be permitted. The agent, thing, fact, event, or phenomenon, to which propensity, will-power, or purpose, is imputed, is always apprehended to act in an environment which is accepted as spiritually inert. There are always opaque facts as well as self-directing agents. Any agent acts through means which lend themselves to his use on other grounds than that of spiritual compulsion, although spiritual compulsion may be a large feature in any given case. The same features of human thinking, the same two complementary methods of correlating facts and handling them for the purposes of knowledge, are similarly in constant evidence in the daily life of men in our own community. The question is, in great part, which of the two bears the greater part in shaping human knowledge at any given time and within any given range of knowledge or of facts. Other features of the growth of knowledge, which are remoter from the point under inquiry, may be of no less consequence to a comprehensive theory of the development of culture and of thought; but it is of course out of the question here to go farther afield. The present inquiry will have enough to do with these two. No other features are correlative with these, and these merit discussion on account of their intimate bearing on the point of view of economics.

The point of interest with respect to these two correlative and complementary habits of thought is the question of how they have fared under the changing exigencies of human culture; in what manner they come, under given cultural circumstances, to share the field of knowledge between them; what is the relative part of each in the composite point of view in which the two habits of thought express themselves at any given cultural stage.

The animistic preconception enforces the apprehension of phenomena in terms generically identical with the terms of personality or individuality. As a certain modern group of psychologists would say, it imputes to objects and sequences an element of habit and attention similar in kind, though not necessarily in degree, to the like spiritual attitude present in the activities of a personal agent. The matter-of-fact preconception, on the other hand, enforces a handling of facts without imputation of personal force or attention, but with an imputation of mechanical continuity, substantially the preconception which has reached a formulation at the hands of scientists under the name of conservation of energy or persistence of quantity. Some appreciable resort to the latter method of knowledge is unavoidable at any cultural stage, for it is indispensable to all industrial efficiency. All technological processes and all mechanical contrivances rest, psychologically speaking, on this ground.

This habit of thought is a selectively necessary consequence of industrial life, and, indeed, of all human experience in making use of the material means of life. It should therefore follow that, in a general way, the higher the culture, the greater the share of the mechanical preconception in shaping human thought and knowledge, since, in a general way, the stage of culture attained depends on the efficiency of industry. The rule, while it does not hold with anything like extreme generality, must be admitted to hold to a good extent; and to that extent it should hold also that, by a selective adaptation of men's habits of thought to the exigencies of those cultural phases that have actually supervened, the mechanical method of knowledge should have gained in scope and range. Something of the sort is borne out by observation.

A further consideration enforces the like view. As the community increases in size, the range of observation of the individuals in the community also increases; and continually wider and more far-reaching sequences of a mechanical kind have to be taken account of. Men have to adapt their own motives to industrial processes that are not safely to be construed in terms of propensity, predilection, or passion. Life in an advanced industrial community does not tolerate a neglect of mechanical fact; for the mechanical sequences through which men, at an appreciable degree of culture, work out their livelihood, are no respecters of persons or of will-power. Still, on all but the higher industrial stages, the coercive discipline of industrial life, and of the scheme of life that inculcates regard for the mechanical facts of industry, is greatly mitigated by the largely haphazard character of industry, and by the great extent to which man continues to be the prime mover in industry. So long as industrial efficiency is chiefly a matter of the handicraftsman's skill, dexterity, and diligence, the attention of men in looking to the industrial process is met by the figure of the workman, as the chief and characteristic factor; and thereby it comes to run on the personal element in industry. But, with or without mitigation, the scheme of life which men perforce adopt under exigencies of an advanced industrial situation shapes their habits of thought on the side of their behavior, and thereby shapes their habits of thought to some extent for all purposes. Each individual is but a single complex of habits of thought, and the same psychical mechanism that expresses itself in one direction as conduct expresses itself in another direction as knowledge.

The habits of thought formed in the one connection, in response to stimuli that call for a response in terms of conduct, must, therefore, have their effect when the same individual comes to respond to stimuli that call for a response in terms of knowledge. The scheme of thought or of knowledge is in good part a reverberation of the scheme of life. So that, after all has been said, it remains true that with the growth of industrial organization and efficiency there must, by selection and by adaptation, supervene a greater resort to the mechanical or dispassionate method of apprehending facts. But the industrial side of life is not the whole of it, nor does the scheme of life in vogue in any community or at any cultural stage comprise industrial conduct alone. The social, civic, military, and religious interests come in for their share of attention, and between them they commonly take up by far the larger share of it. Especially is this true so far as concerns those classes among whom we commonly look for a cultivation of knowledge for knowledge's sake.

The discipline which these several interests exert does not commonly coincide with the training given by industry. So the religious interest, with its canons of truth and of right living, runs exclusively on personal relations and the adaptation of conduct to the predilections of a superior personal agent. The weight of its discipline, therefore, falls wholly on the animistic side. It acts to heighten our appreciation of the spiritual bearing of phenomena and to discountenance a matter-of-fact apprehension of things. The sceptic of the type of Hume has never been in good repute with those who stand closest to the accepted religious truths. The bearing of this side of our culture upon the development of economics is shown by what the mediaeval scholars had to say on economic topics.

The disciplinary effects of other phases of life, outside of the industrial and the religious, is not so simple a matter; but the discussion here approaches nearer to the point of immediate inquiry, - namely, the cultural situation in the eighteenth century, and its relation to economic speculation, - and this ground of interest in the question may help to relieve the topic of the tedium that of right belongs to it.In the remoter past of which we have records, and even in the more recent past, Occidental man, as well as man elsewhere, has eminently been a respecter of persons. Wherever the warlike activity has been a large feature of the community's life, much of human conduct in society has proceeded on a regard for personal force. The scheme of life has been a scheme of personal aggression and subservience, partly in the naive form, partly conventionalised in a system of status. The discipline of social life for the present purpose, in so far as its canons of conduct rest on this element of personal force in the unconventionalised form, plainly tends to the formation of a habit of apprehending and coordinating facts from the animistic point of view.

So far as we have to do with life under a system of status, the like remains true, but with a difference. The regime of status inculcates an unremitting and very nice discrimination and observance of distinctions of personal superiority and inferiority. To the criterion of personal force, or will-power, taken in its immediate bearing on conduct, is added the criterion of personal excellence-in-general, regardless of the first-hand potency of the given person as an agent. This criterion of conduct requires a constant and painstaking imputation of personal value, regardless of fact. The discrimination enjoined by the canons of status proceeds on an invidious comparison of persons in respect of worth, value, potency, virtue, which must, for the present purpose, be taken as putative. The greater or less personal value assigned a given individual or a given class under the canons of status is not assigned on the ground of visible efficiency, but on the ground of a dogmatic allegation accepted on the strength of an uncontradicted categorical affirmation simply.

The canons of status hold their ground by force of preemption. Where distinctions of status are based on a putative worth transmitted by descent from honorable antecedents, the sequence of transmission to which appeal is taken as the arbiter of honor is of a putative and animistic character rather than a visible mechanical continuity. The habit of accepting as final what is prescriptively right in the affairs of life has as its reflex in the affairs of knowledge the formula, *Quid ab omnibus, quid ubique creditur credendum est.* Even this meager account of the scheme of life that characterises a regime of status should serve to indicate what is its disciplinary effect in shaping habits of thought, and therefore in shaping the habitual criteria of knowledge and of reality. A culture whose institutions are a framework of invidious comparisons implies, or rather involves and comprises, a scheme of knowledge whose definitive standards of truth and substantiality are of an animistic character; and, the more undividedly the canons of status and ceremonial honor govern the conduct of the community, the greater the facility with which the sequence of cause and effect is made to yield before the higher claims of a spiritual sequence or guidance in the course of events. Men consistently trained to an unremitting discrimination of honor, worth, and personal force in their daily conduct, and to whom these criteria afford the definitive ground of sufficiency in coordinating facts for the purposes of life, will not be satisfied to fall short of the like definitive ground of sufficiency when they come to coordinate facts for the purposes of knowledge simply.

The habits formed in unfolding his activity in one direction, under the impulse of a given interest, assert themselves when the individual comes to unfold his activity in any other direction, under the impulse of any other interest. If his last resort and highest criterion of truth in conduct is afforded by the element of personal force and invidious comparison, his sense of substantiality or truth in the quest of knowledge will be satisfied only when a like definitive ground of animistic force and invidious comparison is reached. But when such ground is reached he rests content and pushes the inquiry no farther. In his practical life he has acquired the habit of resting his case on an authentic deliverance as to what is absolutely right. This absolutely right and good final term in conduct has the character of finality only when conduct is construed in a ceremonial sense; that is to say, only when life is conceived as a scheme of conformity to a purpose outside and beyond the process of living. Under the regime of status this ceremonial finality is found in the concept of worth or honor. In the religious domain it is the concept of virtue, sanctity, or tabu.

Merit lies in what one is, not in what one does. The habit of appeal to ceremonial finality, formed in the school of status, goes with the individual in his quest of knowledge, as a dependence upon a similarly authentic norm of absolute truth, - a similar seeking of a final term outside and beyond the range of knowledge.The discipline of social and civic life under a regime of status, then, reinforces the discipline of the religious life; and the outcome of the resulting habituation is that the canons of knowledge are cast in the animistic mold and converge to a ground of absolute truth, and this absolute truth is of a ceremonial nature. Its subject-matter is a reality regardless of fact. The outcome, for science, of the religious and social life of the civilisation of status, in Occidental culture, was a structure of quasi-spiritual appreciations and explanations, of which astrology, alchemy, and medieval theology and metaphysics are competent, though somewhat one-sided, exponents. Throughout the range of this early learning the ground of correlation of phenomena is in part the supposed relative potency of the facts correlated. but it is also in part a scheme of status, in which facts are scheduled according to a hierarchical gradation of worth or merit, having only a ceremonial relation to the observed phenomena.

Some elements (some metals, for instance) are noble, others base; some planets, on grounds of ceremonial efficacy, have a sinister influence, others a beneficent one; and it is a matter of serious consequence whether they are in the ascendant, and so on. The body of learning through which the discipline of animism and invidious comparison transmitted its effects to the science of economics was what is known as natural theology, natural rights, moral philosophy, and natural law. These several disciplines or bodies of knowledge had wandered far from the naive animistic standpoint at the time when economic science emerged, and much the same is true as regards the time of the emergence of other modern sciences. But the discipline which makes for an animistic formulation of knowledge continued to hold the primacy in modern culture, although its dominion was never altogether undivided or unmitigated. Occidental culture has long been largely an industrial culture; and, as already pointed out, the discipline of industry, and of life in an industrial community, does not favor the animistic preconception. This is especially true as regards industry which makes large use of mechanical contrivances. The difference in these respects between Occidental industry and science, on the one hand, and the industry and science of other cultural regions, on the other hand, is worth noting in this connection. The result has been that the sciences, as that word is understood in later usage, have come forward gradually, and in a certain rough parallelism with the development of industrial processes and industrial organisation.

It is possible to hold that both modern industry (of the mechanical sort) and modern science center about the region of the North Sea. It is still more palpably true that within this general area the sciences, in the recent past, show a family likeness to the civil and social institutions of the communities in which they have been cultivated, this being true to the greatest extent of the higher or speculative sciences; that is, in that range of knowledge in which the animistic preconception can chiefly and most effectively find application. There is, for instance, in the eighteenth century a perceptible parallelism between the divergent character of British and Continental culture and institutions, on the one hand, and the dissimilar aims of British and Continental speculation, on the other hand. Something has already been said of the difference in preconceptions between the French and the British economists of the eighteenth century.

It remains to point out the correlative cultural difference between the two communities, to which it is conceived that the difference in scientific animus is in great measure due. It is, of course, only the general features, the general attitude of the speculators, that can be credited to the difference in culture. Differences of detail in the specific doctrines held could be explained only on a much more detailed analysis than can be entered on here, and after taking account of facts which cannot here be even allowed for in detail. Aside from the greater resort to mechanical contrivances and the larger scale of organisation in British industry, the further cultural peculiarities of the British community run in the same general direction. British religious life and beliefs had less of the element of fealty personal or discretionary mastery and subservience - and more of a tone of fatalism. The civil institutions of the British had not the same rich personal content as those of the French. The British subject owned allegiance to an impersonal law rather than to the person of a superior.

Relatively, it may be said that the sense of status, as a coercive factor, was in abeyance in the British community. Even in the warlike enterprise of the British community a similar characteristic is traceable. Warfare is, of course, a matter of personal assertion. Warlike communities and classes are necessarily given to construing facts in terms of personal force and personal ends. They are always superstitious. They are great sticklers for rank and precedent, and zealously cultivate those distinctions and ceremonial observances in which a system of status expresses itself. But, while warlike enterprise has by no means been absent from the British scheme of life, the geographical and strategic isolation of the British community has given a characteristic turn to their military relations. In recent times British warlike operations have been conducted abroad. The military class has consequently in great measure been segregated out from the body of the community, and the ideals and prejudices of the class have not been transfused through the general body with the same facility and effect that they might otherwise have had.

The British community at home has seen the campaign in great part from the standpoint of the "sinews of war." The outcome of all these national peculiarities of circumstance and culture has been that a different scheme of life has been current in the British community from what has prevailed on the Continent. There has resulted the formation of a different body of habits of thought and a different animus in their handling of facts. The preconception of causal sequence has been allowed larger scope in the correlation of facts for purposes of knowledge; and, where the animistic preconception has been resorted to, as it always has in the profounder reaches of learning, it has commonly been an animism of a tamer kind. Taking Adam Smith as an exponent of this British attitude in theoretical knowledge, it is to be noted that, while he formulates his knowledge in terms of a propensity (natural laws) working teleologically to an end, the end or objective point which controls the formulation has not the same rich content of vital human interest or advantage as is met with in the Physiocratic speculations. There is perceptibly less of an imperious tone in Adam Smith's natural laws   than in those of the contemporary French economists.

It is true, he sums up the institutions with which he deals in terms of the ends which they should subserve, rather than in terms of the exigencies and habits of life out of which they have arisen; but he does not with the same tone of finality appeal to the end subserved as a final cause through whose coercive guidance the complex of phenomena is kept to its appointed task. Under his hands the restraining, compelling agency retires farther into the background, and appeal is taken to it neither so directly nor on so slight provocation. But Adam Smith is too large a figure to be disposed of in a couple of concluding paragraphs. At the same time his work and the bent which he gave to economic speculation are so intimately bound up with the aims and bias that characterise economics in its next stage of development that he is best dealt with as the point of departure for the Classical School rather than merely as a British counterpart of Physiocracy. Adam Smith will accordingly be considered in immediate connection with the bias of the classical school and the incursion of utilitarianism into economics.

PART II.

Adam Smith's animistic bent asserts itself more plainly and more effectually in the general trend and aim of his discussion than in the details of theory. "Adam Smith's Wealth of Nations is, in fact, so far as it has one single purpose, a vindication of the unconscious law present in the separate actions of men when these actions are directed by a certain strong personal motive.[8] .

Both in the Theory of the Moral Sentiments and in the Wealth of Nations there are many passages that testify to his abiding conviction that there is a wholesome trend in the natural course of things, and the characteristically optimistic tone in which he speaks for natural liberty is but an expression of this conviction. An extreme resort to this animistic ground occurs in his plea for freedom of investment.[9] .

In the proposition that men are "led by an invisible hand," Smith does not fall back on a meddling Providence who is to set human affairs straight when they are in danger of going askew. He conceives the Creator to be very continent in the matter of interference with the natural course of things. The Creator has established the natural order to serve the ends of human welfare; and he has very nicely adjusted the efficient causes comprised in the natural order, including human aims and motives, to this work that they are to accomplish. The guidance of interposition, the invisible hand takes place not by way of interposition, but through a comprehensive scheme of contrivances established from the beginning. For the purpose of economic theory, man is conceived to be consistently self-seeking; but this economic man is a part of the mechanism of nature, and his self-seeking traffic is but a means whereby, in the natural course of things, the general welfare is worked out. The scheme as a whole is guided by the end to be reached, but the sequence of events through which the end is reached is a causal sequence which is not broken into episodically.

The benevolent work of guidance was performed in first establishing an ingenious mechanism of forces and motives capable of accomplishing an ordained result, and nothing beyond the enduring constraint of an established trend remains to enforce the divine purpose in the resulting natural course of things. The sequence of events, including human motives and human conduct, is a causal sequence; but it is also something more, or, rather, there is also another element of continuity besides that of brute cause and effect, present even in the step-by-step process whereby the natural course of things reaches its final term. The presence of such a quasi-spiritual or non-causal element is evident from two (alleged) facts.

---

[8] Bonar, Philosophy and Political Economy, pp. 177, 178.

[9] "Every individual is continually exerting himself to find out the most advantageous employment for whatever capital he can command. It is his own advantage, and not that of the society, which he has in view. But the study of his own advantage naturally, or rather necessarily, leads him to prefer that employment which is most advantageous to the society ... By directing that industry in such a manner as its produce may be of the greatest value, he intends only his own gain; and he is in this, as in many other cases, led by an invisible hand to promote an end which was no part of his intention. Nor is it always the worse for society that it was no part of it. By pursuing his own interest he frequently promotes that of the society more effectually than when he really intends to promote it." Wealth of Nations, Book IV, chap. ii.

(1) The course of things may be deflected from the direct line of approach to that consummate human welfare which is its legitimate end. The natural trend of things may be overborne by an untoward conjuncture of causes. There is a distinction, often distressingly actual and persistent, between the legitimate and the observed course of things. If "natural," in Adam Smith's use, meant necessary, in the sense of causally determined, no divergence of events from the natural or legitimate course of things would be possible. If the mechanism of nature, including man, were a mechanically competent contrivance for achieving the great artificer's design, there could be no such episodes of blundering and perverse departure from the direct path as Adam Smith finds in nearly all existing arrangements. Institutional facts would then be "natural"[10] .

(2) When things have gone wrong, they will right themselves if interference with the natural course ceases; whereas, in the case of a causal sequence simply, the mere cessation of interference will not leave the outcome the same as if no interference had taken place. This recuperative power of nature is of an extra-mechanical character. The continuity of sequence by force of which the natural course of things prevails is, therefore, not of the nature of cause and effect, since it bridges intervals and interruptions in the causal sequence.[11] .

Adam Smith's use of the term "real" in statements of theory - as, for example, "real value," "real price[12] is evidence to this effect. "Natural" commonly has the same meaning as "real" in this connection.[13]

Both "natural" and "real" are placed in contrast with the actual; and, in Adam Smith's apprehension, both have a substantiality different from and superior to facts. The view involves a distinction between reality and fact, which survives in a weakened form in the theories of "normal" prices,

---

[10] The discrepancy between the actual, causally determined situation and the divinely intended consummation is the metaphysical ground of all that inculcation of morality and enlightened policy that makes up so large a part of Adam Smith's work. The like, of course, holds true for all moralists and reformers who proceed on the assumption of a providential order.

[11] "In the political body, however, the wisdom of nature has fortunately made ample provision for remedying many of the bad effects of the folly and injustice of man; in the same manner as it has done in the natural body, for remedying those of his sloth and intemperance." Wealth of Nations, Book IV, chap. ix.

[12] E.g., "the real measure of the exchangeable value of all commodities." Wealth of Nations, Book I, chap. v, and repeatedly in the like connection.

[13] E.g., Book I, chap. vii: "When the price of any commodity is neither more nor less than what is sufficient to pay the rent of the land, the wages of the labor, and the profits of the stock employed in raising, preparing, and bringing it to market, according to their natural rates, the commodity is then sold for what may be called its natural price." "The actual price at which any commodity is commonly sold is called its market price. It may be either
above or below or exactly the same with its natural price."

wages, profits, costs, in Adam Smith's successors. This animistic prepos-session seems to pervade the earlier of his two monumental works in a greater degree than the later. In the Moral Sentiments recourse is had to the teleological ground of the natural order more freely and with percepti-bly greater insistence. There seems to be reason for holding that the ani-mistic preconception weakened or, at any rate, fell more into the back-ground as his later work of speculation and investigation proceeded. The change shows itself also in some details of his economic theory, as first set forth in the Lectures, and afterwards more fully developed in the Wealth of Nations. So, for instance, in the earlier presentation of the matter, "the division of labor is the immediate cause of opulence"; and this division of labor, which is the chief condition of economic well-being, "flows from a direct propensity in human nature for one man to barter with another.[14] .

The "propensity" in question is here appealed to as a natural endow-ment immediately given to man with a view to the welfare of human so-ciety, and without any attempt at further explanation of how man has come by it. No causal explanation of its presence or character is offered. But the corresponding passage of the Wealth of Nations handles the ques-tion more cautiously.[15] .

Other parallel passages might be compared, with much the same effect. The guiding hand has withdrawn farther from the range of human vision. However, these and other like filial expressions of a devout optimism need, perhaps, not be taken as integral features of Adam Smith's economic theo-ry, or as seriously affecting the character of his work as an economist. They are the expression of his general philosophical and theological views, and are significant for the present purpose chiefly as evidences of an animistic and optimistic bent. They go to show what is Adam Smith's accepted ground of finality, - the ground to which all his speculations on human affairs converge; but they do not in any great degree show the teleological bias guiding his formulation of economic theory in detail. The effective working of the teleological bias is best seen in Smith's more detailed han-dling of economic phenomena - in his discussion of what may loosely be called economic institutions - and in the criteria and principles of proce-dure by which he is guided in incorporating these features of economic life into the general structure of his theory.

---

[14] Lectures of Adam Smith (Ed. Cannan, 1896). p. 169.

[15] "This division of labor, from which so many advantages are derived, is not origi-nally the effect of any human wisdom, which foresees and intends that general opulence to which it gives occasion. It is the necessary though very slow and gradu-al consequence of a certain propensity in human nature which has in view no such extensive utility, - the propensity to truck, barter, and exchange one thing for an-other. Whether this propensity be one of those original principles in human nature of which no further account can be given, or whether, as seems more probable, it be the necessary consequence of the faculties of reason and speech, it belongs not to our present subject to inquire." Wealth of Nations, Book I, chap. ii.

A fair instance, though perhaps not the most telling one, is the discussion of the "real and nominal price," and of the "natural and market price" of commodities, already referred to above[16] .

The "real" price of commodities is their value in terms of human life. At this point Smith differs from the Physiocrats, with whom the ultimate terms of value are afforded by human sustenance taken as a product of the functioning of brute nature; the cause of the difference being that the Physiocrats conceived the natural order which works towards the material well-being of man to comprise the nonhuman environment only, whereas Adam Smith includes man in this concept of the natural order, and, indeed, makes him the central figure in the process of production. With the Physiocrats, production is the work of nature: with Adam

Smith, it is the work of man and nature, with man in the foreground. In Adam Smith, therefore, labor the final term in valuation. This "real" value of commodities is the value imputed to them by the economist under the stress of his teleological preconception. It has little, if any, place in the course of economic events, and no bearing on human affairs, apart from the sentimental influence which such a preconception in favor of a "real value" in things may exert upon men's notions of what is the good and equitable course to pursue in their transactions. It is impossible to gauge this real value of goods; it cannot be measured or expressed in concrete terms. Still, if labor exchanges for a varying quality of goods, "it is their value which varies, not that of the labor which purchases them.[17] .

The values which practically attach to goods in men's handling of them are conceived to be determined without regard to the real value which Adam Smith imputes to the goods; but, for all that, the substantial fact with respect to these market values is their presumed approximation to the real values teleologically imputed to the goods under the guidance of inviolate natural laws. The real, or natural, value of articles has no causal relation to the value at which they exchange. The discussion of how values are determined in practice runs on the motives of the buyers and sellers, and the relative advantage enjoyed by the parties to the transaction.[18] .

It is a discussion of a process of valuation, quite unrelated to the "real," or "natural," price of things, and quite unrelated to the grounds on which things are held to come by their real, or natural, price; and yet, when the complex process of valuation has been traced out in terms of human motives and the exigencies of the market, Adam Smith feels that he has only cleared the ground. He then turns to the serious business of accounting

---

[16] Wealth of Nations, Book I, chaps. v.-vii.

[17] Wealth of Nations, Book I, chap. v.

[18] As e.g., the entire discussion of the determination of Wages, Profits and Rent, in Book I, chaps. viii. - xi.

for value and price theoretically, and making the ascertained facts articulate with his teleological theory of economic life.[19]

.The occurrence of the words "ordinary" and "average" in this connection need not be taken too seriously. The context makes it plain that the equality which commonly subsists between the ordinary or average rates, and the natural rates, is a matter of coincidence, not of identity. Not only are there temporary deviations, but there may be a permanent divergence between the ordinary and the natural price of a commodity; as in case of a monopoly or of produce grown under peculiar circumstances of soil or climate.[20] .The natural price coincides with the price fixed by competition, because competition means the unimpeded play of those efficient forces through which the nicely adjusted mechanism of nature works out the design to accomplish which it was contrived. The natural price is reached through the free interplay of the factors of production, and it is itself an outcome of production. Nature, including the human factor, works to turn out the goods; and the natural value of the goods is their appraisement from the standpoint of this productive process of nature.

Natural value is a category of production: whereas, notoriously exchange value or market price is a category of distribution. And Adam Smith's theoretical handling of market price aims to show how the factors of human predilection and human wants at work in the haggling of the market bring about a result in passable consonance with the natural laws that are conceived to govern production. The natural price is a composite result of the blending of the three "component parts of the price of commodities," - the natural wages of laborer, the natural profits of stock, and the natural rent of land; and each of these three components is in its turn the measure of the productive effect of the factor to which it pertains. The further discussion of these shares in distribution aims to account for the facts of distribution on the ground of the productivity of the factors which are held to share the product between them.

---

[19] "There is in every society or neighborhood an ordinary or average rate both of wages and profit in every different employment of labor and stock. The rate is naturally regulated ... partly by the general circumstance of the society ... There is, likewise, in every society or neighborhood an ordinary or average rate of rent, which is regulated, too ... These ordinary or average rates may be called the natural rates of wages, profit, and rent, at the time and place in which they commonly prevail. When the price of any commodity is neither more nor less than what is sufficient to pay the rent of the land, the wages of the labor, and the profits of the stock employed in raising, preparing, and bringing it to market, according to their natural rates, the commodity is then sold for what may be called its natural price." Wealth of Nations, Book I, chap. vii.

[20] "Such commodities may continue for whole centuries together to be sold at this high price; and that part of it which resolves itself into the rent of land is, in this case, the part which is generally paid above its natural rate." Book I, chap. vii.

That is to say, Adam Smith's preconception of a productive natural process as the basis of his economic theory dominates his aims and procedure, when he comes to deal with phenomena that cannot be stated in
terms of production. The causal sequence in the process of distribution is,
by Adam Smith's own showing, unrelated to the causal sequence in the
process of production; but, since the latter is the substantial fact, as
viewed from the standpoint of a teleological natural order, the former
must be stated in terms of the latter before Adam Smith's sense of substantiality, or "reality," is satisfied. Something of the same kind is, of
course, visible in the Physiocrats and in Cantillon. It amounts to an extension of the natural-rights preconception to economic theory. Adam
Smith's discussion of distribution as a function of productivity might be
traced in detail through his handling of Wages, Profits, and Rent; but, since
the aim here is a brief characterisation only, and not an exposition, no
farther pursuit of this point seems feasible. It may, however, be worth
while to point out another line of influence along which the dominance of
the teleological preconception shows itself in Adam Smith. This is the
normalisation of data, in order to bring them into consonance with an
orderly course of approach to the putative natural end of economic life
and development.

The result of this normalisation of data is, on the one and, the use of
what James Steuart calls "conjectural history" in dealing with past phases
of economic life, and, on the other hand, a statement of present-day phenomena in terms of what legitimately ought to be according to the God-
given end of life rather than in terms of unconstrued observation. Account
is taken of the facts (supposed or observed) ostensibly in terms of causal
sequence, but the imputed causal sequence is construed to run on lines of
teleological legitimacy. A familiar instance of this "conjectural history," in
a highly and effectively normalized form, is the account of "that early and
rude state of society which precedes both the accumulation of stock and
the appropriation of land.[21]

It is needless at this day to point out that this "early and rude state," in
which "the whole produce of labor belongs to the laborer," is altogether a
figment. The whole narrative, from the putative origin down, is not only
supposititious, but it is merely a schematic presentation of what should
have been the course of past development, in order to lead up to that ideal
economic situation which would satisfy Adam Smith's preconception.[22] .

As the narrative comes nearer the region of known latter-day facts, the
normalisation of the data becomes more difficult and receives more detailed attention; but the change in method is a change of degree rather

[21] Wealth of Nations, Book I, chap. vi; also chap. viii.

[22] For an instance of how these early phases of industrial development appear,
when not seen in the light of Adam Smith's preconception, see, among others,
Bucher, Entstehung der Volkswirtschaft.

than of kind. In the "early and rude state" the coincidence of the "natural" and the actual course of events is immediate and undisturbed, there being no refractory data at hand; but in the later stages and in the present situation, where refractory facts abound, the coordination is difficult, and the coincidence can be shown only by a free abstraction from phenomena that are irrelevant to the teleological trend and by a laborious interpretation of the rest. The facts of modern life are intricate, and lend themselves to statement in the terms of the theory only after they have been subjected to a "higher criticism." The chapter "Of the Origin and Use of Money"[23] is an elegantly normalised account of the origin and nature of an economic institution, and Adam Smith's further discussion of money runs on the same lines. The origin of money is stated in terms of the purpose which money should legitimately serve in such a community as Adam Smith considered right and good, not in terms of the motives and exigencies which have resulted in the use of money and in the gradual rise of the existing method of payment and accounts. Money is "the great wheel of circulation," which effects the transfer of goods in process of production and the distribution of the finished goods to the consumers. It is an organ of the economic commonwealth rather than an expedient of accounting and a conventional repository of wealth. It is perhaps superfluous to remark that to the "plain man," who is not concerned with the "natural course of things" in a consummate Geldwirtschaft, the money that passes his hand is not a "great wheel of circulation."

"To the Samoyed, for instance, the reindeer which serves him as unit of value is wealth in the most concrete and tangible form. Much the same is true of coin, or even of bank-notes, in the apprehension of unsophisticated people among ourselves to-day. And yet it is in terms of the habits and conditions of life of these "plain people" that the development of money will have to be accounted for if it is to be stated in terms of cause and effect. The few scattered passages already cited may serve to illustrate how Adam Smith's animistic or teleological bent shapes the general structure of his theory and gives it consistency.

The principle of definitive formulation in Adam Smith's economic knowledge is afforded by a putative purpose that does not at any point enter causally into the economic life process which he seeks to know. This formative or normative purpose or end is not freely conceived to enter as an efficient agent in the events discussed, or to be in any way consciously present in the process. It can scarcely be taken as an animistic agency engaged in the process. It sanctions the course of things, and gives legitimacy and substance to the sequence of events, so far as this sequence may be made to square with the requirements of the imputed end. It has therefore a ceremonial or symbolical force only, and lends the discussion a ceremonial competency; although with economists who have been in passable

---

[23] Book I, chap. iv.

agreement with Adam Smith as regards the legitimate end of economic life this ceremonial consistency, or consistency de jure, has for many purposes been accepted as the formulation of a causal continuity in the phenomena that have been interpreted in its terms.

Elucidations of what normally ought to happen, as a matter of ceremonial necessity, have in this way come to pass for an account of matters of fact. But, as has already been pointed out, there is much more to Adam Smith's exposition of theory than a formulation of what ought to be. Much of the advance he achieved over his predecessors consists in a larger and more painstaking scrutiny of facts, and a more consistent tracing out of causal continuity in the facts handled. No doubt, his superiority over the Physiocrats, that characteristic of his work by virtue of which it superseded theirs in the farther growth of economic science, lies to some extent in his recourse to a different, more modern ground of normality, - a ground more in consonance with the body of preconceptions that have had the vogue in later generations.

It is a shifting of the point of view from which the facts are handled; but it comes in great part to a substitution of a new body of preconceptions for the old, or a new adaptation of the old ground of finality, rather than an elimination of all metaphysical or animistic norms of valuation. With Adam Smith, as with the Physiocrats, the fundamental question, the answer to which affords the point of departure and the norm of procedure, is a question of substantiality or economic "reality." With both, the answer to this question is given naively, as a deliverance of common sense. Neither is disturbed by doubts as to this deliverance of common sense or by any need of scrutinising it. To the Physiocrats this substantial ground of economic reality is the nutritive process of Nature. To Adam Smith it is Labor. His reality has the advantage of being the deliverance of the common sense of a more modern community, and one that has maintained itself in force more widely and in better consonance with the facts of latter-day industry.

The Physiocrats owe their preconception of the productiveness of nature to the habits of thought of a community in whose economic life the dominant phenomenon was the owner of agricultural land. Adam Smith owes his preconception in favor of labor to a community in which the obtrusive economic feature of the immediate past was handicraft and agriculture, with commerce as a scarcely secondary phenomenon. So far as Adam Smith's economic theories are a tracing out of the causal sequence in economic phenomena, they are worked out in terms given by these two main directions of activity, - human effort directed to the shaping of the material means of life, and human effort and discretion directed to a pecuniary gain. The former is the great, substantial productive force; the latter is not immediately, or proximately, productive.

[24] .Adam Smith still has too lively a sense of the nutritive purpose of the order of nature freely to extend the concept of productiveness to any activity that does not yield a material increase of the creature comforts. His instinctive appreciation of the substantial virtue of whatever effectually furthers nutrition, even leads him into the concession that "in agriculture nature labors along with man," although the general tenor of his argument is that the productive force with which the economist always has to count is human labor. This recognised substantiality of labor as productive is, as has already been remarked, accountable for his effort to reduce to terms of productive labor such a category of distribution as exchange value. With but slight qualification, it will hold that, in the causal sequence which Adam Smith traces out in his economic theories proper (contained in the first three books of the Wealth of Nations), the causally efficient factor is conceived to be human nature in these two relations, - of productive efficiency and pecuniary gain through exchange. Pecuniary gain - gain in the material means of life through barter - furnishes the motive force to the economic activity of the individual; although productive efficiency is the legitimate, normal end of the community's economic life. To such an extent does this concept of man's seeking his ends through "truck, barter, and exchange" pervade Adam Smith's treatment of economic processes that he even states production in its terms, and says that,, labor was the first price, the original purchase-money, that was paid for all things.[25] .

The human nature engaged in this pecuniary traffic is conceived in somewhat hedonistic terms, and the motives and movements of men are normalised to fit the requirements of a hedonistically conceived order of nature. Men are very much alike in their native aptitudes and propensities;[26] and, so far as economic theory need take account of these aptitudes and propensities, they are aptitudes for the production of the "necessaries and conveniences of life," and propensities to secure as great a share of these creature comforts as may be. Adam Smith's conception of normal human nature - that is to say, the human factor which enters causally in the process which economic theory discusses - comes, on the whole, to this: Men exert their force and skill in a mechanical process of production, and their pecuniary sagacity in a competitive process of distribution, with a view to individual gain in the material means of life. These material means are sought in order to the satisfaction of men's natural wants

---

[24] See Wealth of Nations, Book II, chap. v, "Of the Different Employment of Capitals."

[25] Wealth of Nations, Book I, chap. v. See also the plea for free trade, Book IV, chap. ii: "But the annual revenue of every society is always precisely equal to the exchangeable value of the whole annual produce of its industry, or, rather, is precisely the same thing with that exchangeable value."

[26] "The difference of natural talents in different men is in reality much less than we are aware of." Wealth of Nations, Book I, chap. ii.

through their consumption. It is true, much else enters into men's endeavors in the struggle for wealth, as Adam Smith points out; but this consumption comprises the legitimate range of incentives, and a theory which concerns itself with the natural course of things need take but incidental account of what does not come legitimately in the natural course. In point of fact, there are appreciable "actual," though scarcely "real," departures from this rule. They are spurious and insubstantial departures, and do not properly come within the purview of the stricter theory. And, since human nature is strikingly uniform, in Adam Smith's apprehension, both the efforts put forth and the consumptive effect accomplished may be put in quantitative terms and treated algebraically, with the result that the entire range of phenomena comprised under the head of consumption need be but incidentally considered; and the theory of production and distribution is complete when the goods or the values have been traced to their disappearance in the hands of their ultimate owners.

The reflex effect of consumption upon production and distribution is, on the whole, quantitative only. Adam Smith's preconception of a normal teleological order of procedure in the natural course, therefore, affects not only those features of theory where he is avowedly concerned with building up a normal scheme of the economic process. Through his normalising the chief causal factor engaged in the process, it affects also his arguments from cause to effect.[27] .

What makes this latter feature worth particular attention is the fact that his successors carried this normalisation farther, and employed it with less frequent reference to the mitigating exceptions which Adam Smith notices by the way. The reason for that farther and more consistent normalisation of human nature which gives us the "economic man" at the hands of Adam Smith's successors lies, in great part, in the utilitarian philosophy that entered in force and in consummate form at about the turning of the century. Some credit in the work of normalisation is due also to the farther supersession of handicraft by the "capitalistic" industry that came in at the same time and in pretty close relation with the utilitarian views.

After Adam Smith's day, economics fell into profane hands. Apart from Malthus, who, of all the greater economists, stands nearest to Adam Smith on such metaphysical heads as have an immediate bearing upon the premises of economic science, the next generation do not approach their

---

[27] "Mit diesen philosophischen Ueberzeugungen tritt nun Adam Smith an die Welt der Enfahrung heran, und es ergiebt sich ihm die Richtigkeit der Principien. Der Reiz der Smiths'schen Schriften beruht zum grossen Teile darauf, dass Smith die Principien in so innige Verbindung mit dem Thats δ chlichen gebracht. Hie und da werden dann auch die Principien, was durch diese Verbindung veranlasst wird, an ihren Spitzen etwas abgeschliffen, ihre allzuscharfe Auspr δ gung dadurch vermieden. Nichtsdestoweniger aber bleiben sie stets die leitenden Grundgedanken." Richard Zeyss, *Adam Smith und der Eigennutz* (Tübingen, 1889), p. 110.

subject from the point of view of a divinely instituted, order; nor do they discuss human interests with that gently optimistic spirit of submission that belongs to the economist who goes to his work with the fear of God before his eyes. Even with Malthus the recourse to the divinely sanctioned order of nature is somewhat sparing and temperate. But it is significant for the later course of economic theory that, while Malthus may well be accounted the truest continuer of Adam Smith, it was the undevout utilitarians that became the spokesmen of the science after Adam Smith's time.

There is no wide breach between Adam Smith and the utilitarians, either in details of doctrine or in the concrete conclusions arrived at as regards questions of policy. On these heads Adam Smith might well be classed as a moderate utilitarian, particularly so far as regards his economic work. Malthus has still more of a utilitarian air, - so much so, indeed, that he is not infrequently spoken of as a utilitarian. This view, convincingly set forth by Mr. Bonar,[28] is no doubt well borne out by a detailed scrutiny of Malthus's economic doctrines. His humanitarian bias is evident throughout, and his weakness for considerations of expediency is the great blemish of his scientific work. But, for all that, in order to an appreciation of the change that came over classical economics with the rise of Benthamism, it is necessary to note that the agreement in this matter between Adam Smith and the disciples of Bentham, and less decidedly that between Malthus and the latter, is a coincidence of conclusions rather than an identity of preconceptions.[29] .

With Adam Smith the ultimate ground of economic reality is the design of God, the teleological order; and his utilitarian generalisations, as well as the hedonistic character of his economic man, are but methods of the working out of this natural order, not the substantial and self-legitimating ground. Shifty as Malthus's metaphysics are, much the same is to be said for him.

[30] .Of the utilitarians proper the converse is true, although here, again, there is by no means utter consistency the substantial economic ground is pleasure and pain: the teleological order (even the design of God, where that is admitted) is the method of its working-out. It may be unnecessary here to go into the farther implications, psychological and ethical, which this preconception of the utilitarians involves. And even this much may

---

[28] See, e.g., Malthus and his Work, especially Book III, as also the chapter on Malthus in Philosophy and Political Economy, Book III, Modern Philosophy: Utilitarian Economics, chap. i, "Malthus."

[29] Ricardo is here taken as a utilitarian of the Benthamite color, although he cannot be classed as a disciple of Bentham. His hedonism is but the uncritically accepted metaphysics comprised in the common sense of his time, and his substantial coincidence with Bentham goes to show how well diffused the hedonist preconception was at the time.

[30] Cf. Bonar, Malthus and his Work, pp. 323-336.

seem a taking of excessive pains with a distinction that marks no tangible difference. But a reading of the classical doctrines, with something of this metaphysics of political economy in mind, will show how, and in great part why, the later economists of the classical line diverged from Adam Smith's tenets in the early years of the century, until it has been necessary to interpret Adam Smith somewhat shrewdly in order to save him from heresy.

The post-Bentham economics is substantially a theory of value. This is altogether the dominant feature of the body of doctrines; the rest follows from, or is adapted to, this central discipline. The doctrine of value is of very great importance also in Adam Smith; but Adam Smith's economics is a theory of the production and apportionment of the material, means of life.31 .

With Adam Smith, value is discussed from the point of view of production. With the utilitarians, production is discussed from the point of view of value. The former makes value an outcome of the process of production; the latter make production the outcome of a valuation process. The point of departure with Adam Smith is the "productive power of labor.32 .

With Ricardo it is a pecuniary problem concerned in the distribution of ownership;33 but the classical writers are followers of Adam Smith, and improve upon and correct the results arrived at by him, and the difference of point of view, therefore, becomes evident in their divergence from him, and the different distribution of emphasis, rather than in a new and antagonistic departure. The reason for this shifting of the center of gravity from production to valuation lies, proximately, in Bentham's revision of the "principles" of morals. Bentham's philosophical position is, of course, not a self-explanatory phenomenon, nor does the effect of Benthamism extend only to those who are avowed followers of Bentham; for Bentham is the exponent of a cultural change that affects the habits of thought of the entire community.

The immediate point of Bentham's work, as affecting the habits of thought of the educated community, is the substitution of hedonism (utility) in place of achievement of purpose, as a ground of legitimacy and a guide in the normalisation of knowledge. Its effect is most patent in specu-

---

31 His work is an inquiry into "the Nature and Causes of the Wealth of Nations."

32 "The annual labor of every nation is the fund which originally supplies it with all the necessaries and conveniences of life which it annually consumes, and which consist always either in the immediate produce of that labor or in what is purchases with that produce from other nations." Wealth of Nations, "Introduction and Plan," opening paragraph.

33 "The produce of the earth - all that is derived from its surface by the united application of labor, machinery and capital - is divided among three classes of the community... To determine the laws which regulate this distribution is the principal problem of political economy." Political Economy, Preface.

lations on morals, where it inculcates determinism. Its close connection with determinism in ethics points the way to what may be expected of its working in economics. In both cases the result is that human action is construed in terms of the causal forces of the environment, the human agent being, at the best, taken as a mechanism of commutation, through the workings of which the sensuous effects wrought by the impinging forces of the environment are, by an enforced process of valuation, transmuted without quantitative discrepancy into moral or economic conduct, as the case may be. In ethics and economics alike the subject-matter of the theory is this valuation process that expresses itself in conduct, resulting, in the case of economic conduct, in the pursuit of the greatest gain or least sacrifice.

Metaphysically or cosmologically considered, the human nature into the motions of which hedonistic ethics and economics inquire is an intermediate term in a causal sequence, of which the initial and the terminal members are sensuous impressions and the details of conduct. This intermediate term conveys the sensuous impulse without loss of force to its eventuation in conduct. For the purpose of the valuation process through which the impulse is so conveyed, human nature may, therefore, be accepted as uniform; and the theory of the valuation process may be formulated quantitatively, in terms of the material forces affecting the human sensory and of their equivalents in the resulting activity. In the language of economics, the theory of value may be stated in terms of the consumable goods that afford the incentive to effort and the expenditure undergone in order to procure them. Between these two there subsists a necessary equality; but the magnitudes between which the equality subsists are hedonistic magnitudes, not magnitudes of kinetic energy nor of vital force, for the terms handled are sensuous terms.

It is true, since human nature is substantially uniform, passive, and unalterable in respect of men's capacity for sensuous affection, there may also be presumed to subsist a substantial equality between the psychological effect to be wrought by the consumption of goods, on the one side, and the resulting expenditure of kinetic or vital force, on the other side; but such an equality is, after all, of the nature of a coincidence, although there should be a strong presumption in favor of its prevailing on an average and in the common run of cases. Hedonism, however, does not postulate uniformity between men except in the respect of sensuous cause and effect. The theory of value which hedonism gives is, therefore, a theory of cost in terms of discomfort. By virtue of the hedonistic equilibrium reached through the valuation process, the sacrifice or expenditure of sensuous reality involved in acquisition is the equivalent of the sensuous gain secured.

An alternative statement might perhaps be made, to the effect that the measure of the value of goods is not the sacrifice or discomfort undergone, but the sensuous gain that accrues from the acquisition of the goods; but this is plainly only an alternative statement, and there are special reasons in the economic life of the time why the statement in terms of cost, rather than in terms of "utility," should commend itself to the earlier classical economists. On comparing the utilitarian doctrine of value with earlier theories, then, the case stands somewhat as follows. The Physiocrats and Adam Smith contemplate value as a measure of the productive force that realises itself in the valuable article. With the Physiocrats this productive force is the "anabolism" of

Nature (to resort to a physiological term): with Adam Smith it is chiefly human labor directed to heightening the serviceability of the materials with which it is occupied. Production causes value in either case. The post-Bentham economics contemplates value as a measure of, or as measured by the irksomeness of the effort involved in procuring the valuable goods. As Mr. E. C. K. Gonner has admirably pointed out,[34] Ricardo - and the like holds true of classical economics generally - makes cost the foundation of value, not its cause. This resting of value on cost takes place through a valuation. Any one who will read Adam Smith's theoretical exposition to as good purpose as Mr. Gonner has read Ricardo will scarcely fail to find that the converse is true in Adam Smith's case. But the causal relation of cost to value holds only as regards "natural" or "real" value in Adam Smith's doctrine. As regards market price, Adam Smith's theory does not differ greatly from that of Ricardo on this head. He does not overlook the valuation process by which market price is adjusted and the course of investment is guided, and his discussion of this process runs in terms that should be acceptable to any hedonist.

The shifting of the point of view that comes into economics with the acceptance of utilitarian ethics and its correlate, the associationist psychology, is in great part a shifting to the ground of causal sequence as contrasted with that of serviceability to a preconceived end. This is indicated even by the main fact already cited, - that the utilitarian economists make exchange value the central feature of their theories, rather than the conduciveness of industry to the community's material welfare. Hedonistic exchange value is the outcome of a valuation process enforced by the apprehended pleasure-giving capacities of the items valued.

And in the utilitarian theories of production, arrived at from the standpoint so given by exchange value, the conduciveness to welfare is not the objective point of the argument. This objective point is rather the bearing of productive enterprise upon the individual fortunes of the agents engaged, or upon the fortunes of the several distinguishable classes of beneficiaries comprised in the industrial community; for the great immediate bearing of exchange values upon the life of the collectivity is their bearing upon the distribution of wealth. Value is a category of distribution. The result is that, as is well shown by Mr. Cannan's discussion,

---

[34] In the introductory essay to his edition of Ricardo's Political Economy. See, e.g., paragraphs 9 and 24.

[35] the theories of production offered by the classical economists have been sensibly scant, and have been carried out with a constant view to the doctrines on distribution. An incidental but telling demonstration of the same facts is given by Professor Bucher;[36] and in illustration may be cited Torrens's Essay On the Production of Wealth, which is to a good extent occupied with discussions of value and distribution. The classical theories of production have been theories of the production of "wealth"; and "wealth," in classical usage, consists of material things having exchange value. During the vogue of the classical economics the accepted characteristic by which "wealth" has been defined has been its amenability to ownership. Neither in Adam Smith nor in the Physiocrats is this amenability to ownership made so much of, nor is it in a similar degree accepted as a definite mark of the subject-matter of the science.

As their hedonistic preconception would require, then, it is to the pecuniary side of life that the classical economists give their most serious attention, and it is the pecuniary bearing of any given phenomenon or of any institution that commonly shapes the issue of the argument. The causal sequence about which the discussion centers is a process of pecuniary valuation. It runs on distribution, ownership, acquisition, gain, investment, exchange.[37] .

In this way the doctrines on production come to take a pecuniary coloring; as is seen in a less degree also in Adam Smith, and even in the Physiocrats, although these earlier economists very rarely, if ever, lose touch with the concept of generic serviceability as the characteristic feature of production. The tradition derived from Adam Smith, which made productivity and serviceability the substantial features of economic life, was not abruptly put aside by his successors, though the emphasis was differently distributed by them in following out the line of investigation to which the tradition pointed the way. In the classical economics the ideas of production and of acquisition are not commonly held apart, and very much of what passes for a theory of production is occupied with phenomena of investment and acquisition.

Torrens's Essay is a case in point, though by no means an extreme case. This is as it should be; for to the consistent hedonist the sole motive force concerned in the industrial process is the self-regarding motive of pecuni-

---

[35] Theories of Production and Distribution, 1776-1848.

[36] Entstehung der Volkswirtschaft (second edition). Cf. especially chaps. ii, iii, vi, and vii.

[37] "Even if we put aside all questions which involve a consideration of the effects of industrial institutions in modifying the habits and character of the classes of the community... that enough still remains to constitute a separate science, the mere enumeration of the chief terms of economics - wealth, value, exchange, credit, money, capital, and commodity - will suffice to show." Shirres, Analysis of the Ideas of Economics (London, 1893), pp. 8 and 9.

ary gain, and industrial activity is but an intermediate term between the expenditure or discomfort undergone and the pecuniary gain sought. Whether the end and outcome is an invidious gain for the individual (in contrast with or at the cost of his neighbors), or an enhancement of the facility of human life on the whole, is altogether a by-question in any discussion of the range of incentives by which men are prompted to their work or the direction which their efforts take. The serviceability of the given line of activity, for the life purposes of the community or for one's neighbors, "is not of the essence of this contract." These features of serviceability come into the account chiefly as affecting the vendibility of what the given individual has to offer in seeking gain through a bargain.38

.

In hedonistic theory the substantial end of economic life is individual, gain, and for this purpose production and acquisition may be taken as fairly coincident, if not identical. Moreover, society, in the utilitarian philosophy, is the algebraic sum of the individuals; and the interest of the society is the sum of the interests of the individuals. It follows by easy consequence, whether strictly true or not, that the sum of individual gains is the gain of the society, and that, in serving his own interest in the way of acquisition, the individual serves the collective interest of the community. Productivity or serviceability is, therefore, to be presumed of any occupation or enterprise that looks to a pecuniary gain; and so, by a roundabout path, we get back to the ancient conclusion of Adam Smith, that the remuneration of classes or persons engaged in industry coincides with their productive contribution to the output of services and consumable goods.

A felicitous illustration of the working of this hedonistic norm in classical economic doctrine is afforded by the theory of the wages of superintendence, - an element in distribution which is not much more than suggested in Adam Smith, but which receives ampler and more painstaking attention as the classical body of doctrines reaches a fuller development. The "wages of superintendence" are the gains due to pecuniary management. They are the gains that come to the director of the "business," - not those that go to the director of the mechanical process or to the foreman of the shop.

The latter are wages simply. This distinction is not altogether clear in the earlier writers, but it is clearly enough contained in the fuller development of the theory. The undertaker's work is the management of investment. It is altogether of a pecuniary character, and its proximate aim is "the main chance." If it leads, indirectly, to an enhancement of serviceability or a heightened aggregate output of consumable goods, that is a fortuitous circumstance incident to that heightened vendibility on which the investor's gain depends. Yet the classical doctrine says frankly that the wages

---

38 "If a commodity were in no way useful... it would be destitute of exchangeable value;... (but), possessing utility, commodities derive their exchangeable value from two sources," etc. Ricardo, Political Economy, chap. i, sect I.

of superintendence are the remuneration of superior productivity,[39] and the classical theory of production is in good part a doctrine of investment in which the identity of production and pecuniary gain is taken for granted. The substitution of investment in the place of industry as the central and substantial fact in the process of production is due not to the acceptance of hedonism simply, but rather to the conjunction of hedonism with an economic situation of which the investment of capital and its management for gain was the most obvious feature. The situation which shaped the common-sense apprehension of economic facts at the time was what has since been called a capitalistic system, in which pecuniary enterprise and the phenomena of the market were the dominant and tone-giving facts. But this economic situation was also the chief ground for the vogue of hedonism in economics; so that hedonistic economics may be taken as an interpretation of human nature in terms of the market-place.

The market and the "business world," to which the business man in his pursuit of gain was required to adapt his motives, had by this time grown so large that the course of business events was beyond the control of any one person; and at the same time those far-reaching organisations of invested wealth which have latterly come to prevail and to coerce the market were not then in the foreground. The course of market events took its passionless way without traceable relation or deference to any man's convenience and without traceable guidance towards an ulterior end. Man's part in this pecuniary world was to respond with alacrity to the situation, and so adapt his vendible effects to the shifting demand as to realise something in the outcome. What he gained in his traffic was gained without loss to those with whom he dealt, for they paid no more than the goods were worth to them.

One man's gain need not be another's loss; and, if it is not, then it is net gain to the community. Among the striking remoter effects of the hedonistic preconception, and its working out in terms of pecuniary gain, is the classical failure to discriminate between capital as investment and capital as industrial appliances. This is, of course, closely related to the point already spoken of. The appliances of industry further the production of

---

[39] Cf., for instance, Senior, Political Economy (London, 1872), particularly pp. 88, 89, and 130-135, where the wages of superintendence are, somewhat reluctantly, classed under profits; and the work of superintendence is thereupon conceived as being, immediately or remotely, an exercise of "abstinence" and a productive work. The illustration of the bill-broker is particularly apt. The like view of the wages of superintendence in an article of theory with more than one of the later descendents of the classical line.

goods, therefore capital (invested wealth) is productive; and the rate of its average remuneration marks the degree of its productiveness.[40]

The most obvious fact limiting the pecuniary gain secured by means of invested wealth is the sum invested. Therefore, capital limits the productiveness of industry; and the chief and indispensable condition to an advance in material well-being is the accumulation of invested wealth. In discussing the conditions of industrial improvement, it is usual to assume that "the state of the arts remains unchanged," which is, for all purposes but that of a doctrine of profits per cent., an exclusion of the main fact. Investments may, further, be transferred from one enterprise to another.

Therefore, and in that degree, the means of production are "mobile. "Under the hands of the great utilitarian writers, therefore, political economy is developed into a science of wealth, taking that term in the pecuniary sense, as things amenable to ownership. The course of things in economic life is treated as a sequence of pecuniary events, and economic theory becomes a theory of what should happen in that consummate situation where the permutation of pecuniary magnitudes takes place without disturbance and without retardation. In this consummate situation the pecuniary motive has its perfect work, and guides all the acts of economic man in a guileless, colorless, unswerving quest of the greatest gain at the least sacrifice.

Of course, this perfect competitive system, with its untainted "economic man," is a feat of scientific imagination, and is not intended as a competent expression of fact. It is an expedient of abstract reasoning; and its avowed competency extends only to the abstract principles, the fundamental laws of the science, which hold only so far as the abstraction holds. But, as happens in such cases, having once been accepted and assimilated as real, though perhaps not as actual, it becomes an effective constituent in the inquirer's habits of thought, and goes to shape his knowledge of facts. It comes to serve as a norm of substantiality or legitimacy; and facts in some degree fall under its constraint, as is exemplified by many allegations regarding the "tendency" of things. To this consummation, which Senior speaks of as "the natural state of man,

[41] human development tends by force of the hedonistic character of human nature; and in terms of its approximation to this natural state, therefore, the immature actual situation had best be stated. The pure theory, the "hypothetical science" of Cairnes, " traces the phenomena of the production and distribution of wealth up to their causes, in the principles of

---

[40] Cf. Bohm-Bawerk, Capital and Interest, Books II and IV, as well as the Introduction and chaps. iv and v of Book I. Bohm-Bawerk's discussion bears less immediately on the present point than the similarity of the terms employed would suggest.

[41] Political Economy, p. 87.

human nature and the laws and events - physical, political, and social - of the external world."[42]

But since the principles of human nature that give the outcome in men's economic conduct, so far as it touches the production and distribution of wealth, are but the simple and constant sequence of hedonistic cause and effect, the element of human nature may fairly be eliminated from the problem, with great gain in simplicity and expedition. Human nature being eliminated, as being a constant intermediate term, and all institutional features of the situation being also eliminated (as being similar constants under that natural or consummate pecuniary regime with which the pure theory is concerned), the laws of the phenomena of wealth may be formulated in terms of the remaining factors.

These factors are the vendible items that men handle in these processes of production and distribution and economic laws come, therefore, to be expressions of the algebraic relations subsisting between the various elements of wealth and investment, - capital, labor, land, supply and demand of one and the other, profits, interest, wages. Even such items as credit and population become dissociated from the personal factor, and figure in the computation as elemental factors acting and reacting though a permutation of values over the heads of the good people whose welfare they are working out. To sum up: the classical economics, having primarily to do with the pecuniary side of life, is a theory of a process of valuation.

But since the human nature at whose hands and for whose behoof the valuation takes place is simple and constant in its reaction to pecuniary stimulus, and since no other feature of human nature is legitimately present in economic phenomena than this reaction to pecuniary stimulus, the value concerned in the matter is to be overlooked or eliminated; and the theory of the valuation process then becomes a theory of the pecuniary interaction of the facts valued. It is a theory of valuation with the element of valuation left out, - a theory of life stated in terms of the normal paraphernalia of life. In the preconceptions with which classical economics set out were comprised the remnants of natural rights and of the order of nature, infused with that peculiarly mechanical natural theology that made its way into popular vogue on British ground during the eighteenth century and was reduced to a neutral tone by the British penchant for the commonplace - stronger at this time than at any earlier period.

The reason for this growing penchant for the commonplace, for the explanation of things in causal terms, lies partly in the growing resort to mechanical processes and mechanical prime movers in industry, partly in the (consequent) continued decline of the aristocracy and the priesthood, and partly in the growing density of population and the consequent greater

---

[42] Character and Logical Method of Political Economy (New York, 1875), p. 71. Cairnes may not be altogether representative of the high tide of classicism, but his characterisation of the science is none the less to the point.

specialisation and wider organisation of trade and business. The spread of the discipline of the natural sciences, largely incident to the mechanical industry, counts in the same direction; and obscurer factors in modern culture may have had their share.

The animistic preconception was not lost, but it lost tone; and it partly fell into abeyance, particularly so far as regards its avowal. It is visible chiefly in the unavowed readiness of the classical writers to accept as imminent and definitive any possible outcome which the writer's habit or temperament inclined him to accept as right and good. Hence the visible inclination of classical economists to a doctrine of the harmony of interests, and their somewhat uncircumspect readiness to state their generalisations in terms of what ought to happen according to the ideal requirements of that consummate Geldwirtschaft to which men "are impelled by the provisions of nature[43] .

By virtue of their hedonistic preconceptions, their habituation to the ways of a pecuniary culture, and their unavowed animistic faith that nature is in the right, the classical economists knew that the consummation to which, in the nature of things, all things tend, is the frictionless and beneficent competitive system. This competitive ideal, therefore, affords the normal, and conformity to its requirements affords the test of absolute economic truth. The standpoint so gained selectively guides the attention of the classical writers in their observation and apprehension of facts, and they come to see evidence of conformity or approach to the normal in the most unlikely places.

Their observation is, in great part, interpretative, as observation commonly is. What is peculiar to the classical economists in this respect is their particular norm of procedure in the work of interpretation. And, by virtue of having achieved a standpoint of absolute economic normality, they became a "deductive" school, so called, in spite of the patent fact that they were pretty consistently employed with an inquiry into the causal sequence of economic phenomena. The generalisation of observed facts becomes a normalisation of them, a statement of the phenomena in terms of their coincidence with, or divergence from, that normal tendency that makes for the actualisation of the absolute economic reality.

This absolute or definitive ground of economic legitimacy lies beyond the causal sequence in which the observed phenomena are conceived to be interlinked. It is related to the concrete facts neither as cause nor as effect in any such way that the causal relation may be traced in a concrete instance. It has little causally to do either with the "mental" or with the "physical" data with which the classical economist is avowedly employed. Its relation to the process under discussion is that of an extraneous - that is to say, a ceremonial - legitimation. The body of knowledge gained by its help and under its guidance is, therefore, a taxonomic science. So, by way

[43] Senior, Political Economy, p. 87.

of a concluding illustration, it may be pointed out that money, for instance, is normalised in terms of the legitimate economic tendency. It becomes a measure of value and a medium of exchange.

It has become primarily an instrument of pecuniary commutation, instead of being, as under the earlier normalisation of Adam Smith, primarily a great wheel of circulation for the diffusion of consumable goods. The terms in which the laws of money, as of the other phenomena of pecuniary life, are formulated, are terms which connote its normal function in the life history of objective values as they live and move and have their being in the consummate pecuniary situation of the "natural" state. To a similar work of normalisation we owe those creatures of the myth-maker, the quantity theory and the wages-fund.

PART III.

In what has already been said, it has appeared that the changes which have supervened in the preconceptions of the earlier economists constitute a somewhat orderly succession. The feature of chief interest in this development has been a gradual change in the received grounds of finality to which the successive generations of economists have brought their theoretical output, on which they have been content to rest their conclusions, and beyond which they have not been moved to push their analysis of events or their scrutiny of phenomena. There has been a fairly unbroken sequence of development in what may be called the canons of economic reality; or, to put it in other words, there has been a precession of the point of view from which facts have been handled and valued for the purpose of economic science.

The notion which has in its time prevailed so widely, that there is in the sequence of events a consistent trend which it is the office of the science to ascertain and turn to account, - this notion may be well founded or not. But that there is something of such a consistent trend in the sequence of the canons of knowledge under whose guidance the scientist works is not only a generalisation from the past course of things, but lies in the nature of the case; for the canons of knowledge are of the nature of habits of thought, and habit does not break with the past, nor do the hereditary aptitudes that find expression in habit vary gratuitously with the mere lapse of time. What is true in this respect, for instance, in the domain of law and institutions is true, likewise, in the domain of science. What men have learned to accept as good and definitive for the guidance of conduct and of human relations remains true and definitive and unimpeachable until the exigencies of a later, altered situation enforce a variation from the norms and canons of the past, and so give rise to a modification of the habits of thought that decide what is, for the time, right in human conduct.

So in good and science the ancient ground of finality remains a valid test of scientific truth until the altered exigencies of later life enforce habits of thought that are not wholly in consonance with the received notions as to what constitutes the ultimate, self-legitimating term - the substantial reality - to which knowledge in any given case must penetrate. This ultimate term or ground of knowledge is always of a metaphysical character. It is something in the way of a preconception, accepted uncritically, but applied in criticism and demonstration of all else with which the science is concerned. So soon as it comes to be criticised, it is in a way to be superseded by a new, more or less altered formulation; for criticism of it means that it is no longer fit to survive unaltered in the altered complex of habits of thought to which it is called upon to serve as fundamental principle. It is subject to natural selection and selective adaptation, as are other conventions.

The underlying metaphysics of scientific research and purpose, therefore, changes gradually and, of course, incompletely, much as is the case with the metaphysics underlying the common law and the schedule of civil rights. As in the legal framework the now avowedly useless and meaningless preconceptions of status and caste and precedent are even yet at the most metamorphosed and obsolescent rather than overpassed, - witness the facts of inheritance, vested interests, the outlawry of debts through lapse of time, the competence of the State to coerce individuals into support of a given, policy - so in the science the living generation has not seen an abrupt and traceless disappearance of the metaphysics that fixed the point of view of the early classical political economy. This is true even for those groups of economists who have most incontinently protested against the absurdity of the classical doctrines and methods. In Professor Marshall's words, "There has been no real breach of continuity in the development of the science," but, while there has been no breach, there has none the less been change, - more far-reaching change than some of us are glad to recognise; for who would not be glad to read his own modern views into the convincing words of the great masters. Seen through modern eyes and without effort to turn past gains to modern account, the metaphysical or preconceptional furniture of political economy as it stood about the middle of this century may come to look quite curious. The two main canons of truth on which the science proceeded, and with which the inquiry is here concerned, were: (a) a hedonistic - associational psychology, and (b) an uncritical conviction that there is a meliorative trend in the course of events, apart from the conscious ends of the individual members of the community. This axiom of a meliorative developmental trend fell into shape as a belief in an organic or quasi-organic (physiological)[44] life process on the part of the economic community or of the nation; and this belief carried with it something of a constraining sense of self realising cycles of growth, maturity and decay in the life history of nations or communities. Neglecting what may for the immediate purpose be negligible in this outline of fundamental tenets, it will bear the following construction. (a) On the ground of the hedonistic or associational psychology, all spiritual continuity and any consequent teleological

---

[44] So, e.g., Roscher, Comte, the early socialists, J. S. Mill, and later Spencer, Schaeffle, Wagner.

trend is tacitly denied so far as regards individual conduct, where the later psychology, and the sciences which build on this later psychology, insist upon and find such a teleological trend at every turn. (b) Such a spiritual or quasi-spiritual continuity and teleological trend is uncritically affirmed as regards the non-human sequence or the sequence of events in the affairs of collective life, where the modern sciences diligently assert that nothing of the kind is discernible, or that, if it is discernible, its recognition is beside the point, so far as concerns the purposes of the science.

This position, here outlined with as little qualification as may be admissible, embodies the general metaphysical ground of that classical political economy that affords the point of departure for Mill and Cairnes,, and also for Jevons. And what is to be said of Mill and Cairnes in this connection will apply to the later course of the science, though with a gradually lessening force. By the middle of the century the psychological premises of the science are no longer so neat and succinct as they were in the days of Bentham and James Mill. At J.S. Mill's hands, for instance, the naively quantitative hedonism of Bentham is being supplanted by a sophisticated hedonism, which makes much of an assumed qualitative divergence between the different kinds of pleasures that afford the motives of conduct. This revision of hedonistic dogma, of course, means a departure from the strict hedonistic ground. Correlated with this advance more closely in the substance of the change than in the assignable dates, is a concomitant improvement - at least, set forth as an improvement - upon the received associational psychology, whereby "similarity" is brought in to supplement "contiguity" as a ground of connection between ideas.

This change is well shown in the work of J. S. Mill and Bain. In spite of all the ingenuity spent in maintaining the associational legitimacy of this new article of theory, it remains a patent innovation and a departure from the ancient standpoint. As is true of the improved hedonism, so it is true of the new theory of association that it is no longer able to construe the process which it discusses as a purely mechanical process, a concatenation of items simply. Similarity of impressions implies a comparison of impressions by the mind in which the association takes place, and thereby it implies some degree of constructive work on the part of the perceiving subject. The perceiver is thereby construed to be an agent in the work of perception; therefore, he must be possessed of a point of view and an end dominating the perceptive process. To perceive the similarity, he must be guided by an interest in the outcome, and must "attend." The like applies to the introduction of qualitative distinctions into the hedonistic theory of conduct. Apperception in the one case and discretion in the other cease to be the mere registration of a simple and personally uncolored sequence of permutations enforced by the factors of the external world. There is implied a spiritual - that is to say, active - "teleological" continuity of process on the part of the perceiving or of the discretionary agent, as the case may be. It is on the ground of their departure from the stricter hedonistic premises that Mill and, after him, Cairnes, are able, for instance, to offer their improvement upon the earlier doctrine of cost of production as determining value.

Since it is conceived that the motives which guide men in their choice of employments and of domicile differ from man to man and from class to class, not only in degree, but in kind, and since varying antecedents, of heredity and of habit, variously influence men in their choice of a manner of life, therefore the mere quantitative pecuniary stimulus cannot be depended on to decide the outcome without recourse. There are determinable variations in the alacrity with which different classes or communities respond to the pecuniary stimulus; and in so far as this condition prevails, the classes or communities in question are non-competing. Between such non-competing groups the norm that determines values is not the unmitigated norm of cost of production taken absolutely, but only taken relatively. The formula of cost of production is therefore modified into a formula of reciprocal demand. This revision of the cost-of-production doctrine is extended only sparingly, and the emphasis is thrown on the pecuniary circumstances on which depend the formation and maintenance of non-competing groups.

Consistency with the earlier teaching is carefully maintained, so far as may be; but extra-pecuniary factors are, after all, even if reluctantly, admitted into the body of the theory. So also, since there are higher and lower motives, higher and lower pleasures, - as well as motives differing in degree, - it follows that an unguided response even to the mere quantitative pecuniary stimuli may take different directions, and so may result in activities of widely differing outcome. Since activities set up in this way through appeal to higher and lower motives are no longer conceived to represent simply a mechanically adequate effect of the stimuli, working under the control of natural laws that tend to one beneficent consummation, therefore the outcome of activity set up even by the normal pecuniary stimuli may take a form that may or may not be serviceable to the community. Hence laissez-faire ceases to be a sure remedy for the ills of society. Human interests are still conceived normally to be at one; but the detail of individual conduct need not, therefore, necessarily serve these generic human interests.[45].

Therefore, other inducements than the unmitigated impact of pecuniary exigencies may be necessary to bring about a coincidence of class or individual endeavor with the interests of the community. It becomes incumbent on the advocate of laissez-faire to "prove his minor premise." It is no

---

[45] "Let us not confound the statement that human interests are at one with the statement that class interests are at one. The latter I believe to be as false as the former is true ... But accepting the major premises of the syllogism, that the interests of human beings are fundamentally the same, how as to the minor - how as to the assumption that people know their interests in the sense in which they are identical with the interests of others, and that they spontaneously follow them in this sense?" - Cairnes, Essays in Political Economy (London, 1873), p. 245. This question cannot consistently be asked by an adherent of the stricter hedonism.

longer self-evident that Interests left to themselves tend to harmonious combinations, and to the progressive preponderance of the general good[46] .

The natural-rights preconception begins to fall away as soon as the hedonistic mechanics have been seriously tampered with. Fact and right cease to coincide, because the individual in whom the rights are conceived to inhere has come to be something more than the field of intersection of natural forces that work out in human conduct. The mechanics of natural liberty - that assumed constitution of things by force of which the free hedonistic play of the laws of nature across the open field of individual choice is sure to reach the right outcome - is the hedonistic psychology, and the passing of the doctrine of natural rights and natural liberty whether as a premise or as a dogma, therefore coincides with the passing of that mechanics of conduct on the validity of which the theoretical acceptance of the dogma depends.

It is, therefore, something more than a coincidence that the half-century which has seen the disintegration of the hedonistic faith and of the associational psychology has also seen the dissipation, in scientific speculations, of the concomitant faith in natural rights and in that benign order of nature of which the natural-rights dogma is a corollary. It is, of course, not hereby intended to say that the later psychological views and premises imply a less close dependence of conduct on environment than do the earlier ones. Indeed, the reverse may well be held to be true. The pervading characteristic of later thinking is the constant recourse to a detailed analysis of phenomena in causal terms. The modern catchword, in the present connection, is "response to stimulus," but the manner in which this response is conceived has changed. The fact, and ultimately the amplitude, at least in great part, of the reaction to stimulus, is conditioned by the forces in impact; but the constitution of the organism, as well as its attitude at the moment of impact, in great part decides what will serve as a stimulus, as well as what the manner and direction of the response will be. The later psychology is biological, as contrasted with the metaphysical psychology of hedonism. It does not conceive the organism as a causal hiatus.

The causal sequence in the "reflex arc" is, no doubt, continuous; but the continuity is not, as formerly, conceived in terms of spiritual substance transmitting a shock: it is conceived in terms of the life activity of the organism. Human conduct, taken as the reaction of such an organism under stimulus, may be stated in terms of tropism, involving, of course, a very close-knit causal sequence between the impact and the response, but at the same time imputing to the organism a habit of life and a self-directing and selective attention in meeting the complex of forces that make up its environment. The selective play of this tropismatic complex that consti-

---

46 Bastiat, quoted by Cairnes, Essays, p. 319.

tutes the organism's habit of life under the impact of the forces of the environment counts as discretion.

So far, therefore, as it is to be placed in contrast with the hedonistic phase of the older psychological doctrines, the characteristic feature of the newer conception is the recognition of a selectively self-directing life process in the agent. While hedonism seeks the causal determinant of conduct in the (probable) outcome of action, the later conception seeks this determinant in the complex of propensities that constitutes man a functioning agent, that is to say, a personality. Instead of pleasure ultimately determining what human conduct shall be, the tropismatic propensities that eventuate in conduct ultimately determine what shall be pleasurable. For the purpose in hand, the consequence of the transition to the altered conception of human nature and its relation to the environment is that the newer view formulates conduct in terms of personality, whereas the earlier view was content to formulate it in terms of its provocation and its by-product.

Therefore, for the sake of brevity, the older preconceptions of the science are here spoken of as construing human nature in inert terms, as contrasted with the newer, which construes it in terms of functioning. It has already appeared above that the second great article of the metaphysics of classical political economy the belief in a meliorative trend or a benign order of nature - is closely connected with the hedonistic conception of human nature; but this connection is more intimate and organic than appears from what has been said above.

The two are so related as to stand or fall together, for the latter is but the obverse of the former. The doctrine of a trend in events imputes purpose to the sequence of events; that is, it invests this sequence with a discretionary, teleological character, which asserts itself in a constraint over all the steps in the sequence by which the supposed objective point is reached. But discretion touching a given end must be single, and must alone cover all the acts by which the end is to be reached. Therefore, no discretion resides in the intermediate terms through which the end is worked out. Therefore, man being such an intermediate term, discretion cannot be imputed to him without violating the supposition. Therefore, given an indefeasible meliorative trend in events, man is but a mechanical intermediary in the sequence.

It is as such a mechanical intermediate term that the stricter hedonism construes human nature.[47].

Accordingly, when more of teleological activity came to be imputed to man, less was thereby allowed to the complex of events. Or it may be put

---

[47] It may be remarked, by the way, that the use of the differential calculus and similar mathematical expedients in the discussion of marginal utility and the like, proceeds on the psychological ground, and that the theoretical results so arrived at are valid to the full extent only if this hedonistic psychology is accepted.

in the converse form: When less of a teleological continuity came to be imputed to the course of events, more was thereby imputed to man's life process. The latter form of statement probably suggests the direction in which the causal relation runs, more nearly than the former. The change whereby the two metaphysical premises in question have lost their earlier force and symmetry, therefore, amounts to a (partial) shifting of the seat of putative personality from inanimate phenomena to man. It may be mentioned in passing, as a detail lying perhaps afield, yet not devoid of significance for latter-day economic speculation, that this elimination of personality, and so of teleological content, from the sequence of events, and its increasing imputation to the conduct of the human agent, is incident to a growing resort to an apprehension of phenomena in terms of process rather than in terms of outcome, as was the habit in earlier schemes of knowledge.

On this account the categories employed are, in a gradually increasing degree, categories of process, - "dynamic" categories. But categories of process applied to conduct, to discretionary action, are teleological categories: whereas categories of process applied in the case of a sequence where the members of the sequence are not conceived to be charged with discretion, are, by the force of this conception itself, non-teleological, quantitative categories. The continuity comprised in the concept of process as applied to conduct is consequently a spiritual, teleological continuity, whereas the concept of process under the second head, the non-teleological sequence, comprises a continuity of a quantitative, causal kind, substantially the conservation of energy. In its turn the growing resort to categories of process in the formulation of knowledge is probably due to the epistemological discipline of modern mechanical industry, the technological exigencies of which enforce a constant recourse to the apprehension of phenomena in terms of process, differing therein from the earlier forms of industry, which neither obtruded visible mechanical process so constantly upon the apprehension nor so imperatively demanded an articulate recognition of continuity in the processes actually involved.

The contrast in this respect is still more pronounced between the discipline of modern life in an industrial community and the discipline of life under the conventions of status and exploit that formerly prevailed. To return to the benign order of nature, or the meliorative trend, - its passing, as an article of economic faith, was not due to criticism leveled against it by the later classical economists on grounds of its epistemological incongruity. It was tried on its merits, as an alleged account of facts; and the weight of evidence went against it. The belief in a self-realising trend bad no sooner reached a competent and exhaustive statement - e.g., at Bastiat's hands, as a dogma of the harmony of interests specifically applicable to the details of economic life than it began to lose ground. With his usual concision and incisiveness, Cairnes completed the destruction of Bastiat's special dogma, and put it forever beyond a rehearing. But Cairnes is not a destructive critic of the classical political economy, at least not in intention: he is an interpreter and continuer - perhaps altogether the clearest and truest continuer - of the classical teaching.

While he confuted Bastiat and discredited Bastiat's peculiar dogma, he did not thereby put the order of nature bodily out of the science. He qualified and improved it, very much as Mill qualified and improved the tenets of the hedonistic psychology. As Mill and the ethical speculation of his generation threw more of personality into the hedonistic psychology, so Cairnes and the speculators on scientific method (such as Mill and Jevons) attenuated the imputation of personality or teleological content to the process of material cause and effect. The work is of course, by no means, an achievement of Cairnes alone; but he is, perhaps, the best exponent of this advance in economic theory. In Cairnes's, redaction this foundation of the science became the concept of a colorless normality. It was in Cairnes's time the fashion for speculators in other fields than the physical sciences to look to those sciences for guidance in method and for legitimation of the ideals of scientific theory which they were at work to realize. More than that, the large and fruitful achievements of the physical sciences had so far taken men's attention captive as to give an almost instinctive predilection for the methods that had approved themselves in that field.

The ways of thinking which had on this ground become familiar to all scholars occupied with any scientific inquiry, had permeated their thinking on any subject whatever. This is eminently true of British thinking. It had come to be a commonplace of the physical sciences that "natural laws" are of the nature of empirical generalisations simply, or even of the nature of arithmetical averages. Even the underlying preconception of the modern physical sciences - the law of the conservation of energy, or persistence of quantity - was claimed to be an empirical generalisation, arrived at inductively and verified by experiment.

It is true the alleged proof of the law took the whole conclusion for granted at the start, and used it constantly as a tacit axiom at every step in the argument which was to establish its truth; but that fact serves rather to emphasise than to call in question the abiding faith which these empiricists had in the sole efficacy of empirical generalisation. Had they been able overtly to admit any other than an associational origin of knowledge, they would have seen the impossibility of accounting on the mechanical grounds of association for the premise on which all experience of mechanical fact rests. That any other than a mechanical origin should be assigned to experience, or that any other than a so-conceived empirical ground was to be admitted for any general principle, was incompatible with the prejudices of men trained in the school of the associational psychology, however widely they perforce departed from this ideal in practice.

Nothing of the nature of a personal element was to be admitted into these fundamental empirical generalisations; and nothing, therefore, of the nature of a discretionary or teleological movement was to be comprised in the generalisations to be accepted as "natural laws." Natural laws must in no degree be imbued with personality, must say nothing of an ulterior end; but for all that they remained "laws" of the sequences subsumed under them. So far is the reduction to colorless terms carried by Mill, for instance, that he formulates the natural laws as empirically ascertained sequences simply, even excluding or avoiding all imputation of

causal continuity, as that term is commonly understood by the unsophisticated. In Mill's ideal no more of organic connection or continuity between the members of a sequence is implied in subsuming them under a
law of causal relationship than is given by the ampersand. He is busied
with dynamic sequences, but he persistently confines himself to static
terms.

Under the guidance of the associational psychology, therefore, the extreme of discontinuity in the deliverances of inductive research is aimed at
by those economists Mill and Cairnes, being taken as typical - whose
names have been associated with deductive methods in modern science.
With a fine sense of truth they saw that the notion of causal continuity, as
a premise of scientific generalisation, is an essentially metaphysical postulate; and they avoided its treacherous ground by denying it, and construing causal sequence to mean a uniformity of co-existences and succes-
sions simply. But, since a strict uniformity is nowhere to be observed at
first hand in the phenomena with which the investigator is occupied, it
has to be found by a laborious interpretation of the phenomena and a
diligent abstraction and allowance for disturbing circumstances, whatever
may be the meaning of a disturbing circumstance where causal continuity
is denied. In this work of interpretation and expurgation the investigator
proceeds on a conviction of the orderliness of the natural sequence.
"Natura non facit saltum": a maxim which has no meaning within the
stricter limits of the associational theory of knowledge.

Before anything can be said as to the orderliness of the sequence, a point
of view must be chosen by the speculator, with respect to which the sequence in question does or does not fulfill this condition of orderliness;
that is to say, with respect to which it is a sequence. The endeavor to avoid
all metaphysical premises fails here as everywhere. The associationists, to
whom economics owes its transition from the older classical phase to the
modern or quasi-classical, chose as their guiding point of view the metaphysical postulate of congruity, - in substance, the "similarity" of the associationist theory of knowledge. This must be called their proton pseudos, if
associationism pure and simple is to be accepted. The notion of congruity
works out in laws of resemblance and equivalence, in both of which it is
plain to the modern psychologist that a metaphysical ground of truth,
antecedent to and controlling empirical data, is assumed. But the use of
the postulate of congruence as a test of scientific truth has the merit of
avoiding all open dealing with an imputed substantiality of the data handled, such as would be involved in the overt use of the concept of causation. The data are congruous among themselves, as items of knowledge;
and they may therefore be handled in a logical synthesis and concatenation on the basis of this congruence alone, without committing the scientist to an imputation of a kinetic or motor relation between them.

The metaphysics of process is thereby avoided, in appearance. The sequences are uniform or consistent with one another, taken as articles of
theoretical synthesis simply, and so they become elements of a system or
discipline of knowledge in which the test of theoretical truth is the congruence of the system with its premises. In all this there is a high-wrought

appearance of matter-of-fact and all metaphysical subjection of a non-empirical or non-mechanical standard of reality or substantiality is avoided in appearance. The generalisations which make up such a system of knowledge are, in this way, stated in terms of the system itself; and when a competent formulation of the alleged uniformities has been so made in terms of their congruity or equivalence with the prime postulates of the system, the work of theoretical inquiry is done. The concrete premises from which proceeds the systematic knowledge of this generation of economists are certain very concise assumptions concerning human nature, and certain slightly less concise generalisations of physical fact[48] presumed to be mechanically empirical generalisations. These postulates afford the standard of normality. Whatever situation or course of events can be shown to express these postulates without mitigation is normal; and wherever a departure from this normal course of things occurs, it is due to disturbing causes, that is to say, to causes not comprised in the main premises of the science, - and such departures are to be taken account of by way of qualification. Such departures and such qualification are constantly present in the facts to be handled by the science; but, being not congruous with the underlying postulates, they have no place in the body of the science. The laws of the science, that which makes up the economist's theoretical knowledge, are laws of the normal case. The normal case does not occur in concrete fact. These laws are, therefore, in Cairnes's terminology, "hypothetical" truths; and the science is a "hypothetical" science.

They apply to concrete facts only as the facts are interpreted and abstracted from, in the light of the underlying postulates. The science is, therefore, a theory of the normal case, a discussion of the concrete facts of life in respect of their degree of approximation to the normal case. That is to say, it is a taxonomic science. Of course, in the work actually done by these economists this standpoint of rigorous normality is not consistently maintained; nor is the unsophisticated imputation of causality to the facts under discussion consistently avoided. The associationist postulate, that causal sequence means empirical uniformity simply, is in great measure forgotten when the subject-matter of the science is handled in detail. Especially is it true that in Mill the dry light of normality is greatly relieved by a strong common sense.

But the great truths or laws of the science remain hypothetical laws; and the test of scientific reality is congruence with the hypothetical laws, not coincidence with matter-of-fact events. The earlier, more archaic metaphysics of the science, which saw in the orderly correlation and sequence of events a constraining guidance of an extra-causal, teleological kind, in this way becomes a metaphysics of normality which asserts no extra-causal constraint over events, but contents itself with establishing correla-

---

[48] See, e.g., Cairnes, Character and Logical Method (New York), p. 71.

tions, equivalencies, homologies, and theories concerning the conditions of an economic equilibrium. The movement, the process of economic life, is not overlooked, and it may even be said that it is not neglected, but the pure theory, in its final deliverances, deals not with the dynamics, but with the statics of the case. The concrete subject-matter of the science is, of course, the process of economic life, - that is unavoidably the case, - and in so far the discussion must be accepted as work bearing on the dynamics of the phenomena discussed; but even then it remains true that the aim of this work in dynamics is a determination and taxis of the outcome of the process under discussion rather than a theory of the process as such.

The process is rated in terms of the equilibrium to which it tends or should tend, not conversely. The outcome of the process, taken in its relation of equivalence within the system, is the point at which the inquiry comes to rest. It is not primarily the point of departure for an inquiry into what may follow. The science treats of a balanced system rather than of a proliferation. In this lies its characteristic difference from the later evolutionary sciences. It is this characteristic bent of the science that leads its spokesman, Cairnes, to turn so kindly to chemistry rather than to the organic sciences, when he seeks an analogy to economics among the physical sciences [49] . ,

What Cairnes has in mind in his appeal to chemistry is, of course, the received, extremely taxonomic (systematic) chemistry of his own time, not the tentatively genetic theories of a slightly later day. It may seem that in the characterisation just offered of the standpoint of normality in economics there is too strong an implication of colorlessness and impartiality. The objection holds as regards much of the work of the modern economists of the classical line. It will hold true even as to much of Cairnes's work, but it cannot be admitted as regards Cairnes's ideal of scientific aim and methods. The economists whose theories Cairnes received and developed, assuredly did not pursue the discussion of the normal case with an utterly dispassionate animus. They had still enough of the older teleological metaphysics left to give color to the accusation brought against them that they were advocates of laissez-faire.

The preconception of the utilitarians, - in substance the natural-rights preconception, - that unrestrained human conduct will result in the greatest human happiness, retains so much of its force in Cairnes's time as is implied in the then current assumption that what is normal is also right. The economists, and Cairnes among them, not only are concerned to find out what is normal and to determine what consummation answers to the normal, but they also are at pains to approve that consummation. It is this somewhat uncritical and often unavowed identification of the normal with the right that gives colorable ground for the widespread vulgar preju-

---

[49] Character and Logical Method, p. 62.

dice, to which Cairnes draws attention,[50] that political economy "sanctions" one social arrangement and "condemns" another. And it is against
this uncritical identification of two essentially unrelated principles or categories that Cairnes's essay on "Political Economy and Laissez-faire," and
in good part also that on Bastiat, are directed. But, while this is one of the
many points at which Cairnes has substantially advanced the ideals of the
science, his own concluding argument shows him to have been but half-
way emancipated from the prejudice, even while most effectively combat-
ing it.[51] It is needless to point out that the like prejudice is still present in
good vigor in many later economists who have had the full benefit of
Cairnes's teachings on this head.[52] ,

Considerable as Cairnes's achievement in this matter undoubtedly was,
it effected a mitigation rather than an elimination of the untenable metaphysics against which he contended. The advance in the general point of
view from animistic teleology to taxonomy is shown in a curiously succinct manner in a parenthetical clause of Cairnes's in the chapter on
Normal Value.[53] .

With his acceptance of the later point of view involved in the use of the
new term, Cairnes becomes the interpreter of the received theoretical results. The received positions are not subjected to a destructive criticism.
The aim is to complete them where they fall short and to cut off what may
be needless or what may run beyond the safe ground of scientific generalisation. In his work of redaction, Cairnes does not avow - probably he is not
sensible of - any substantial shifting of the point of view or any change in
the accepted ground of theoretic reality. But his advance to an unteleological taxonomy none the less changes the scope and aim of his theoretical
discussion. The discussion of Normal Value may be taken in illustration.

Cairnes is not content to find (with Adam Smith) that value will "naturally" coincide with or be measured by cost of production, or even (with Mill)
that cost of production must, in the long run, "necessarily" determine
value. "This is to take a much too limited view of the range of this phenomenon.[54] .

He is concerned to determine not only this general tendency of values to
a normal, but all those characteristic circumstances as well which condi-

---

[50] Essays in Political Economy, pp. 260-264.

[51] See especially Essays, pp. 263, 264.

[52] It may be interesting to point out that the like identification of the categories of
normality and right gives the dominant note of Mr. Spencer's ethical and social
philosophy, and that later economists of the classical and social philosophy to be
Spencerians.

[53] "Normal value (called by Adam Smith and Ricardo "natural value," and by Mill
"necessary value," but best expressed, it seems to me, by the term which I have
used)." Leading Principles (New York), p. 45.

[54] Leading Principles, p. 45.

tion this tendency and which determine the normal to which values tend. His inquiry pursues the phenomena of value in a normal economic system rather than the manner and rate of approach of value relations to a teleologically or hedonistically defensible consummation. It therefore becomes an exhaustive but very discriminating analysis of the circumstances that bear upon market values, with a view to determine what circumstances are normally present; that is to say, what circumstances conditioning value are commonly effective and at the same time in consonance with the premises of economic theory, These effective conditions, in so far as they are not counted anomalous and, therefore, to be set aside in the theoretical discussion, are the circumstances under which a hedonistic valuation process in any modern industrial community is held perforce to take place, - the circumstances which are held to enforce a recognition and rating of the pleasure-bearing capacity of facts. They are not, as under the earlier cost-of-production doctrines, the circumstances which determine the magnitude of the forces spent in the production of the valuable article. Therefore, the normal (natural) value is no longer (as with Adam Smith, and even to some extent with his classical successors) the primary or initial fact in value theory, the substantial fact of which the market value is an approximate expression and by which the latter is controlled.

The argument does not, as formerly, set out from that expenditure of personal force which was once conceived to constitute the substantial value of goods, and then construe market value to be an approximate and uncertain expression of this substantial fact. The direction in which the argument runs is rather the reverse of this. The point of departure is taken from the range of market values and the process of bargaining by which these values are determined. This latter is taken to be a process of discrimination between various kinds and degrees of discomfort, and the average or consistent outcome of such a process of bargaining constitutes normal value.

It is only by virtue of a presumed equivalence between the discomfort undergone and the concomitant expenditure, whether of labor or of wealth, that the normal value so determined is conceived to be an expression of the productive force that goes into the creation of the valuable goods. Cost being only in uncertain equivalence with sacrifice or discomfort, as between different persons, the factor of cost falls into the background; and the process of bargaining, which is in the foreground, being a process of valuation, a balancing of individual demand and supply, it follows that a law of reciprocal demand comes in to supplant the law of cost. In all this the proximate causes at work in the determination of values are plainly taken account of more adequately than in earlier cost-of-production doctrines; but they are taken account of with a view to explaining the mutual adjustment and interrelation of elements in a system rather than to explain either a developmental sequence or the working out of a fore-ordained end.

This revision of the cost-of-production doctrine, whereby it takes the form of a law of reciprocal demand, is in good part effected by a consistent reduction of cost to terms of sacrifice, - a reduction more consistently carried through by Cairnes than it had been by earlier hedonists, and extended by Cairnes's successors with even more far-reaching results. By this step the doctrine of cost is not only brought into closer accord with the neo-hedonistic premises, in that it in a greater degree throws the stress upon the factor of personal discrimination, but it also gives the doctrine a more general bearing upon economic conduct and increases its serviceability as a comprehensive principle for the classification of economic phenomena. In the further elaboration of the hedonistic theory of value at the hands of Jevons and the Austrians the same principle of sacrifice comes to serve as the chief ground of procedure. ,

Of the foundations of later theory, in so far as the postulates of later economists differ characteristically from those of Mill and Cairnes, little can be said in this place. Nothing but the very general features of the later development can be taken up; and even these general features of the existing theoretic situation can not be handled with the same confidence as the corresponding features of a past phase of speculation. With respect to writers of the present or the more recent past the work of natural selection, as between variants of scientific aim and animus and between more or less divergent points of view, has not yet taken effect; and it would be over-hazardous to attempt an anticipation of the results of the selection that lies in great part yet in the future. As regards the directions of theoretical work suggested by the names of

Professor Marshall, Mr. Cannan, Professor Clark, Mr. Pierson, Austrian Professor Loria, Professor Schmoller, the group, - no off-hand decision is admissible as between these candidates for the honor, or, better, for the work, of continuing the main current of economic speculation and inquiry. No attempt will here be made even to pass a verdict on the relative claims of the recognised two or three main "schools" of theory, beyond the somewhat obvious finding that, for the purpose in hand, the so-called Austrian school is scarcely distinguishable from the neo-classical, unless it be in the different distribution of emphasis. The divergence between the modernised classical views, on the one hand, and the historical and Marxist schools, on the other hand, is wider, - so much so, indeed, as to bar out a consideration of the postulates of the latter under the same head of inquiry with the former.

The inquiry, therefore, confines itself to the one line standing most obviously in unbroken continuity with that body of classical economics whose life history has been traced in outline above. And, even for this phase of modernised classical economics, it seems necessary to limit discussion, for the present, to a single strain, selected as standing peculiarly close to the classical source, at the same time that it shows unmistakable adaptation to the later habits of thought and methods of knowledge. For this later development in the classical line of political economy, Mr. Keynes's book may fairly be taken as the maturest exposition of the aims and ideals of the science; while Professor Marshall excellently exemplifies the best work that is being done under the guidance of the classical antecedents. As, after a lapse of a dozen or fifteen years from Cairnes's days of full conviction,

Mr. Keynes interprets the aims of modern economic science, it has less of the "hypothetical" character assigned it by Cairnes; that is to say, it confines its inquiry less closely to the ascertainment of the normal case and the interpretative subsumption of facts under the normal. It takes fuller account of the genesis and developmental continuity of all features of modern economic life, gives more and closer attention to institutions and their history. This is, no doubt, due, in part at least, to impulse received from German economists; and in so far it also reflects the peculiarly vague and bewildered attitude of protest that characterises the earlier expositions of the historical school. To the same essentially extraneous source is traceable the theoretic blur embodied in Mr. Keynes's attitude of tolerance towards the conception of economics as a "normative" science having to do with "economic ideals", or an "applied economics" having to do with "economic precepts."[55].

An inchoate departure from the consistent taxonomic ideals shows itself in the tentative resort to historical and genetic formulations, as well as in Mr. Keynes's pervading inclination to define the scope of the science, not by exclusion of what are conceived to be non-economic phenomena, but by disclosing a point of view from which all phenomena are seen to be economic facts. The science comes to be characterised not by the delimitation of a range of facts, as in Cairnes,[56] but as an inquiry into the bearing which all facts have upon men's economic activity. It is no longer that certain phenomena belong within the science, but rather that the science is concerned with any and all phenomena as seen from the point of view of the economic interest. Mr. Keynes does not go fully to the length which this last proposition indicates. He finds[57] that political economy "treats of the phenomena arising out of the economic activities of mankind in society"; but, while the discussion by which he leads up to this definition might be construed to say that all the activities of mankind in society have an economic bearing, and should therefore come within the view of the science, Mr. Keynes does not carry out his elucidation of the matter to that broad conclusion. Neither can it be said that modern political economy has, in practice, taken on the scope and character which this extreme position would assign it. The passage from which the above citation is taken is highly significant also in another and related bearing, and it is at the same time highly characteristic of the most effective modernised classical economics. The subject matter of the science has come to be the "economic activities" of mankind, and the phenomena in which these activities manifest themselves. So Professor Marshall's work, for instance, is, in aim, even if not always in achievement, a theoretical handling of human activity in its economic bearing, - an inquiry into the multiform phases and ramifica-

---

[55] Scope and Method of Political Economy (London, 1891), chaps. i and ii.
[56] Character and Logical Method; e.g., Lecture II, especially pp. 53, 54, 71.
[57] Scope and Method of Political Economy, chap. iii, particularly p. 97.

tions of that process of valuation of the material means of life by virtue of which man is an economic agent. And still it remains an inquiry directed to the determination of the conditions of an equilibrium of activities and a quiescent normal situation. It is not in any eminent degree an inquiry into cultural or institutional development as affected by economic exigencies or by the economic interest of the men whose activities are analysed and portrayed.

Any sympathetic reader of Professor Marshall's great work - and that must mean every reader - comes away with a sense of swift and smooth movement and interaction of parts; but it is the movement of a consummately conceived and self-balanced mechanism, not that of a cumulatively unfolding process or an institutional adaptation to cumulatively unfolding exigencies. The taxonomic bearing is, after all, the dominant feature. It is significant of the same point that even in his discussion of such vitally dynamic features of the economic process as the differential effectiveness of different laborers or of different industrial plants, as well as of the differential advantages of consumers,

Professor Marshall resorts to an adaptation of so essentially taxonomic a category as the received concept of rent. Rent is a pecuniary category, a category of income, which is essentially a final term, not a category of the motor term, work or interest[58].

It is not a factor or a feature of the process of industrial life, but a phenomenon of the pecuniary situation which emerges from this process under given conventional circumstances. However far-reaching and various the employment of the rent concept in economic theory has been, it has through all permutations remained, what it was to begin with, a rubric in the classification of incomes. It is a pecuniary, not an industrial category. In so far as resort is had to the rent concept in the formulation of a theory of the industrial process, - as in Professor Marshall's work, - it comes to a statement of the process in terms of its residue. Let it not seem presumptuous to say that great and permanent as is the value of Professor Marshall's exposition of quasi-rents and the like, the endeavor which it involves to present in terms of a concluded system what is of the nature of a fluent process has made the exposition unduly bulky, unwieldy, and inconsequent. There is a curious reminiscence of the perfect taxonomic day in Mr. Keynes's characterisation of political economy as a "positive science," "the sole province of which is to establish economic uniformities"; [59] and, in this resort to the associationist expedient of defining a natural

---

[58] "Interest" is, of course, here used in the sense which it has in modern psychological discussion.

[59] Scope and Method of Political Economy, p. 46.

law as a "uniformity," Mr. Keynes is also borne out by Professor Marshall.[60]

But this and other survivals of the taxonomic terminology, or even of the taxonomic canons of procedure, do not binder the economists of the modern school from doing effective work of a character that must be rated as genetic rather than taxonomic. Professor Marshall's work in economics is not unlike that of Asa Gray in botany, who, while working in great part within the lines of "systematic botany" and adhering to its terminology, and on the whole also to its point of view, very materially furthered the advance of the science outside the scope of taxonomy. Professor Marshall shows an aspiration to treat economic life as a development; and, at least superficially, much of his work bears the appearance of being a discussion of this kind. In this endeavor his work is typical of what is aimed at by many of the later economists. The aim shows itself with a persistent recurrence in his Principles. His chosen maxim is, "Natura non facit saltum," - a maxim that might well serve to designate the prevailing attitude of modern economists towards questions of economic development as well as towards questions of classification or of economic policy. His insistence on the continuity of development and of the economic structure of communities is a characteristic of the best work along the later line of classical political economy. All this gives an air of evolutionism to the work. Indeed, the work of the neo-classical economics might be compared, probably without offending any of its adepts, with that of the early generation of Darwinians, though such a comparison might somewhat shrewdly have to avoid any but superficial features. Economists of the present day are commonly evolutionists, in a general way.

They commonly accept, as other men do, the general results of the evolutionary speculation in those directions in which the evolutionary method has made its way. But the habit of handling by evolutionist methods the facts with which their own science is concerned has made its way among the economists to but a very uncertain degree. The prime postulate of evolutionary science, the preconception constantly underlying the inquiry, is the notion of a cumulative causal sequence; and writers on economics are in the habit of recognising that the phenomena with which they are occupied are subject to such a law of development. Expressions of assent to this proposition abound. But the economists have not worked out or hit upon a method by which the inquiry in economics may consistently be conducted under the guidance of this postulate. Taking Professor Marshall as exponent, it appears that, while the formulations of economic theory are not conceived to be arrived at by way of an inquiry into the developmental variation of economic institutions and the like, the theorems ar-

---

[60] Principles of Economics, Vol. 1, Book 1, chap. vi, sect. 6, especially p. 105 (3rd edition).

rived at are held, and no doubt legitimately, to apply to the past,[61] and with due reserve also to the future, phases of the development. But these theorems apply to the various phases of the development not as accounting for the developmental sequence, but as limiting the range of variation. They say little, if anything, as to the order of succession, as to the derivation and the outcome of any given phase, or as to the causal relation of one phase of any given economic convention or scheme of relations to any other. They indicate the conditions of survival to which any innovation is subject, supposing the innovation to have taken place, not the conditions of variational growth. The economic laws, the" statements of uniformity," are therefore, when construed in an evolutionary bearing, theorems concerning the superior or the inferior limit of persistent innovations, as the case may be[62] .

It is only in this negative, selective bearing that the current economic laws are held to be laws of developmental continuity; and it should be added that they have hitherto found but relatively scant application at the hands of the economists, even for this purpose. Again, as applied to economic activities under a given situation, as laws governing activities in equilibrium, the economic laws are, in the main, laws of the limits within which economic action of a given purpose runs. They are theorems as to the limits which the economic (commonly the pecuniary) interest imposes upon the range of activities to which the other life interests of men incite, rather than theorems as to the manner and degree in which the economic interest creatively shapes the general scheme of life. In great part they formulate the normal inhibitory effect of economic exigencies rather than the cumulative modification and diversification of human activities through the economic interest, by initiating and guiding habits of life and of thought.

This, of course, does not go to say that economists are at all slow to credit the economic exigencies with a large share in the growth of culture; but, while claims of this kind are large and recurrent, it remains true that the laws which make up the framework of economic doctrine are, when construed as generalisations of causal relation, laws of conservation and selection, not of genesis and proliferation. The truth of this, which is but a commonplace generalisation, might be shown in detail with respect to such fundamental theorems as the laws of rent, of profits, of wages, of the increasing or diminishing returns of industry, of population, of competitive prices, of cost of production. In consonance with this quasi-evolutionary tone of the neo-classical political economy, or as an expression of it, comes the further clarified sense that nowadays attaches to the

[61] See, e.g., Professor Marshall's "Reply" to Professor Cunningham in the Economic Journal for 1892, pp. 508-513.

[62] This is well illustrated by what Professor Marshall says of the Ricardian law of rent in his "Reply" cited above.

terms "normal" and economic "laws." The laws have gained in colorless-ness, until it can no longer be said that the concept of normality implies approval of the phenomena to which it is applied.[63] .

They are in an increasing degree laws of conduct, though they still con-tinue to formulate conduct in hedonistic terms; that is to say, conduct is construed in terms of its sensuous effect, not in terms of its teleological content. The light of the science is a drier light than it was, but it continues to be shed upon the accessories of human action rather than upon the process itself. The categories employed for the purpose of knowing this economic conduct with which the scientists occupy themselves are not the categories under which the men at whose hands the action takes place themselves apprehend their own action at the instant of acting. Therefore, economic conduct still continues to be somewhat mysterious to the econ-omists; and they are forced to content themselves with adumbrations whenever the discussion touches this central, substantial fact. All this, of course, is intended to convey no dispraise of the work done, nor in any way to disparage the theories which the passing generation of economists have elaborated, or the really great and admirable body of knowledge which they have brought under the hand of the science; but only to indi-cate the direction in which the inquiry in its later phases - not always with full consciousness - is shifting as regards its categories and its point of view.

The discipline of life in a modern community, particularly the industrial life, strongly reinforced by the modern sciences, has divested our knowledge of non-human phenomena of that fullness of self-directing life that was once imputed to them, and has reduced this knowledge to terms of opaque causal sequence. It has thereby narrowed the range of discre-tionary, teleological action to the human agent alone; and so it is compel-ling our knowledge of human conduct, in so far as it is distinguished from the non-human, to fall into teleological terms. Foot-pounds, calories, ge-ometrically progressive procreation, and doses of capital, have not been supplanted by the equally uncouth denominations of habits, propensities, aptitudes, and conventions, nor does there seem to be any probability that they will be; but the discussion which continues to run in terms of the former class of concepts is in an increasing degree seeking support in con-cepts of the latter class.

---

[63] See, e.g., Marshall, Principles, Book I, chap. vi, sect. 6, pp. 105-108. The like dis-passionateness is visible in most other modern writers on theory; as, e.g., Clark, Cannan, and the Austrians.

Chapter 2

The Limitations of Marginal Utility

The limitations of the marginal-utility economics are sharp and characteristic. It is from first to last a doctrine of value, and in point of form and method it is a theory of valuation. The whole system, therefore, lies within the theoretical field of distribution, and it has but a secondary bearing on any other economic phenomena than those of distribution - the term being taken in its accepted sense of pecuniary distribution, or distribution in point of ownership. Now and again an attempt is made to extend the use of the principle of marginal utility beyond this range, so as to apply it to questions of production, but hitherto without sensible effect, and necessarily so. The most ingenious and the most promising of such attempts have been those of Mr. Clark, whose work marks the extreme range of endeavor and the extreme degree of success in so seeking to turn a postulate of distribution to account for a theory of production. But the outcome has been a doctrine of the production of values, and value, in Mr. Clark's as in other utility systems, is a matter of valuation; which throws the whole excursion back into the field of distribution.

Similarly, as regards attempts to make use of this principle in an analysis of the phenomena of consumption, the best results arrived at are some formulation of the pecuniary distribution of consumption goods. Within this limited range marginal utility theory is of a wholly statical character. It offers no theory of a movement of any kind, being occupied with the adjustment of values to a given situation. Of this, again, no more convincing illustration need be had than is afforded by the work of Mr. Clark, which is not excelled in point of earnestness, perseverance, or insight. For all their use of the term "dynamic", neither Mr. Clark nor any of his associates in this line of research have yet contributed anything at all appreciable to a theory of genesis, growth, sequence, change, process, or the like, in economic life. They have had something to say as to the bearing which given economic changes, accepted as premises, may have on economic valuation, and so on distribution; but as to the causes of change or the unfolding sequence of the phenomena of economic life they have had nothing to say hitherto; nor can they, since their theory is not drawn in causal terms but in terms of teleology.

In all this the marginal utility school is substantially at one with the classical economics of the nineteenth century, the difference between the two being that the former is confined within narrower limits and sticks more consistently to its teleological premises. Both are teleological, and neither can consistently admit arguments from cause to effect in the formulation of their main articles of theory. Neither can deal theoretically with phenomena of change, but at the most only with rational adjustment to change which may be supposed to have supervened. To the modern scientist the phenomena of growth and change are the most obtrusive and

most consequential facts observable in economic life. For an understanding of modern economic life the technological advance of the past two
centuries - e.g., the growth of the industrial arts - is of the first importance;
but marginal utility theory does not bear on this matter, nor does this matter bear on marginal utility theory. As a means of theoretically accounting
for this technological movement in the past or in the present, or even as a
means of formally, technically stating it as an element in the current economic situation, that doctrine and all its works are altogether idle.

The like is true for the sequence of change that is going forward in the
pecuniary relations of modern life; the hedonistic postulate and its propositions of differential utility neither have served nor can serve an inquiry
into these phenomena of growth, although the whole body of marginal
utility economics lies within the range of these pecuniary phenomena. It
has nothing to say to the growth of business usages and expedients or to
the concomitant changes in the principles of conduct which govern the
pecuniary relations of men, which condition and are conditioned by these
altered relations of business life or which bring them to pass. It is characteristic of the school that whatever an element of the cultural fabric, an
institution or any institutional phenomenon, is involved in the facts with
which the theory is occupied, such institutional facts are taken for granted, denied, or explained away. If it is a question of price, there is offered an
explanation of how exchanges may take place with such effect as to leave
money and price out of the account.

If it is a question of credit, the effect of credit extension on business traffic is left on one side and there is an explanation of how the borrower and
lender cooperate to smooth out their respective income streams of consumable goods or sensations of consumption. The failure of the school in
this respect is consistent and comprehensive. And yet these economists
are lacking neither in intelligence nor in information. They are, indeed, to
be credited, commonly, with a wide range of information and an exact
control of materials, as well as with a very alert interest in what is going on;
and apart from their theoretical pronouncements the members of the
school habitually profess the sanest and most intelligent views of current
practical questions, even when these questions touch matters of institutional growth and decay .The infirmity of this theoretical scheme lies in its
postulates, which confine the inquiry to generalizations of the teleological
or "deductive" order.

These postulates, together with the point of view and logical method
that follow from them, the marginal utility school shares with other economists of the classical line - for this school is but a branch or derivative of
the English classical economists of the nineteenth century. The substantial
difference between this school and the generality of classical economists
lies mainly in the fact that in the marginal utility economics the common
postulates are more consistently adhered to at the same time that they are
more neatly defined and their limitations are more adequately realized.
Both the classical school is general and its specialized variant, the marginal utility school, in particular, take as their common point of departure the
traditional psychology of the early nineteenth century hedonists, which is

accepted as a matter of course or of common notoriety and is held quite uncritically. The central and well defined tenet so held is that of the hedonistic calculus. Under the guidance of this tenet and of the other psychological conceptions associated and consonant with it, human conduct is conceived of and interpreted as a rational response to the exigencies of the situation in which mankind is placed; as regards economic conduct it is such a rational and unprejudiced response to the stimulus of anticipated pleasure and pain - being, typically and in the main, a response to the promptings of anticipated pleasure, for the hedonists of the nineteenth century and of the marginal utility school are in the main of an optimistic temper.

(1*) Mankind is, on the whole and normally, (conceived to be) clearsighted and farsighted in its appreciation of future sensuous gains and losses, although there may be some (inconsiderable) difference between men in this respect. Men's activities differ, therefore, (inconsiderably) in respect of the alertness of the response and the nicety of adjustment of irksome pain cost to apprehended future sensuous gain; but, on the whole, no other ground or line or guidance of conduct than this rationalistic calculus falls properly within the cognizance of the economic hedonists. Such a theory can take account of conduct only in so far as it is rational conduct, guided by deliberate and exhaustively intelligent choice - wise adaption to the demands of the main chance. The external circumstances which condition conduct are variable, of course, and so they will have a varying effect upon conduct; but their variation is, in effect, construed to be of such a character only as to vary the degree of strain to which the human agent is subject by contact with these external circumstances.

The cultural elements involved in the theoretical scheme, elements that are of the nature of institutions, human relations governed by use and wont in whatever kind and connection, are not subject to inquiry but are taken from granted as pre-existing in a finished, typical form and as making up a normal and definite economic situation, under which and in terms of which human intercourse is necessarily carried on. This cultural situation comprises a few large and simple articles of institutional furniture, together with their logical implications or corollaries; but it includes nothing of the consequences or effects caused by these institutional elements. The cultural elements so tacitly postulated as immutable conditions precedent to economic life are ownership and free contract, together with such other features of the scheme of natural rights as are implied in the exercise of these. These cultural products are, for the purpose of the theory, conceived to be given a priori in unmitigated force.

They are part of the nature of things; so that there is no need of accounting for them or inquiring into them, as to how they have come to be such as they are, or how and why they have changed and are changing, or what effect all this may have on the relations of men who live by or under this cultural situation. Evidently the acceptance of these immutable premises, tacitly, because uncritically and as a matter of course, by hedonistic economics gives the science a distinctive character and places it in contrast with other sciences whose premises are of a different order. As has already been indicated, the premises in question, so far as they are peculiar to the hedonistic economics, are (a) a certain institutional situation, the substantial feature of which is the natural right of ownership, and (b) the hedonistic calculus.

The distinctive character given to this system of theory by these postulates and by the point of view resulting from their acceptance may be summed up broadly and concisely in saying that the theory is confined to the ground of sufficient reason instead of proceeding on the ground of efficient cause. The contrary is true of modern science, generally (except mathematics), particularly of such sciences as have to do with the phenomena of life and growth. The difference may seem trivial. It is serious only in its consequences. The two methods of inference - from sufficient reason and from efficient cause - are out of touch with one another and there is no transition from one to the other; no method of converting the procedure or the results of the one into those of the other. The immediate consequence is that the resulting economic theory is of a teleological character - "deductive" or "a priori" as it is often called - instead of being drawn in terms of cause and effect.

The relation sought by this theory among the facts with which it is occupied is the control exercised by future (apprehended) events over present conduct. Current phenomena are dealt with as conditioned by their future consequences; and in strict marginal-utility theory they can be dealt with only in respect of their control of the present by consideration of the future. Such a (logical) relation of control or guidance between the future and the present of course involves an exercise of intelligence, a taking thought, and hence an intelligent agent through whose discriminating forethought the apprehended future may affect the current course of events; unless, indeed, one were to admit something in the way of a providential elements, the relation of sufficient reason runs by way of the interested discrimination, the forethought, of an agent who takes thought of the future and guides his present activity by regard for this future. The relation of sufficient reason runs only from the (apprehended) future into the present, and it is solely of an intellectual, subjective, personal, teleological character and force; while the relation of cause and effect runs only in the contrary direction, and it is solely of an objective, impersonal materialistic character and force.

The modern scheme of knowledge, on the whole, rests for its definitive ground, on the relation of cause and effect; the relation of sufficient reason being admitted only provisionally and as a proximate factor in the analysis, always with the unambiguous reservation that the analysis must ultimately come to rest in terms of cause and effect. The merits of this scientific animus, of course, do not concern the present argument. Now, it happens that the relation of sufficient reason enters very substantially into human conduct. It is this element of discriminating forethought that distinguishes human conduct from brute behavior. And since the economist's subject of inquiry is this human conduct, that relation necessarily comes in for a large share of his attention in any theoretical formulation of economic phenomena, whether hedonistic or otherwise. But while modern science at large has made the causal relation the sole ultimate ground of theoretical formulation; and while the other sciences that deal with human life admit the relation of sufficient reason as a proximate, supplementary, or intermediate ground, subsidiary, and subservient to the argument from cause and effect; economics has had the misfortune - as seen from the scientific point of view - to let the former supplant the latter.

It is, of course, true that human conduct is distinguished from other natural phenomena by the human faculty for taking thought, and any science that has to do with human conduct must face the patent fact that the details of such conduct consequently fall into the teleological form; but it is the peculiarity of the hedonistic economics that by force of its postulated its attention is confined to this teleological bearing of conduct alone. It deals with this conduct only in so far as it may be construed in rationalistic, teleological terms of calculation and choice. But it is at the same time no less true that human conduct, economic or otherwise, is subject to the sequence of cause and effect, by force of such elements as habituation and conventional requirements. But facts of this order, which are to modern science of graver interest than the teleological details of conduct, necessarily fall outside the attention of the hedonistic economist, because they cannot be construed in terms of sufficient reason, such as his postulates demand, or be fitted into a scheme of teleological doctrines.

There is, therefore, no call to impugn these premises of the marginal-utility economics within their field. They commend themselves to all serious and uncritical persons at first glance. They are principles of action which underlie the current, business-like scheme of economic life, and as such, as practical grounds of conduct, they are not to be called in question without questioning the existing law and order. As a matter of course, men order their lives by these principles and, practically, entertain no question of their stability and finality. That is what is meant by calling them institutions; they are settled habits of thought common to the generality of men. But it would be mere absent mindedness in any student of civilization therefore to admit that these or any other human institutions have this stability which is currently imputed to them or that they are in this way intrinsic to the nature of things.

The acceptance by the economists of these or other institutional elements as given and immutable limits their inquiry in a particular and decisive way. It shuts off the inquiry at the point where the modern scientific interest sets in. The institutions in question are no doubt good for their purpose as institutions, but they are not good as premises for a scientific inquiry into the nature, origin, growth, and effects of these institutions and of the mutations which they undergo and which they bring to pass in the community's scheme of life. To any modern scientist interested in economic phenomena, the chain of cause and effect in which any given phase of human culture is involved, as well as the cumulative changes wrought in the fabric of human conduct itself by the habitual activity of mankind, are matters of more engrossing and more abiding interest than the method of inference by which an individual is presumed invariably to balance pleasure and pain under given conditions that are presumed to be normal and invariable. The former are questions of the life-history of the race or the community, questions of cultural growth and of the fortunes of generations; while the latter is a question of individual casuistry in the face of a given situation that may arise in the course of this cultural growth.

The former bear on the continuity and mutations of that scheme of conduct whereby mankind deals with its material means of life; the latter, if it is conceived in hedonistic terms, concerns a disconnected episode in the sensuous experience of an individual member of such a community. In so far as modern science inquires into the phenomena of life, whether inanimate, brute, or human, it is occupied about questions of genesis and cumulative change, and it converges upon a theoretical formulation in the shape of a life-history drawn in causal terms. In so far as it is a science in the current sense of the term, any science, such as economics, which has to do with human conduct, becomes a genetic inquiry into the human scheme of life; and where, as in economics, the subject of inquiry is the conduct of man in his dealings with the material means of life, the science is necessarily an inquiry into the life-history of material civilization, on a more or less extended or restricted plan.

Not that the economist's inquiry isolates material civilization from all other phases and bearings of human culture, and so studies the motions of an abstractly conceived "economic man." On the contrary, no theoretical inquiry into this material civilization in its causal, that is to say, its genetic, relations to other phases and bearings of the cultural complex; without studying it as it is wrought upon by other lines of cultural growth and as working its effects in these other lines. But in so far as the inquiry is economic science, specifically, the attention will converge upon the scheme of material life and will take in other phases of civilization only in their correlation with the scheme of material civilization. Like all human culture this material civilization is a scheme of institutions - institutional fabric and institutional growth. But institutions are an outgrowth of habit. The growth of culture is a cumulative sequence of habituation, and the ways and means of it are the habitual response of human nature to exigencies that vary incontinently, cumulatively, but with something of a consistent sequence in the cumulative variations that so go forward, - incontinently, because each new move creates a new situation which induces a further new variation in the habitual manner of response; cumulatively, because each new situation is a variation of what has gone before it and embodies as causal factors all that has been effected by what went before; consistently, because the underlying traits of human nature (propensities, aptitudes, and what not) by force of which the response takes place, and on the ground of which the habituation takes effect, remain substantially unchanged.

Evidently an economic inquiry which occupies itself exclusively with the movements of this consistent, elemental human nature under given, stable institutional conditions - such as is the case with the current hedonistic economics - can reach statical results alone; since it makes abstraction from those elements that make for anything but a statical result. On the other hand an adequate theory of economic conduct, even for statical purposes, cannot be drawn in terms of the individual simply - as is the case in the marginal-utility economics - because it cannot be drawn in terms of the underlying traits of human nature simply; since the response that goes to make up human conduct takes place under institutional norms and only under stimuli that have an institutional bearing; for the situation that provokes and inhibits action in any given case is itself in great part of institutional, cultural derivation.

Then, too, the phenomena of human life occur only as phenomena of the life of a group or community; only under stimuli due to contact with the group and only under the (habitual) control exercised by canons of conduct imposed by the group's scheme of life. Not only is the individual's conduct hedged about and directed by his habitual relations to his fellows in the group, but these relations, being of an institutional character, vary as the institutional scheme varies. The wants and desires, the end and aim, the ways and means, the amplitude and drift of the individual's conduct are functions of an institutional variable that is of a highly complex and wholly unstable character.

The growth and mutations of the institutional fabric are an outcome of the conduct of the individual members of the group, since it is out of the experience of the individuals, through the habituation of individuals, that institutions arise; and it is in this same experience that these institutions act to direct and define the aims and end of conduct. It is, of course, on individuals that the system of institutions imposes those conventional standards, ideals, and canons of conduct that make up the community's scheme of life. Scientific inquiry in this field, therefore, must deal with individual conduct and must formulate its theoretical results in terms of individual conduct. But such an inquiry can serve the purposes of a genetic theory only if and in so far as this individual conduct is attended to in those respects in which it counts toward habituation, and so toward change (or stability) of the institutional fabric, on the one hand, and in those respects in which it is prompted and guided by the received institutional conceptions and ideals on the other hand.

The postulates of marginal utility, and the hedonistic preconceptions generally, fail at this point in that they confine the attention to such bearings of economic conduct as are conceived not to be conditioned by habitual standards and ideals and to have no effect in the way of habituation.

They disregard or abstract from the causal sequence of propensity and habituation in economic life and exclude from theoretical inquiry all such interest in the facts of cultural growth, in order to attend to those features of the case that are conceived to be idle in this respect. All such facts of institutional force and growth are put on one side as not being germane to pure theory; they are to be taken account of, if at all, by afterthought, by a more or less vague and general allowance for inconsequential disturbances due to occasional human infirmity. Certain institutional phenomena, it is true, are comprised among the premises of the hedonists, as has been noted above; but they are included as postulates a priori. So the institution of ownership is taken into the inquiry not as a factor of growth or an element subject to change, but as one of the primordial and immutable facts of the order of nature, underlying the hedonistic calculus. Property, ownership, is presumed as the basis of hedonistic discrimination and it is conceived to be given in its finished (nineteenth-century) scope and force. There is not thought either of a conceivable growth of this definitive nineteenth-century institution out of a cruder past or of any conceivable cumulative change in the scope and force of ownership in the present or future.

Nor is it conceived that the presence of this institutional element in men's economic relations in any degree affects or disguises the hedonistic calculus, or that its pecuniary conceptions and standards in any degree standardize, color, mitigate, or divert the hedonistic calculator from the direct and unhampered quest of the net sensuous gain. While the institution of property is included in this way among the postulates of the theory, and is even presumed to be ever-present in the economic situation, it is allowed to have no force in shaping economic conduct, which is conceived to run its course to its hedonistic outcome as if no such institutional factor intervened between the impulse and its realization. The institution of property, together with all the range of pecuniary conceptions that belong under it and that cluster about it, are presumed to give rise to no habitual or conventional canons of conduct or standards of valuation, no proximate ends, ideals, or aspirations.

All pecuniary notions arising from ownership are treated simply as expedients of computation which mediate between the pain-cost and the pleasure-gain of hedonistic choice, without lag, leak, or friction; they are conceived simply as the immutably correct, God-given notation of the hedonistic calculus. The modern economic situation is a business situation, in that economic activity of all kinds is commonly controlled by business considerations. The exigencies of modern life are commonly pecuniary exigencies. That is to say they are exigencies of the ownership of property. Productive efficiency and distributive gain are both rated in terms of price. Business considerations are considerations of price, and pecuniary exigencies of whatever kind in the modern communities are exigencies of price. The current economic situation is a price system. Economic institutions in the modern civilized scheme of life are (prevailing) institutions of the price system. The accountancy to which all phenomena of modern economic life are amenable is an accountancy in terms of price; and by the current convention there is no other recognized scheme of accountancy, no other rating, either in law or in fact, to which the facts of modern life are held amenable.

Indeed, so great and pervading a force has this habit (institution) of pecuniary accountancy become that it extends, often as a matter of course, to many facts which properly have no pecuniary bearing and no pecuniary magnitude, as, e.g., works of art, science, scholarship, and religion. More or less freely and fully, the price system dominates the current common sense in its appreciation and rating of these non-pecuniary ramifications of modern culture; and this in spite of the fact that, on reflection, all men of normal intelligence will freely admit that these matters lie outside the scope of pecuniary valuation. Current popular taste and the popular sense of merit and demerit are notoriously affected in some degree by pecuniary considerations. It is a matter of common notoriety, not to be denied or explained away, that pecuniary ("commercial") tests and standards are habitually made use of outside of commercial interests proper. Precious stones, it is admitted, even by hedonistic economists, are more esteemed than they would be if they were more plentiful and cheaper.

A wealthy person meets with more consideration and enjoys a larger measure of good repute than would fall to the share of the same person with the same habit of mind and body and the same record of good and evil deeds if he were poorer. It may well be that this current "commerciali-zation" of taste and appreciation has been overstated by superficial and hasty critics of contemporary life, but it will not be denied that there is a modicum of truth in the allegation. Whatever substance it has, much or little, is due to carrying over into other fields of interest the habitual con-ceptions induced by dealing with and thinking of pecuniary matters. These "commercial" conceptions of merit and demerit are derived from business experience.

The pecuniary tests and standards so applied outside of business trans-actions and relations are not reducible to sensuous terms of pleasure and pain. Indeed, it may, e.g., be true, as is commonly believed, that the con-templation of a wealthy neighbor's pecuniary superiority yields painful rather than pleasurable sensations as an immediate result; but it is equally true that such a wealthy neighbor is, on the whole, more highly regarded and more considerately treated than another neighbor who differs from the former only in being less enviable in respect of wealth. It is the institu-tion of property that gives rise to these habitual grounds of discrimination, and in modern times, when wealth is counted in terms of money, it is in terms of money value that these tests and standards of pecuniary excel-lence are applied. This much will be admitted. Pecuniary institutions in-duce pecuniary habits of thought which affect men's discrimination out-side of pecuniary matters; but the hedonistic interpretation alleges that such pecuniary habits of thought do not affect men's discrimination in pecuniary matters.

Although the institutional scheme of the price system visibly dominates the modern community's thinking in matters that lie outside the econom-ic interest, the hedonistic economists insist, in effect, that this institution-al scheme must be accounted of no effect within that range of activity to which it owes its genesis, growth, and persistence. The phenomena of business, which are peculiarly and uniformly phenomena of price, are in the scheme of the hedonistic theory reduced to non-pecuniary hedonistic terms and the theoretical formulation is carried out as if pecuniary con-ceptions had no force within the traffic in which such conceptions origi-nate. It is admitted that preoccupation with commercial interests has "commercialised" the rest of modern life, but the "commercialization" of commerce is not admitted. Business transactions and computations in pecuniary terms, such as loans, discounts, and capitalisation, are without hesitation or abatement converted into terms of hedonistic utility, and conversely. It may be needless to take exception to such conversion from pecuniary into sensuous terms, for the theoretical purpose for which it is habitually make; although, if need were, it might not be excessively difficult to show that the whole hedonistic basis of such a conversion is a psychological misconception.

But it is to the remoter theoretical consequences of such a conversion that exception is to be taken. In making the conversion abstraction is made from whatever elements do not lend themselves to its terms; which amounts to abstracting from precisely those elements of business that have an institutional force and that therefore would lend themselves to scientific inquiry of the modern kind - those (institutional) elements whose analysis might contribute to an understanding of modern business and of the life of the modern business community as contrasted with the assumed primordial hedonistic calculus. The point may perhaps be made clearer. Money and the habitual resort to its use are conceived to be simply the ways and means by which consumable goods are acquired, and therefore simply a convenient method by which to procure the pleasurable sensations of consumption; these latter being in hedonistic theory the sole and overt end of all economic endeavor.

Money values have therefore no other significance than that of purchasing power over consumable goods, and money is simply an expedient of computation. Investment, credit extensions, loans of all kinds and degrees, with payment of interest and the rest, are likewise taken simply as intermediate steps between the pleasurable sensations of consumption and the efforts induced by the anticipation of these sensations, other bearings of the case being disregarded. The balance being kept in terms of the hedonistic consumption, no disturbance arises in this pecuniary traffic so long as the extreme terms of this extended hedonistic equation - pain-cost and pleasure-gain - are not altered, what lies between these extreme terms being merely algebraic notation employed for convenience of accountancy. But such is not the run of the facts in modern business. Variation of capitalization, e.g., occur without its being practicable to refer them to visibly equivalent variations either in the state of the industrial arts or in the sensations of consumption.

Credit extensions tend to inflation of credit, rising prices, overstocking of markets, etc., likewise without a visible or securely traceable correlation in the state of the industrial arts or in the pleasures of consumption; that is to say, without a visible basis in those material elements to which the hedonistic theory reduces all economic phenomena. Hence the run of the facts, in so far, must be thrown out of the theoretical formulation. The hedonistically presumed final purchase of consumable goods is habitually not contemplated in the pursuit of business enterprise. Business men habitually aspire to accumulate wealth in excess of the limits of practicable consumption, and the wealth so accumulated is not intended to be converted by a final transaction of purchase into consumable goods or sensations of consumption. Such commonplace facts as these, together with the endless web of business detail of a like pecuniary character, do not in hedonistic theory raise a question as to how these conventional aims, ideals, aspirations, and standards have come into force or how they affect the scheme of life in business or outside of it; they do not raise the questions because such questions cannot be answered in the terms which the hedonistic economists are content to use, or, indeed, which their premises permit them to use.

The question which arises is how to explain the facts away; how theoretically to neutralize them so that they will not have to appear in the theory, which can then be drawn indirect and unambiguous terms of rational hedonistic calculation. They are explained away as being aberrations due to oversight or lapse of memory on the part of business men, or to some failure of logic or insight. Or they are construed and interpreted into the rationalistic terms of the hedonistic calculus by resort to an ambiguous use of the hedonistic concepts. So that the whole "money economy", with all the machinery of credit and the rest, disappears in a tissue of metaphors to reappear theoretically expurgated, sterilized, and simplified into a "refined system of barter", culminating in a net aggregate maximum of pleasurable sensations of consumption.

But since it is in just this unhedonistic, unrationalistic pecuniary traffic that the tissue of business life consists, since it is this peculiar conventionalism of aims and standards that differentiates the life of the modern business community from any conceivable earlier or cruder phase of economic life; since it is in this tissue of pecuniary intercourse and pecuniary concepts, ideals, expedients, and aspirations that the conjunctures of business life arise and run their course of felicity and devastation; since it is here that those institutional changes take place which distinguish one phase or era of the business community's life from any other; since the growth and change of these habitual, conventional elements make the growth and character of any business era or business community; any theory of business which sets these elements aside or explains them away misses the main facts which it has gone out to seek.

Life and its conjunctures and institutions being of this complexion, however much that state of the case may be depreciated, a theoretical account of the phenomena of this life must be drawn in these terms in which the phenomena occur. It is not simply that the hedonistic interpretation of modern economic phenomena is inadequate or misleading; if the phenomena are subjected to the hedonistic interpretation in the theoretical analysis they disappear from the theory; and if they would bear the interpretation in fact they would disappear in fact. If, in fact, all the conventional relations and principles of pecuniary intercourse were subject to such a perpetual rationalized, calculating revision, so that each article of usage, appreciation, or procedure must approve itself de novo on hedonistic grounds of sensuous expediency to all concerned at every move, it is not conceivable that the institutional fabric would last over night.

Chapter 3

Fisher's Capital and Income

The Nature of Capital and Income[1] is of that class of books that have kept the guild of theoretical economists content to do nothing toward "the increase and diffusion of knowledge" during the past quarter of a century. Of this class

Mr. Fisher's work is of the best - thoughtful, painstaking, sagacious, exhaustive, lucid, and tenaciously logical. What it lacks is the breath of life; and this lack it shares with the many theoretical productions of the Austrian diversion as well as of the economists of more strictly classical antecedents. Not that Mr. Fisher's work falls short of the mark set by those many able men who have preceded him in this field. No reader of Mr. Fisher can justly feel disappointed in his performance of the difficult task which he sets himself. The work performs what it promises and does it in compliance with all the rules of the craft. But it does not set out substantially to extend the theory or to contribute to the sum of knowledge, either by bringing hitherto refractory phenomena into the organised structure of the science, or by affording farther or more comprehensive insight into the already familiar processes of modern economic life. Consistently with its aim, it is a work of taxonomy, of definition and classification; and it is carried through wholly within the limits imposed by this its taxonomic aim.

There are many shrewd observations on the phenomena of current business, and much evidence of an extensive and intimate acquaintance with such facts of modern culture as are still awaiting scientific treatment at the hands of the economists (e.g., in chapters v and vi, "Capital Accounts" and "Capital Summation", as also in chapters viii, ix, xiii, xiv, "Income Accounts", "Income Summation", "Value of Capital", "Earnings and Income", "The Risk Element"). But the facts of observation so drawn into the discussion are chiefly drawn in to illustrate or fortify an argument, somewhat polemical, not as material calling for theoretical explanation. As affects the development of the theory, these observations and this information run along on the side and are not allowed to disturb the argument in its secure march toward its taxonomic goal. There is no intention here to decry taxonomy, of course. Definition and classification are as much needed in economics as they are in those other sciences which have already left the exclusively taxonomic standpoint behind.

The point of criticism, on this head, is that this class of economic theory differs from the modern sciences in being substantially nothing but definition and classification. Taxonomy for taxonomy's sake, definition and

---

[1] The Nature of Capital and Income, by Irving Fisher, New York, 1906.

classification for the sake of definition and classification, meets no need of modern science. Work of this class has no value and no claims to consideration except so far as it is of use to the science in its endeavor to know and explain the processes of life. This test of usefulness applies even more broadly in economics and similar sciences of human conduct than in the natural sciences, commonly so-called. It is on this head, as regards the serviceability of his taxonomic results, that Mr. Fisher's work falls short. A modern science has to do with the facts as they come to hand, not with putative phenomena warily led out from a primordial metaphysical postulate, such as the "hedonic principle". To meet the needs of science, therefore, such modern concepts as "capital" and "income" must be defined by observation rather than by ratiocination.

Observation will not yield such a hard-and-fast definition of the term as is sought by Mr. Fisher and his co-disputants, a definition which shall mark off a pecuniary concept by physical distinctions, which shall be good for all times and places and all economic situations, ancient and modern, whether there is investment of capital or not "Capital" is a concept much employed by modern men of affairs. If it were not for the use of the concept in economic affairs - its growing use for a century past - the science would not be concerned about the meaning of the term today. It is this use of the concept in the conduct of affairs that obtrudes it upon the attention of economists; and it is, primarily at least, for a better knowledge of these pecuniary affairs, in which the concept of capital plays so large a part, that a better knowledge of the concept itself is sought. As it plays its part in these affairs of business, the concept of capital is, substantially, a habit of thought of the men engaged in business, more or less closely defined in practice by the consensus of usage in the business community.

A serviceable definition of it therefore, for the use of modern science, can be got only by observation of the current habits of thought of business men. This painfully longwinded declaration of what must appear to be a patent truism so soon as it is put in words may seem a gratuitous insistence on a stale commonplace. But it is an even more painfully tedious fact that the current polemics about "the capital concept" goes on year after year without recognition of this patent truism. What may help to cover, rather than to excuse, the failure of many economists to resort to observation for a knowledge of what the term "capital" means is the fact, adverted to by the way in various writers, that business usage of the term is not uniform and stable; it does not remain the same from generation to generation; and it cannot, at least as regards present usage, be identified and defined by physical marks.

The specific marks of the concept - the characteristics of the category - in the common usage are not physical marks, and the categories with which it is, in usage, related and contrasted are not categories that admit of definition in material terms; because it is, in usage, a pecuniary concept and stands in pecuniary relations and contrasts with other categories. It is a pecuniary term, primarily a term of investment, and as such, as a habit of thought of the men who have to do with pecuniary affairs, it necessarily changes in response to the changes going forward in the pecuniary situation and in the methods of conducting pecuniary affairs. "Capital", is the usage of current business, undoubtedly has not precisely the same meaning as it had in the corresponding usage of half a century ago; and it is safe to say that it will not retain its present meaning, unimpaired and unimproved, in the usage of ten years hence; nor does it cover just the same details in one connection as in another. Yet business men know what the term means to them. With all its shifting ambiguities, they know it securely enough for their use. The concept has sufficient stability and precision to serve their needs; and, if the economist is to deal with the phenomena of modern life in which this concept serves a use of first-rate importance, he must take the term and the concept as he finds them. It is idle fatigue to endeavor to normalise them into a formula which may suit his prepossessions but which is not true to life.

The mountain will not come to Mahomet. It is not for its idiosyncrasies that Mr. Fisher's analysis and formulation of the "capital concept" merits particular attention, but because it is the most elaborate outcome of classificatory economics to this date. Except for certain minor features - important, no doubt, within the school - his definition of capital is by no means a wide departure. It is only worked out more consistently, painstakingly, and circumspectly than has hitherto been done. Some of these special features peculiar to Mr. Fisher's position have been carefully and very ably discussed by Mr. Fetter.[2] .

The merits of the discussion of these matters between the critic and his author, with the incidental balancing of accounts, need not detain the present argument. Nor need particular attention here be given to the points in dispute so far as regards their consistency with the general body of theory upheld by Mr. Fisher and other economists who cultivate the classificatory science. But there are some details of the "nature of capital" as set forth by Mr. Fisher - and in large part assented to by Mr. Fetter and others of the life way of thinking - that require particular attention as regards their adequacy for other purposes than that of a science of classification.(1) In the general definition of "capital" (e.g., pp. 51-53, 66-68, 324), the concept is made to comprise all wealth (in its relation to future income); and "wealth" has, in the same as well as in earlier pages, been defined "to signify material objects owned by human beings," which, in turn, includes all persons, as well as other material objects. As an aggregate, therefore, as an outcome of a comprehensive "capital summation," "capital" comprises the material universe in so far as the material universe may be turned to use by man (see p. 328). This general definition includes too much and too little.

---

[2] Journal of Political Economy, March, 1907, "The Nature of Capital and Income". See also Mr. Fisher's reply in the same journal, July, 1907, "Professor Fetter on Capital and Income."

A serviceable definition of capital, one that shall answer to the concept as it is found in practice in the habits of thought of business men, will not include persons. Hitherto, there is no question, the distinction between the capitalist and his capital is not disregarded by practical men, except possibly by way of an occasional affectation of speech; and it is highly improbable that, at any point in the calculable future, business men can come habitually to confuse these two disparate concepts. Modern business proceeds on the distinction. It is only in pulpit oratory that a man's person is legitimately spoken of as an item of his assets. And as for a business man's capitalizing other persons, the law does not allow it, even in the form of peonage. There are also other material objects "under the dominion of man" which are not currently thought of as items of capital.

There are apparently two many perplexities of the mechanical classification which constrain Mr. Fisher to include the person of the owner among the owner's assets as capital: (a) Contrary to business usage, he is required by his premises to exclude immaterial wealth because it is not amenable to classification by mechanical tests, and it is therefore necessary to find some roundabout line of approach to such elements as good will, and the like;[3] and (b) persons are conceived to yield income (in the sense of Mr. Fisher's definition of "income" presently to be noted), and since capital is held to be anything which yields "income" - indeed "capital" is such by virtue of its yielding "income" - persons are included under "capital" by force of logic, though contrary to fact.(2) As has already been indicated in passing, "immaterial wealth", or "intangible assets", is excluded from "capital" in Mr. Fisher's analysis. Indeed, the existence of intangible assets is denied. The phrase is held to be an untoward misnomer for certain classes of property rights in material objects which are not wholly owned by the individual to whom these property rights inure. An important part of these incomplete property rights are rights of quasi-ownership in other persons, or claims to services performed by such persons. This denial of immaterial wealth

Mr. Fisher intends as a salutary correction of current business usage (see p. 39); and he takes pains to show how, by a cumbersome ratiocination (see chapter ii, sections 6-10), the term "intangible assets" may be avoided without landing the theory in the instant confusion which a simple denial of the concept would bring about. As a correction of current usage the attempted exclusion of intangible assets from "capital" does not seem a wise innovation. It cripples the definition for the purposes which alone would make a definition worth while. The concept of intangible assets is present in current usage on no such doubtful or precarious tenure as could be canceled by a bit of good advice. Its vogue is growing and its use is becoming more secure and more definite. The habit and the necessity of taking account, under one name or another, of the various immaterial

_____

[3] See chapter ii, section 6, pp. 24-31; also section 10.

items of wealth classed as intangible assets counts for more and more in the conduct of affairs; and any theory that aims to deal with the actualities of modern business will have to make its peace with the term or terms by which these elements of capital are called, however wrong-headed a habit it may be conceived to be. The men of affairs find the concept serviceable, or rather they find it forced upon them, and the theorist of affairs cannot afford to dispense with a concept which is so large a constituent in the substance of affairs.

But the fault of the definition at this point is more serious than the mere exclusion of a serviceable general term which might be avoided by a circumlocution. "Intangible assets" is not simply a convenient general term covering certain more or less fluctuating property rights in certain material items of wealth.

The elements of capital so designated are chiefly of the nature of differential advantages of a given business man, or a given concern, as against another. But they are capitalised in the same way as tangible items of wealth are capitalised, and in large part they are covered by negotiable securities, indistinguishable, and in most cases inseparable from, securities representing tangible assets. So, being blended in the process of capitalisation with the tangible assets, the securities based on the intangible assets create claims of ownership co-ordinate with those based on the material items and enter, in practice, into "capital summation" on the same footing as other items of wealth. Hence they become a basis of credit extensions, serving to increase the aggregate claims of creditors beyond what the hypothecable material wealth of the debtors would satisfy. Hence, in a period of general liquidation, when the differential advantages of the various concerns greatly contract, the legitimate claims of creditors come greatly to exceed the paying capacity of debtors, and the collapse of the credit system follows.

The failure of classical theory to give an intelligent account of credit and crises is in great part due to the habitual refusal of economists to recognise intangible assets, and Mr. Fisher's argument is, in effect, an accentuation of this ancient infirmity of the classical theory. It may be added that differential competitive advantages cannot be added together to make an aggregate even apart from the tangible items of "capital wealth", since the advantage of one concern is the disadvantage of another. These assets come forth, grow great, and decay, according to the advance or decline of the strategic advantage achieved by given individuals or business concerns. Their "summation" is a spurious summation, in the main, since they represent competitive advantages, in the main; and their capitalisation adds a spurious volume to the aggregate property rights of the community. So that it follows from the capitalisation of these items of differential wealth, particularly when they are covered by vendible securities, that the aggregate property rights of the community come to exceed the aggregate wealth of the community.[4] .

This is, of course, a sufficiently grave trait of the modern business situation, but the effect of Mr. Fisher's contention is to deny its existence by the turn of a phrase and to put economic theory back where it stood before the modern situation had arisen. There are other turns in modern business affairs traceable to the vogue of this concept of "intangible assets," but this illustration of its grave consequences should be a sufficient caution to any taxonomist who endeavors to simplify his scheme of definition by denying inconvenient facts. The point is perhaps sufficiently plain from what has been said, but it will bear specific mention that the apparent success of Mr. Fisher's analysis of intangible assets (pp. 32-40, 96-97) is due to his not going beyond the first move. So soon as the actualities of business complication and the cumulative effects of capitalisation are taken into account, it is evident that, with the best intentions,

Mr. Fisher's explanation of intangible assets as a roundabout claim to certain concrete (tangible) items of wealth will not serve. The treatment of credit suffers from a like unwillingness to accept the facts of observation or to look farther than the first move in an analysis. This shortsightedness of the taxonomic economist is a logical consequence of the hedonistic postulates of the school, not a personal peculiarity of the present or any other author. As to Mr. Fisher's definition and handling of the second concept with which the book is occupied - income - much the same is true as of the discussion of capital. Income is re-defined with a close adherence to the logic of that hedonistic-taxonomic system of theory for which he speaks. The concept of income here offered is more tenaciously consistent with the logical run of current classificatory economics, perhaps, than any that has been offered before. It is the perfect flower of economic taxonomy, and it shows, as no previous exposition of the kind has shown, the inherent futility of this class of work for other than purely taxonomic ends.

The concept of income, like that of capital, is well at home in current business usage; and professedly, it is the concept of income as it plays its part in the affairs of business that occupies the author's attention. But here, again, as before, the definition - "the nature of income" - is not worked out from observation of current facts, with an endeavor to make the demarcation of the concept square with the habitual apprehension of the phenomena of income in the business community. Taken at its current import, as the concept is taken in the run of business and in the economic affair of any community of men dominated by the animus of business enterprise, there can be no question but that "income" is a pecuniary concept; it is money income, or is as an element which is convertible into

---

[4] Contrary to Mr. Fisher's elaborate doctrine of property rights as defined by mechanical limits. - Chapter ii.

terms of money income and amenable to the pecuniary scheme of accountancy.

As a business proposition, nothing that cannot be rated in terms of money income is to be accounted income at all; which is the same as saying that no definition which goes beyond or behind the pecuniary concept can be a serviceable definition of income for modern use. There may be something beyond or behind this pecuniary concept which it may be desirable to reach and discuss for some other purpose more or less germane to the affairs of modern life; but such a something, whatever its nature, cannot be called "income" in the same sense in which that term is employed in modern business usage. When the term is applied to such an extra-pecuniary or praetor-pecuniary concept, such as an extension of the term is a rhetorical license; it is a figure of speech which is bound to work confusion in any argument or analysis that deals with the two inconvertible concepts. "Income" in modern usage, is a business concept; "psychic income" is not; and, as Mr. Fisher is in an eminently good position to admit, the two are incommensurable, or rather disparate, magnitudes. The one cannot be reduced to terms of the other. This state of the case may be deprecated, but it cannot be denied; and it is no service to the science of modern economic life to confuse this distinction by running the two under one technical term.

Chapter xiv ("Earnings and Income"), and more particularly the latter sections of the chapter, illustrate how far from facts one may be led by a consistent adherence to Mr. Fisher's hedonistic working-out of the concept of income. "To regard 'savings' as income is essentially to regard an increase of capital as income" (pp. 244-253). Now, apart from the hedonistic prepossession, there is, of course, no reason for not regarding such an increase of capital as income. The two ideas - "income" and "increase of capital" - are by no means mutually exclusive in the current usage; and ordinarily, so long as the terms are taken in their current (pecuniary) meaning, such an increase of capital would unhesitatingly be rated as income to the owner. The need of making "income" and "increase of capital" mutually exclusive categories is a need incident to a mechanically drawn scheme of classification, and it disappears so soon as classification for classification's sake is given up.

It is traceable to a postulated (hedonistic) principle presumed to rule men and things, not to observation of the run of facts in modern life. Indeed, even in Mr. Fisher's analysis the distinction goes into abeyance for a while where, in the doctrine of "capital value" (chapter xiii, especially section 11, and chapter xviii, section 2) the facts will absolutely not tolerate its being kept up. The hedonistic taxonomy breaks down at this juncture. And the fact is significant that this point of doctrine - viz., that capital considered as a magnitude of value "is the discounted value of the expected income" - is the latest and most highly prized advance in economic theory to whose initiation Mr. Fisher's writings give him a defensible claim.[5] .

The day when Bentham's conception of economic life was serviceable for the purposes of contemporary science lies about one hundred years back, and Mr. Fisher's reduction of "income" to "psychic income" is late by that much. The absolute merits of the hedonistic conception of economic theory need not be argued here. It was a far-reaching conception, and its length of life has made it a grand conception. But great as may be the due of courtesy to that conception for the long season of placid content which economic theory has spent beneath its spreading chestnut tree, yet the fact is not to be overlooked that is scheme of accountancy is not that of the modern business community. The logic of economic life in a modern community runs in terms of pecuniary, not of hedonistic magnitudes. Mr. Fisher's farthest advance, his definition and handling of "capital value" involves the breaking down of the classical hedonistic taxonomy; and the breakdown is typical of the best work done by the school. This move of the classifiers is, of course, nothing sudden; nor is it an accident. It means, in substance, only that the modern facts have increasingly shown themselves incompatible with the mechanical scheme of classical definitions, and that this discrepancy between the facts and the received categories has finally forced a breaking away from the old categories.

The whole voluminous discussion of the capital concept, for the past twenty years or so, has, indeed, turned about this discrepancy between business practice and the hedonistic classification by means of which economists have tried to deal with this business practice. All expedients of classification, definition, refinement, and interpretation of technical phrases have been tried, except the surrender of the main position - that economic conduct must be read in terms of the hedonistic calculus.[6] .

Under the stress of this controversy of interpretation, the hedonistic concept of capital as a congeries of "productive goods" has gradually and reluctantly, but hitherto not wholly, been replaced by something more serviceable. But this gain in serviceability has been won - in so far as the achievement may be spoken of in the past tense - at some cost to the hedonistic point of view. Such serviceability as the newly achieved interpretation of the capital concept has, it has because, and only so far as, it substitutes a pecuniary for a hedonistic construction of the phenomena of capitalisation. Among those who speak for the new (pecuniary) construction is Mr. Fisher, although he is not by any means the freest of those who are breaking away. His position is, no doubt, deprecated by many taxonomic economists as being an irreverently, brutally iconoclastic innovation, quite indefensible on taxonomic grounds; but, after all, as Mr. Fetter

---

[5] Cf. Journal of Political Economy, papers cited above.

[6] The argument will return to the hedonistic calculus presently to show how the logic of this calculus has forced the theory at certain points.

has shown in more courteous words,[7] it is an equivocal, or perhaps rather an irresolute position at the best. "Capital", in the classical definition, was, as required by the hedonistic point of view, a congeries of what has latterly been named "productive goods." From such a concept of capital, which is hopelessly and increasingly out of touch with business usage, the theorists have been straining away; and Mr. Fisher has borne a large part in the speculations that are leading up to the emancipation of theorists from the chore work required by that white elephant. But he is not content formally to give up the heirloom; although, as Mr. Fetter indicates, he now makes little use of it except for parade. He offers two correlate definitions of capital: "capital wealth", i.e., productive goods, and "capital value", i.e., pecuniary capital.[8] .

The former of these, the authentic hedonistic concept, shortly drops out of the discussion, although it does not drop out so tracelessly as Mr. Fetter's criticism may suggest. The argument then proceeds, almost throughout, on the concept of "capital value".

[9] .But there is a recurrent, and, one is tempted to say, dutiful, reminder that this "capital value", or capitalisation of values, is to be taken as the value of a congeries of tangible objects (productive goods); whereby a degree of taxonomic consistency with the authentic past and with the hedonistic postulate is formally maintained, and whereby also, dutifully and authentically, intangible assets are excluded from the capital concept, as already indicated above. Capital value is "simply the present worth of the future income from the specified capital.[10] (p. 202); but this capital value, it is held, is always the value of tangible items (including persons).It is the uncanny office of the critic to deal impersonally with his author's work as an historical phenomenon. Under cover of this license it may be pardonable to speak badly and broadly of the logic of this retention of the authentic postulate that physically productive goods (including persons) alone are to be included in the capitalisation out of which capital value emerges. And what is here said in this connection is not to be taken as a presumptuous make-believe of reproducing the sequence of ideas by which Mr. Fisher has arrived to trace the logical sequence between the main hedonistic body of theory and the historical outcome of its development at this point. In the classical-Austrian scheme of theory the center and circum-

---

[7] Journal of Political Economy, as above, pp. 143-144.

[8] Pp. 66-67, 327, and elsewhere.

[9] Mr. Fetter, in advance of Mr. Fisher in the position taken if not in priority of departure, advocates discarding the older (authentic hedonistic) concept, in form as well as in fact.

[10] In this and similar passages Mr. Fisher appears to be in search of a more competent phrase, which has been used, but which he apparently has not met with - "putative earning-capacity." Certain infirmities of such a definition, whether under one phrase or another, for the taxonomic purpose, will be indicated presently.

ference of economic life is the production of what a writer on ethics has called "pleasant feeling." Pleasant feeling is produced only by tangible, physical objects (including persons), acting somehow upon the sensory. The inflow of pleasant feeling is "income" - "psychic income" net and positive.

The purpose of capital is to serve this end - the increase of pleasant feeling - and things are capital, in the authentic hedonistic scheme, by as much as they serve this end. Capital, therefore, must be tangible, material goods, since only tangible goods will stimulate the human sensory pleasantly. Intangible assets, being not physical, do not impinge upon the sensory; therefore they are not capital. Since they unavoidably are thrown prominently on the screen in the show of modern life, they must, consistently with the hedonistic conception, be explained away by construing them in terms of some authentic category of tangible items. There is a second line of approach to the same conclusion comprised in the logical scheme of hedonistic economics, more cogent on practical grounds than that sketched above and perhaps of equally convincing metaphysical force. The hedonistic (classical-Austrian) economics is a system of taxonomic science - a science of normalities. Its office is the definition and classification of "normal" phenomena, or, perhaps better, phenomena as they occur in the normal case.

And in this normal case, when and so far as the laws of nature work out their ends unvitated, nature does all things well. This is also according to the ancient and authentic canons of taxonomic science. In the hedonistically normal scheme of life wasteful, disserviceable, or futile acts have no place.[11].

The current competitive, capitalistic business scheme of life is normal, when rightly seen in the hedonistic light. There is not (normally) in it anything of a wasteful, disserviceable, or futile character. Whatever phenomena do not fit into the scheme of normal economic life, as tested by the hedonistic postulate, are to be taken account of by way of exception. If there are discrepancies, in the way of waste, disserviceability, or futility, e.g., they are not inherent in the normal scheme and they do not call for incorporation in the theory of the situation in which they occur, except for interpretative elimination and correction. In this course the hedonistic economics, with its undoubting faith that whatever (normally) is, is right, simply follows the rule of all authentic taxonomic science.

As indicated above, the normal end of capital, as of all the multifarious phenomena of economic life, is the production of pleasure and the prevention of pain; and in the Benthamite system of theory - which includes the classical-Austrian economics - the normal end of the life of man in

---

[11] Cf., e.g., Clark, Essentials of Economic Theory, passim. - "Each man who gets in a normal way, any income at all performs one or more productive functions" etc. - p. 92.

society, economic and otherwise, is the greatest happiness of the greatest number. Such may not be the outcome in any given actual situation, but in so far as such is not the outcome the situation departs from the normal; and such departures from the normal do not properly concern the (hedonistic) "science" of economics, but fall authentically to the care of the "art" of economics, whose concern it is to find correctives for these, essentially sporadic, aberrations.

Under the rule of normal serviceability nothing can be included in the theoretically right "capital summation" which does not go to swell the aggregate of hedonistic "services" to man - nothing which is not "productive", in the sense of increasing the well-being of mankind at large. Persons may, indeed they "normally" should always, be productive in this sense, and persons, therefore, should properly be included in the capital summation.[12] .

---

[12] What is to be done, theoretically, with persons leading disserviceable or futile lives, "undesirable citizens", does not clearly appear. They are undesirable, but they are of the human breed and so are presumably to be included in the normal human aggregate whose "greatest number" are elected for the "greatest happiness" by the (normally) benevolent laws of nature. The suggestion is, of course, obvious that they should be deducted from the gross aggregate of items - i.e., algebraically added in as negative magnitudes - so as to leave a net algebraic sum of positively serviceable capital goods, including persons. The like might apparently be done with impersonal material items which are wastefully or noxiously employed. But the converse suggestion is at least equally cogent, that such disserviceable items, personal and impersonal, are simply abnormal, aberrant, exceptional, and that therefore they simply drop tracelessly out of the theoretical scheme, so as to the theoretically correct "summation" as large as it would be had these disserviceable negative times items not been present. That is to say, the theoretically correct net aggregate serviceability is the same as the gross serviceability; since the negative quantities actually present among the aggregate of items are not normally present, and are, therefore, theoretically non-existent. There is a third alternative. The abnormal disserviceable items being indubitably present in fact, and some part of them being present with the hedonistically sacred stamp of the human breed, it may be that, in the apprehension of the adepts, should this problem of taxonomy present itself to them, at least so much of the disserviceable productive goods as are human beings should be counted in; but, since they are persons, and since it is the normal estate of man to be serviceable to his fellows, they should be theoretically counted as normally serviceable, and therefore included in the net aggregate of serviceability at the magnitude of serviceability normally imputable to them. What rule should guide in fixing the true magnitude of imputed normal serviceability for such disserviceable persons in such a case is a further problem of taxonomy which would take the present argument too far afield. This much seems clear, however, that under this third alternative the net aggregate serviceability to be imputed to the sum of capital goods (including persons) should exceed the actual aggregate serviceability by the addition of an amount approximately equal to the disservice rendered by the disserviceable persons in question.

In this normalised scheme of economic life all claims represented by negotiable instruments, e.g., must be led back, as is done by Mr. Fisher,[13] to
tangible items of serviceable goods; and in its application to the concrete
case, the actual situation, if follows from this rule that all such instruments
are, normally, evidences of the ownership of such tangible items as serve
the material needs of mankind at large. It follows also that there are, normally, no items of differential serviceability included among the property
rights covered by negotiable instruments; that in the hedonistic theory of
business there are no differential advantages and no differential or competitive gains; that the gain of each business man is, at the most, simply
the sum of his own contributions to the aggregate of services that maintain the life and happiness of the community. This optimistic light shed on
the business situation by the hedonistic postulate is one of the most valued, and for the wise quietist assuredly the most valuable, of the theoretical results following from the hedonistic taxonomy. And this optimistic
light will fail with the surrender of the authentic position that capital is a
congeries of physically productive goods.

But while this light lasts the hedonistic economist is able to say that, although the scheme of economic life contemplated by him as normal is a
competitive system, yet the gains of the competitors are in no degree of a
competitive character; no one (normally) gains at the cost of another or at
the cost of the community at large; nor does any one (normally) turn any
part of his equipment of capital goods to use for a competitive or differential advantage. In this light, the competitive struggle is seen to work out as,
in effect, a friendly rivalry in the service of mankind at large, with an eye
single to the greatest happiness of the greatest number. If intangible assets
are recognised by the theory this comforting outlook on the business situation fails, because intangible assets are, in the main, of a differential effect only. Hence they are excluded by the logic of the hedonistic taxonomy.
Returning to a point left uncovered above (p. 120), it may be in place to
look more narrowly into the definition of capital as 'capital value" arrived
at by Mr. Fisher, ably spoken for by Mr. Fetter, and apparently in train to be
accepted by many economists interested in questions of theory.[14] .

On its face this formulation seems definite, tangible, and stable enough.
Such a concept appears to serve the needs of business traffic. But it is a

---

[13] Chapter ii, especially sections 4-9, and pp. 93-96

[14] The value of capital is the discounted value of the expected income" (p. 328). "It is
found by discounting (or 'capitalising') the value of the income expected from the
wealth of property." (p. 330). "Capital today may be defined as economical wealth
expressed in terms of the general unit of value." (Fetter, Principles of Economics, p.
115) ... "every good becoming capital when it is capitalised, that is, when the totality
of its uses is expressed as a present sum of values." (Ibid. p. 116) It has elsewhere
been characterised as "capitalisation of putative earning capacity." The latter is
perhaps the more serviceable definition, being nearer to the concept of capital current in the business community.

more delicate question, and more to the present purpose, whether the definition has the requisite stability and mechanical precision for the purposes of a taxonomy such as Mr. Fisher's, which seeks to set up mutually exclusive categories of things distinguished from one another by statistically determined lines of demarcation. The question obtrudes itself, as regards this putative value of expected income: Whose imputation of value is to be accepted?

Value, of course, is a fact of imputation; and it may seem a ready solution to say that the decision in this question of appraisement is rendered by a consensus of imputation between or among the parties concerned in the capitalisation. This consensus would be shown concretely by market quotations of securities, and it would be shown in generalised form by the familiar diagrams offered by all taxonomists of the marginal-utility school. But, concretely, there is not always a consensus of imputations as to the expected value of a given flow of income; in the case of unlisted securities, as well as of other capitalisable property in like case, the appeal to a consensus fails. And, in point of taxonomic theory, the marginal-utility curves apply to the case in hand only when and in so far as the property in question is the subject of a bargain; and, further, the diagrams of intersections and the like are of no avail for the cases, frequent enough in practice, where bargains are struck at the same time for different lots of the same line of goods at different heights on the ordinate. It is only by virtue of broad and untenable generalisations concerning the haggling of the market that the diagrams appear to cover a general proposition as to the actual value of property. The upshot of the matter is that a given block of capital need not, in practice it frequently does not, have one particular value at a given time; no more than a given expected flow of income need have one particular value alone imputed to it by all, or by a consensus of, the various parties in interest. A summary review of an actual case taken from current business traffic may illustrate some of the difficulties of arriving, in detail, at such a definite and stable determination of capital value as will serve the needs of "capital summation" as expounded by Mr. Fisher. A relatively small and inconspicuous corporation managed by two men, A and B, had for a series of years been doing a successful, conservative business in one of the necessaries of life, and had achieved an enviable reputation for efficiency and reliability; that is to say, it had accumulated a large and valuable body of "good will."

The only form of securities outstanding was common stock, unlisted, and held by relatively few stockholders. During the late winter and spring of the present year (1907), the managers of the company gathered from the course of the market that business in their line would probably slacken off appreciably in the immediate future, with small change of a prompt recovery. They determined to sell out and withdraw to another line of business, not similarly dependent on prices. To this end they set about buying in all the stock of their company, A-B, with a view to selling out the going concern to another corporation, C-D, whose appraisement of the future (imputation of value) was apparently more sanguine than their own. The outstanding shares of stock were bought in, during a period of

some six weeks, by A and B bargaining separately with the several stockholders as opportunity offered, at prices ranging from about 105 to about
125.

Meantime, negotiation had been going forward with company C-D for
the sale of the concern as a whole on the basis of an inventory of the plant,
including the stock of goods on hand. Both the plant and the stock of
goods were somewhat extensive and scattered. With the inventory as a
basis the concern was sold at an aggregate price which included a fair allowance for the intangible assets (good will) of the going concern. The
inventory was taken on the basis of the last previous monthly price-
current, and the transfer to C-D took place on that basis. As counted on by
A-B, and as apparently not counted on by C-D, the next succeeding
monthly price-current showed a decline in the market value of the stock of
goods on hand of some nine or ten percent; and the subsequent course of
the market, as well as of the volume of traffic in this line of business, has
been of the same complexion. The transfer of the concern, all told, from A-
B to C-D took place at figures which aggregated an advance of some 25
percent over the cost to A and B, counting the stock of the corporation at
an average of the prices paid by them for such shares of stock as they
bought in from other stockholders, which was rather more than one-half
of all the outstanding stock.

The question now is:

What, for purposes of "capital summation", should be taken as the basis
of the capital value of corporation A-B last spring, say, at the date of the
transfer to C-D, or at any date during the buying in of the outstanding
stock? During all this time the "capital value" must have been something
over 100 percent of the nominal capital, since none of the stock was
bought at less than 105. But the shares of stocks were bought in, slattering-
ly, from 105 to 125, with an average in the neighborhood of 115; while the
aggregate price of the going concern at the same time seems to have been
in the neighborhood of 140 percent of the nominal capitalisation. Should
the last transaction in the purchase of stock from day to day, running uncertainly between 105 and 125, be construed to revise the 'capital value" of
the concern to that date? This would make the "capital value" skip capri-
ciously back and forth within the 20 points of the margin, in attendance
upon the last previous "consensus of imputation" between a given seller
and one or the other of the two buyers.

The final average of, say, 115, had not at that time been established, so
that that figure could not be taken as a basis during the interval. Or should
the stipulated price of the going concern rule the case, in the face of these
transactions taking place at figures incompatible with it? Again, at the date
of the transfer to C-D, was the "capital value" immediately before the
transfer the (indefinite) rating given by the then owners, A and B; and was
it, the next minute, to be counted at the price paid by C-D; or, at the nominal capitalisation; or, at the (indefinite) figure at which C-D might have
been willing to sell? What further serves to muddle the whole question is
the fact that the transfer price of the going concern had been agreed upon

between A-B and C-D before the whole amount of the outstanding stock had been bought in by A-B.

This case, which is after all sufficiently commonplace, offers a chance for further refinements of confusion, but what has been said may serve to illustrate the point in question. The difficulty, it will be noticed, is a difficulty of classification, not of business procedure. There are no difficulties of mutual intelligibility among the various parties engaged in the transactions. The difficulties arise when it is attempted to define the phenomena for some (taxonomic) purpose not germane to the transactions in question, and to draw lines of demarcation that are of no effect in the business affairs in which these phenomena arise. The resulting confusion marks a taxonomic infirmity in the proposed capital concept, due to an endeavor to reach a definition from a metaphysical postulate (of hedonism) not comprised among the postulates on which business traffic proceeds.

This fable teaches that it is a wise hedonist who keeps his capital concept clear of all entanglement with 'capital value", and, more particularly, with the live business notion of capitalised earning-capacity.

Chapter 4
Fisher's Rate of Interest

There is less novelty, either in the course of the argument or in the results achieved, in the Rate of Interest1 than in Mr. Fisher's earlier volume
on the Nature of Capital and Income. Substantially the whole of it lies
within the accustomed lines of that marginal-utility school of economics
for which its author has so often and so convincingly spoken. It is true to
the canons of the school, even to the point of making the usual error of
logic in the usual place. But while it makes no material innovation, beyond
a new distribution of emphasis among the factors held by the school to
determine the rate of interest, it carries out the analysis of these determi-
nants with unexampled thoroughness and circumspection, such, indeed,
it may fairly be hoped, as will close the argument, on the main heads of
the theory at least, within the school. There is all the breadth and facility of
command over materials, which Mr. Fisher's readers have learned to ex-
pect, such as to make the book notable even among a group of writers to
whom such facility seems native. If fault is to be found with this exposition
of the marginal-utility doctrines it is scarcely to be sought in details of fact
or unauthorised discrepancies of logic.

Exception may be taken to the argument as a whole, but scarcely from
the accepted ground of the marginal-utility school. Nor should that remnant of the classical school which has not yet given its adherence to the
marginal-utility doctrines readily find fault with an exposition which finds
its foundations in so good and authentic a utilitarian theorist as John Rae.
The theory of interest arrived at is the so-called "agio" or discount theory,
already familiar to Mr. Fisher's readers and substantially in accord with
the like theory spoken for by Bohm-Bawerk. Mr. Fisher takes issue with
Bohm-Bawerk on the one grave and far-famed point of doctrine concerning the "Roundabout Process". And on this head, I apprehend, it will be
conceded that the later writer occupies the stronger and more consistent
position, whatever exceptions may be taken to his line of argument in refutation of the doctrine in dispute. In his critical survey of competing and
inadequate interest theories, occupying the first four chapters of the volume, this doctrine of the roundabout process comes in for more serious
attention than all the rest; and justly so, since it is an alien in the school - a
heresy which has been brought in by oversight.

Leaving on one side for the moment all question as to the merits of this
doctrine, it may readily be shown not to belong in the same explanation of

---

1 The Rate of Interest: Its Nature, Determination and Relation to Economic Phenomena, By Irving Fisher, New York, 1908.

interest with the agio theory, at least not as a proposition correlative with the theorem about the differential preference for present over future income. Interest and the rate of interest is a matter of value, therefore to be explained in terms of valuation, and so in terms of marginal utility with the scheme of value theory for which Mr. Fisher and Bohm-Bawerk are spokesmen no analysis of a value phenomenon can be brought to a conclusion until it is stated in terms of marginal utility. All fundamental proposition, all theorems of the first order in this theoretical scheme must be stated in these terms, since these terms alone are ultimate. Facts of a different order bear on any question of value, in this scheme, only as they bear on the process of valuation, which is matter to be stated in terms of marginal utility. This scheme of theory is a branch of applied psychology - of that school of psychology which was in vogue in the early nineteenth century; whereas the roundabout process is not a psychological phenomenon - at least not of the same class with the doctrines of marginal utility. It is a technological matter.

The roundabout process has a bearing on the rate of interest, therefore, only as it bears on the main theorem concerning the preference for present over future income; that is to say, the doctrine of the greater productivity of the roundabout process is, at the best, a secondary proposition, subsidiary to the main theorem. The valuations out of which the rate of interest emerges take account of various circumstances affecting the desirability of present as contrasted with future goods; among these circumstances may be the greater productivity of the roundabout process; but this is as near to the core of the problem as that phenomenon can be brought. The problem of the rate of interest in the marginal-utility system is a problem of applied psychology, more precisely a problem of the hedonistic calculus; whereas the alleged greater productivity of the roundabout process is a technological phenomenon, an empirical generalisation concerning the mechanical efficiency of given industrial ways and means.

As an explanation of interest the doctrine of the roundabout process belongs among the productivity theories, as Mr. Fisher has indicated: and as such it cannot be admitted as a competent, or indeed a relevant, explanation of interest in a system of theory whose purpose is to formulate a scheme of economic conduct in terms of the hedonistic calculus. It is quite conceivable that in some other system of economic theory, worked out for some other purpose than the hedonistic explanation of value, the roundabout process might be brought into the central place in a doctrine of interest; but such a doctrine would have as its theoretical core, upon which the theorist's attention should be concentrated, the physical production of that increment of wealth that is presumed to go to interest, rather than the pecuniary determination of the rate of interest through which this increment is distributed among its claimants.

Such a doctrine would belong in a theory of production, or of industry, not in a theory of distribution, or of business. But the marginal-utility system is primarily a theoretical scheme of production; and, therefore, in so far as it is or aims to be primarily a theory of business traffic, not of the processes of industry, particularly not of technological efficiency or of technological changes. This is well shown, e.g., in Mr. Fisher's discussion of invention (ch. x, ch. xi, sec. 4, ch. xvii, sec. 6). Apart from all question of consistency or conclusiveness within the premises of the marginal-utility school, the test to which Mr. Fisher's theory of interest must finally be brought is the question of its adequacy as an explanation of interest in modern business. Mr. Fisher has recognised this, and the most painstaking and most admirable portions of the volume are those which discuss interest as involved in current business transactions (e.g., ch. xii-xvi).

In modern life distribution takes place almost wholly in pecuniary terms and by means of business transactions. In so far as it does not, e.g., in the distribution of consumable goods within the household or in the distributive use of public utilities, it does not bear sensibly on any question of interest, particularly does it not bear immediately as a determinant on the rate of interest. Interest, as demanding the attention of the modern economist, is eminently a pecuniary phenomenon, and its rate is a question of business adjustments. It is in the business community and under the guidance and incitement of business exigencies that the rate is determined. The rate of interest in any other bearing in modern life is wholly subordinate and subsidiary. It is therefore an inversion of the logical sequence when Mr. Fisher, with others of the school, explains pecuniary interest and its rate by appeal to non-pécuniary factors. But such are the traditions of the school, and such a line of analysis is imposed by their premises.

As has been remarked above, Mr. Fisher's development of the doctrine of interest is true to these premises and traditions to a degree of nicety never excelled by any of the adepts. These premises or postulates on which the marginal-utility scheme rests are derived from the English classical economists, and through them from the hedonistic philosophy of the earlier decades of the last century. According to the hedonistic postulates the end and incentive is necessarily the pleasurable sensations to be derived from the consumption of goods, what Mr. Fisher calls "enjoyable income" or "psychic income", and for reasons set forth in his analysis (ch. vi), it is held that, on the whole, men prefer present to future consumption.

This is the beginning of economic (marginal-utility) wisdom; but it is also the end of the wisdom of marginal utility. To these elemental terms it has been incumbent on all marginal-utility theorists to reduce their formulations of economic phenomena. And from the acceptance of these limitations follow several characteristic excrescences and incongruities in Mr. Fisher's theory, presently to be spoken of. To save argument it may be conceded that the hedonistic interpretation of human conduct is fundamentally sound. It is not requisite for the purpose in hand to discard that postulate, however frail it might prove on closer scrutiny. But if it be granted that the elemental motive force of economic life is the hedonistic calculus it does not follow that the same elemental calculus of preference for present over future sensations of consumption is to be directly appealed to in explanation of a phenomenon so far from elementary as the rate of interest. In point of historical fact anything like a consistent rate of interest emerges into the consciousness of mankind only after business traffic has reached some appreciable degree of development; and this development of business enterprise has taken place only on the basis and within the lines of the so-called "money economy", and virtually only on that higher stage of the money economy specifically called a "credit economy." Indeed interest is, strictly, a phenomenon of credit transactions alone.

But a money economy and the consequent credit transactions which give rise to the phenomena of interest can emerge only on the basis afforded by the mature development of the institution of property. The whole matter lies within the range of a definite institutional situation which is to be found only during a relatively brief phase of civilisation that has been preceded by thousands of years of cultural growth during which the existence of such a thing as interest was never suspected. In short, interest is a business proposition and is to be explained only in terms of business, not in terms of livelihood, as Mr. Fisher aims to do. Business may be intimately concerned with livelihood, it may even be that in modern life business activity is the sole or chief method of getting a livelihood, but the two are not convertible terms, as Mr. Fisher's argument would require; neither are business gains convertible with the sensations of consumption, as his argument would also require.

The reason why these terms are not convertible, and therefore the reason why an argument proceeding on their convertibility or equivalence must reach a fallacious outcome, is that a growth of institutions intervenes between the two - granting that the hedonistic calculus is the primary incentive and guide of economic activity. In economic life, as in other lines of human conduct, habitual modes of activity and relations have grown up and have by convention settled into a fabric of institutions. These institutions, and the usual concepts involved in them, have a prescriptive, habitual force of their own, although it is not necessary at every move to ravel out and verify the intricate web of precedents, accidents, compromises, indiscretions, and appetites, out of which in the course of centuries the current cultural situation has arisen. If the contrary were true, if men universally acted not on the conventional grounds and values afforded by the fabric of institutions, but solely and directly on the grounds and values afforded by the unconventionalised propensities and aptitudes of hereditary human nature, then there would be no institutions and no culture.

But the institutional structure of society subsists and men live within its lines, with more or less questioning, it is true, but with more acquiescence than dissent. Business proceeds on the ground afforded by the institution of property, more particularly of property as rated in terms of money values. The rate of interest is one of the phenomena involved in this business traffic, and its theoretical explanation must run in terms of business, and so in terms of money. When the question is removed from this institutional basis and is pushed back to the grounds on which property and money are conceived to rest, it ceases to be a question of interest and becomes a detail of the analysis of the phenomena of value. But value, as understood by living economists, has no existence apart from the institution of property - since it is concerned with the exchange of property. Interest is a pecuniary concept having no validity (except by force of an ambiguity) outside of the pecuniary relations of the business community, and to construe it in other, presumably more elementary, terms is to explain it away by dissolving it into the elements out of which it is remotely derived, or rather to which it is presumed to be remotely related.

The phenomena of modern business, including the rate of interest, can no more be handled in non-pecuniary terms than human physiology can be handled in terms of the amphioxus. The difference is that between explaining current facts and endeavouring to explain them away. There is (probably) no science except economics in which such an endeavor to explain the phenomena of an institution in terms of one class of the rudiments which have afforded the point of departure for the growth of the institution would be listened to with any degree of civility. The philologists, for example, have various infirmities of their own, but they would have little patience with a textual critic who should endeavor to reduce the Homeric hymns to terms of those onomatopoetic sounds out of which it is presumed that human speech has grown.

What fortune would have overtaken E. B. Tylor's Researches into the Development of Mythology, Philosophy, Religion, Language, Art and Custom, if he had set out to explain away the facts and show these institutions are of no effect because he knows something about the remote sources from which they have come? Scientific vagaries of that heroic stature are not unknown among ethnologists, but it is to be noted to the credit of the craft that they are known vagaries. Mr. Fisher's theory of the rate of interest suffers from the same oversight of this difference between explaining facts and explaining them away, as do the common run of marginal-utility doctrines. So, since interest is to be formulated in terms of consumptive hedonism, instead of in business concepts, and since price is to be formulated in the same terms, there arises an unavoidable confusion between the two, as appears in the discussion of "Appreciation and Interest" (ch. v, and elsewhere).

In the main, this discussion belongs properly in a theory of prices. Appreciation and depreciation of the standard of payments may of course - so far as they are foreseen - affect the rate of interest; but they are, after all, phenomena of price. Business transactions run in terms of money. Interest is rated in money and paid with a view to money gain. Many contingencies bear on the changes of such gain, and changes of price are notoriously among those contingencies. Speculative buying and selling look to this contingency chiefly, and may look to such a change in the price of the goods bought or sold as shall offset the interest on the funds tied up in the speculation, but the rate of interest does not thereby come to be conceived or stated in terms of the advance or decline of the price of goods.

Appreciation and depreciation, if foreseen, are circumstances to be taken into account by lender and borrower very much as the productivity of the roundabout process (if that doctrine be allowed) will be taken into account in making the rate of interest. But this state of the case does not make either of these phenomena a rate of interest; nor does it reduce interest to a technological matter on the one hand or to a variation of prices on the other hand. Now and again, especially in ch. xiv (pp. 276-285), Mr.

Fisher cites facts showing that neither investment nor interest are counted in terms of livelihood or in the sensations of consumption, and showing also that questions of livelihood touch these phenomena only uncertainly and incidentally. He well shows (a) that business men habitually do not (adequately) appreciate variations in the commodity-value of money, and (b) that with rising prices they simply do business at a high money profit and are content to pay a high rate of interest without suspecting that all this has any connection with the "commodity interest" of Mr. Fisher. (Cf. the passages cited from Baxter and from Jevons).

But his hedonistic preconceptions lead him to take note of this state of things as exceptional and anomalous, whereas, of course, it is the rule. It is not only the rule, but there is no avoiding it so long as business is done in terms of money, and in the absence of a foregone conclusion these facts should persuade any observer that money value has an institutional force in the counsels of business men. This chapter (xiv), and in good part the succeeding one, explain interest without support from or reference to Mr. Fisher's "agio" theory, although they are offered as an "inductive verification" of that theory. Except for the author's recurrent intimations, nothing in this inductive verification bears on, or leans on, the doctrine of a preference for present over future income. Not only so, but chapter xiv, incidentally helped out by various passages elsewhere, goes far to disprove that the rate of interest is a matter of the preference for present over future income, taking "income" in Mr. Fisher's sense of the term.

There is a strikingly ingenuous passage in ch. xv, (p. 315): "For him [the farmer] the lowest ebb is in the fall, when gathering and marketing his crops cause him a sudden expenditure of labor or of money for the labor of others. To tide him over this period he may need to borrow ... The rate of interest tends upward." The farmer, in other words, bids up the rate of interest when his crops are in hand or are coming in; particularly just after he has secured them, when he is required to meet certain pecuniary obligations. But the farmer's crops are his "income" in the case assumed, and when his income has come in, at this springtide of his income stream, his preference for present over future goods should logically be at its lowest, and, indeed, there need be little question but such is the case.

There is also no doubt that the farmer is willing to bid high for funds at this period; and the reason seems to be that then the fresh access of income enables him to bid high, at the same time that he needs the funds to meet pecuniary obligations. His need of borrowing is due to the necessity of marketing his crops and so "realising" on them; that is to say, it is a business or pecuniary need, not a matter of smoothing out the income stream. Farming is a business venture in modern times, and the end of business is gain in terms of money. The cycle of business enterprise closes with a sale, a conversion of "income" into money values, not conversely, and the farmer is under more or less pecuniary pressure to bring this pecuniary cycle to a close.

Chapter 5

Professor Clark's Economics

For some time past economists have been looking with lively anticipation for such a comprehensive statement of Mr. Clark's doctrines as is now offered. The leading purpose of the present volume[1] is "to offer a brief and provisional statement of the more general laws of progress"; although it also comprises a more abridged restatement of the laws of "Economic Statics" already set forth in fuller form in his Distribution of Wealth. Though brief, this treatise is to be taken as systematically complete, as including in due correlation all the "essentials" of Mr. Clark's theoretical system. As such, its publication is an event of unusual interest and consequence. Mr. Clark's position among this generation of economists is a notable and commanding one. No serious student of economic theory will, or can afford to, forego a pretty full acquaintance with his development of doctrines. Nor will any such student avoid being greatly influenced by the position which Mr. Clark takes on any point of theory on which he may speak, and many look confidently to him for guidance where it is most needed. Very few of those interested in modern theory are under no obligations to him. He has, at the same time, in a singular degree the gift of engaging the affections as well as the attention of students in his field. Yet the critic is required to speak impersonally of Mr. Clark's work as a phase of current economic theory.

In more than one respect Mr. Clark's position among economists recalls the great figures in the science a hundred years ago. There is the same rigid grasp of the principles, the "essentials," out of which the broad theorems of the system follow in due sequence and correlation; and like the leaders of the classical era, while Mr. Clark is always a theoretician, never to be diverted into an inconsistent makeshift, he is moved by an alert and sympathetic interest in current practical problems. While his aim is a theoretical one, it is always with a view to the theory of current affairs; and his speculations are animated with a large sympathy and an aggressive interest in the amelioration of the lot of man.

His relation to the ancient adepts of the science, however, is something more substantial than a resemblance only. He is, by spiritual consanguinity, a representative of that classical school of thought that dominated the science through the better part of the nineteenth century. This is peculiarly true of Mr. Clark, as contrasted with many of those contemporaries who have fought for the marginal-utility doctrines. Unlike these spokesmen of

---

[1] The Essentials of Economic Theory, as Applied to Modern Problems of Industry and Public Policy. By John Bates Clark. New York: The Macmillan Company, 1907.

the Austrian wing, he has had the insight and courage to see the continuity between the classical position and his own, even where he advocates drastic changes in the classical body of doctrines. And although his system of theory embodies substantially all that the consensus of theorists approves in the Austrian contributions to the science, yet he has arrived at his position on these heads not under the guidance of the Austrian school, but, avowedly, by an unbroken development out of the position given by the older generation of economists[2] .

Again, in the matter of the psychological postulates of the science, he accepts a hedonism as simple, unaffected, and uncritical as that of Jevons Or of James Mill. In this respect his work is as true to the canons of the classical school as the best work of the theoreticians of the Austrian observance. There is the like unhesitating appeal to the calculus of pleasure and pain as the indefeasible ground of action and solvent of perplexities, and there is the like readiness to reduce all phenomena to terms of a "normal," or "natural," scheme of life constructed on the basis of this hedonistic calculus. Even in the ready recourse to "conjectural history," to use Stuart's phrase, Mr. Clark's work is at one with both the early classical and the late (Jevons-Austrian) marginal-utility school. It has the virtues of both, coupled with the graver shortcomings of both. But, as his view exceeds theirs in breadth and generosity, so his system of theory is a more competent expression of current economic science than what is offered by the spokesmen of the Jevons-Austrian wing. It is as such, as a competent and consistent system of current economic theory, that it is here intended to discuss Mr. Clark's work, not as a body of doctrines peculiar to Mr. Clark or divergent from the main current. Since hedonism came to rule economic science, the science has been in the main a theory of distribution - distribution of ownership and of income. This is true both of the classical school and of those theorists who have taken an attitude of ostensible antagonism to the classical school. The exceptions to the rule are late and comparatively few, and they are not found among the economists who accept the hedonistic postulate as their point of departure. And, consistently with the spirit of hedonism, this theory of distribution has centered about] a doctrine of exchange value (or price) and has worked out its scheme of (normal) distribution in terms of (normal) price. The normal economic community, upon which theoretical interest has converged, is a business community, which centers about the market, and whose scheme of life is a scheme of profit and loss. Even when some considerable attention is ostensibly devoted to theories of consumption and production, in these systems of doctrine the theories are constructed in terms of owner-

---

[2] Cf., e.g. The Distribution of Wealth, p. 376, note.

ship, price, and acquisition, and so reduce themselves in substance to doctrines of distributive acquisition[3] .

In this respect Mr. Clark's work is true to the received canons. The "Essentials of Economic Theory" are the essentials of the hedonistic theory of distribution, with sundry reflections on related topics. The scope of Mr. Clark's economics, indeed, is even more closely limited by concepts of distribution than many others, since he persistently analyses production in terms of value, and value is a concept of distribution. As Mr. Clark justly observes (p. 4), "The primitive and general facts concerning industry ... need to be known before the social facts can profitably be studied." In these early pages of the treatise, as in other works of its class, there is repeated reference to that more primitive and simple scheme of economic life out of which the modern complex scheme has developed, and it is repeatedly indicated that in order to an understanding of the play of forces in the more advanced stages of economic development and complication, it is necessary to apprehend these forces in their unsophisticated form as they work out In the simple scheme prevalent on the plane of primitive life. Indeed, to a reader not well acquainted with Mr. Clark's scope and method of economic theorising, these early pages would suggest that he is Preparing for something in the way of a genetic study, - a study of economic institutions approached from the side of their origins.

It looks as if the intended line of approach to the modern situation might be such as an evolutionist would choose, who would set out with showing what forces are at work in the primitive economic community, and then trace the cumulative growth and complication of these factors as they presently take form in the institutions of a later phase of the development. Such, however, is not Mr. Clark's intention. The effect of his recourse to "primitive life" is simply to throw into the foreground, in a highly unreal perspective, those features which lend themselves to interpretation in terms of the normalised competitive system. The best excuse that can be offered for these excursions into "primitive life" is that they have substantially nothing to do with the main argument of the book, being of the nature of harmless and graceful misinformation. In the primitive economic situation - that is to say, in savagery and the lower barbarism - there is, of course, no "solitary hunter," living either in a cave or otherwise, and there is no man who "makes by his own labor all the goods that he uses," etc.

It is, in effect, a highly meretricious misrepresentation to speak in this connection of "the economy of a man who works only for himself," and say that "the inherent productive power of labor and capital is of vital concern to him," because such a presentation of the matter overlooks the main facts in the case in order to put the emphasis on a feature which is of negligible consequence. There is no reasonable doubt but that, at least

---

[3] See, e.g., J. S. Mill, Political Economy, Book I; Marshall, Principles of Economics, Vol. I, Books II-V.

since mankind reached the human plane, the economic unit has been not a "solitary hunter," but a community of some kind; in which, by the way, women seem in the early stages to have been the most consequential factor instead of the man who works for himself. The 4' capital" possessed by such a community - as, e.g., a band of California "Digger" Indians - was a negligible quantity, more valuable to a collector of curios than to any one else, and the loss of which to the "Digger" squaws would mean very little. What was of "vital concern" to them, indeed, what the life of the group depended on absolutely, was the accumulated wisdom of the squaws, the technology of their economic situation.[4] .

The loss of the basket, digging-stick, and mortar, simply as physical objects, would have signified little, but the conceivable loss of the squaw's knowledge of the soil and seasons, of food and fiber plants, and of mechanical expedients, would have meant the present dispersal and starvation of the community. This may seem like taking Mr. Clark to task for an inconsequential gap in his general information on Digger Indians, Eskimos, and palaeolithic society at large. But the point raised is not of negligible consequence for economic theory, particularly not for any theory of "economic dynamics" that turns in great part about questions of capital and its uses at different stages of economic development.

In the primitive culture the quantity and the value of mechanical appliances is relatively slight; and whether the group is actually possessed of more or less of such appliances at a given time is not a question of first-rate importance. The loss of these objects - tangible assets - would entail a transient inconvenience. But the accumulated, habitual knowledge of the ways and means involved in the production and use of these appliances is the outcome of long experience and experimentation; and, given this body of commonplace technological information, the acquisition and employment of the suitable apparatus is easily arranged. The great body of commonplace knowledge made use of in industry is the product and heritage of the group. In its essentials it is known by common notoriety, and the "capital goods" needed for putting this commonplace technological knowledge to use are a slight matter, - practically within the reach of every one. Under these circumstances the ownership of "capital-goods" has no great significance, and, as a practical fact, interest and wages are unknown, and the "earning power of capital" is not seen to be "governed by a specific power of productivity which resides in capital-goods." But the situation changes, presently, by what is called an advance "in the industrial arts."

The "capital" required to put the commonplace knowledge to effect grows larger, and so its acquisition becomes an increasingly difficult matter. Through "difficulty of attainment" in adequate quantities, the apparatus and its ownership become a matter of consequence; increasingly so,

---

[4] Cf., e.g., such an account as Barrows, Ethno-botany of the Coahuilla Indians.

until presently the equipment required for an effective pursuit of industry comes to be greater than the common man can hope to acquire in a lifetime. The commonplace knowledge of ways and means, the accumulated experience of mankind, is still transmitted in and by the body of the community at large; but, for practical purposes, the advanced "state of the industrial arts" has enabled the owners of goods to corner the wisdom of the ancients and the accumulated experience of the race. Hence "capital," as it stands at that phase of the institution's growth contemplated by Mr. Clark. The "natural" system of free competition, or, as it was once called, "the obvious and simple system of natural liberty," is accordingly a phase of the development of the institution of capital; and its claim to immutable dominion is evidently as good as the like claim of any other phase of cultural growth.

The equity, or "natural justice," claimed for it is evidently just and equitable only in so far as the conventions of ownership on which it rests continue to be a secure integral part of the institutional furniture of the community; that is to say, so long as these conventions are part and parcel of the habits of thought of the community; that is to say, so long as these things are currently held to be just and equitable. This normalised present, or "natural," state of Mr. Clark, is, as near as may be, Senior's "Natural State of Man,"- the hypothetically perfect competitive system; and economic theory consists in the definition and classification of the phenomena of economic life in terms of this hypothetical competitive system. Taken by itself, Mr. Clark's dealing with the past development might be passed over with slight comment, except for its negative significance, since it has no theoretical connection with the present, or even with the "natural" state in which the phenomena of economic life are assumed to arrange themselves in a stable, normal scheme. But his dealings with the future, and with the present in so far as the present situation is conceived to comprise "dynamic" factors, is of substantially the same kind. With Senior's "natural state of man" as the baseline of normality in things economic, questions of present and future development are treated as questions of departure from the normal, aberrations and excesses which the theory does not aim even to account for.

What is offered in place of theoretical inquiry when these "positive perversions of the natural forces themselves" are taken up (e.g., in chapters xxii.-xxix.) is an exposition of the corrections that must be made to bring the situation back to the normal static state, and solicitous advice as to what measures are to be taken with a view to this beneficent end. The problem presented to Mr. Clark by the current phenomena of economic development is: how can it be stopped or, failing that, how can it be guided and minimised. Nowhere is there a sustained inquiry into the dynamic character of the changes that have brought the present (deplorable) situation to pass, nor into the nature and trend of the forces at work in the development that is going forward in this situation. None of this is covered by Mr. Clark's use of the word "dynamic." All that it covers in the way of theory (chapters xii.-xxi.) is a speculative inquiry as to how the equilibrium re-established itself when one or more of the quantities involved increases or decreases. Other than quantitative changes are not noticed, except as provocations to homiletic discourse. Not even the causes and the scope of the quantitative changes that may take place in the variables are allowed to fall within the scope of the theory of economic dynamics.

So much of the volume, then, and of the system of doctrines of which the volume is an exposition, as is comprised in the later eight chapters (pp. 372-554), is an exposition of grievances and remedies, with only sporadic intrusions of theoretical matter, and does not properly constitute a part of the theory, whether static or dynamic. There is no intention here to take exception to Mr. Clark's outspoken attitude of disapproval toward certain features of the current business situation or to quarrel with the remedial measures which he thinks proper and necessary. This phase of his work is spoken of here rather to call attention to the temperate but uncompromising tone of Mr. Clark's writings as a spokesman for the competitive system, considered as an element in the Order of Nature, and to note the fact that this is not economic theory[5] .

The theoretical section specifically scheduled as Economic Dynamics (chapters xii.-xxi.), on the other hand, is properly to be included under the caption of Statics. As already remarked above, it presents a theory of equilibrium between variables. Mr. Clark is, indeed, barred out by his premises from any but a statical development of theory. To realise the substantially statical character of his Dynamics, it is only necessary to turn to his chapter xii. (Economic Dynamics). "

A highly dynamic condition, then, is one in which the economic organism changes rapidly and yet, at any time in the course of its changes, is relatively near to a certain static model" (p. 196). "The actual shape of society at any one time is not the static model of that time; but it tends to conform to it; and in a very dynamic society is more nearly like it than it would be in one in which the forces of change are less active" (p. 197). The more "dynamic" the society, the nearer it is to the static model; until in an ideally dynamic society, with a frictionless competitive system, to use Mr. Clark's figure, the static state would be attained, except for an increase in size,- that is to say, the ideally perfect "dynamic" state would coincide with the "static" state. Mr. Clark's conception of a dynamic state reduces itself to a conception of an imperfectly static state, but in such a sense that the

---

[5] What would be the scientific rating of the work of a botanist who should spend his energy in devising ways and means to neutralize the ecological variability of plant, or of a physiologist who conceived it the end of his scientific endeavors to rehabilitate the vermiform appendix or the pineal eye, or to denounce and penalize the imitative coloring of the Viceroy butterfly? What scientific interest would attach to the matter if Mr. Loeb, e.g., should devote a few score pages to canvassing the moral responsibilities incurred by him in his parental relation to his partheno-genetically developed sea-urchin eggs? Those phenomena which Mr. Clark characterizes as "positive perversions" may be distasteful and troublesome, perhaps, but "the economic necessity of doing what is legally difficult" is not of the "essentials of theory."

more highly and truly "dynamic" condition is thereby the nearer to a static condition. Neither the static nor the dynamic state, in Mr. Clark's view, it should be remarked, is a state of quiescence. Both are states of more or less intense activity, the essential difference being that in the static state the activity goes on in perfection, without lag, leak, or friction; the movement of parts being so perfect as not to disturb the equilibrium. The static state is the more "dynamic" of the two.

The "dynamic" condition is essentially a deranged static condition: whereas the static state is the absolute perfect, "natural" taxonomic norm of competitive life. This dynamic-static state may vary in respect of the magnitude of the several factors which hold one another in equilibrium, but these are none other than quantitative variations. The changes which Mr. Clark discusses under the head of dynamics are all of this character, changes in absolute or relative magnitude of the several factors comprised in the equation. But, not to quarrel with Mr. Clark's use of the term "static" and "dynamic," it is in place to inquire into the merits of this class of economic science apart from any adventitious shortcomings. For such an inquiry Mr. Clark's work offers peculiar advantages. It is lucid, concise, and unequivocal, with no temporising euphemisms and no politic affectations of sentiment. Mr. Clark's premises, and therewith the aim of his inquiry, are the standard ones of the classical English school (including the Jevons-Austrian wing). This school of economics stands on the pre-evolutionary ground of normality and natural law," which the great body of theoretical science occupied in the early nineteenth century. It is like the other theoretical sciences that grew out of the rationalistic and humanitarian conceptions of the eighteenth century in that its theoretical aim is taxonomy - definition and classification - with the purpose of subsuming its data under a rational scheme of categories which are presumed to make up the Order of Nature.

This Order of Nature, or realm of Natural Law, is not the actual run of material facts, but the facts so interpreted as to meet the needs of the taxonomist in point of taste, logical consistency, and sense of justice. The question of the truth and adequacy of the categories is a question as to the consensus of taste and predilection among the taxonomists; i.e., they are an expression of trained human nature touching the matter of what ought to be. The facts so interpreted make up the "normal," or "natural," scheme of things, with which the theorist has to do. His task is to bring facts within the framework of this scheme of "natural" categories.

Coupled with this scientific purpose of the taxonomic economist is the pragmatic purpose of finding and advocating the expedient course of policy. On this latter head, again, Mr. Clark is true to the animus of the school. The classical school, including Mr. Clark and his contemporary associates in the science, is hedonistic and utilitarian - hedonistic in its theory and utilitarian in its pragmatic ideals and endeavors. The hedonistic postulates on which this line of economic theory is built up are of a statical scope and character, and nothing but statical theory (taxonomy) comes out of their development.[6].

These postulates, and the theorems drawn from them, take account of none but quantitative variations, and quantitative variation alone does not give rise to cumulative change, which proceeds on changes in kind. Economics of the line represented at its best by Mr. Clark has never entered this field of cumulative change. It does not approach questions of the class which occupy the modern sciences,- that is to say, questions of genesis, growth, variation, process (in short, questions of a dynamic import),- but confines its interest to the definition and classification of a mechanically limited range of phenomena.

Like other taxonomic sciences, hedonistic economics does not, and cannot, deal with phenomena of growth except so far as growth is taken in the quantitative sense of a variation in magnitude, bulk, mass, number, frequency. In its work of taxonomy this economics has consistently bound itself, as Mr. Clark does, by distinctions of a mechanical, statistical nature, and has drawn its categories of classification on those grounds.

Concretely, it is confined, in substance, to the determination of and refinements upon the concepts of land, labor, and capital, as handed down by the great economists of the classical era, and the correlate concepts of rent, wages, interest and profits. Solicitously, with a painfully meticulous circumspection, the normal, mechanical metes and bounds of these several concepts are worked out, the touchstone of the absolute truth aimed at being the hedonistic calculus. The facts of use and wont are not of the essence of this mechanical refinement. These several categories are mutually exclusive categories, mechanically speaking. The circumstance that the phenomena covered by them are not mechanical facts is not allowed to disturb the pursuit of mechanical distinctions among them. They nowhere overlap, and at the same time between them they cover all the facts with which this economic taxonomy is concerned. Indeed, they are in logical consistency, required to cover them. They are hedonistically "natural" categories of such taxonomic force that their elemental lines of cleavage run through the facts of any given economic situation, regardless of use and wont, even where the situation does not permit these lines of cleavage to be seen by men and recognised by use and wont; so that, e.g., a gang of Aleutian Islanders slushing about in the wrack and surf with rakes and

---

[6] It is a notable fact that even the genius of Herbert Spencer could extract nothing but taxonomy from his hedonistic postulates; e.g., his Social Statics. Spencer is both evolutionist and hedonist, but it is only by recourse to other factors, alien to the rational hedonistic scheme, such as habit, delusions, use and disuse, sporadic variation, environmental forces, that he is able to achieve anything in the way of genetic science, since it is only by this recourse that lie is enabled to enter the field of cumulative change within which the modern post-Darwinian sciences live and move and have their being.

magical incantations for the capture of shell-fish are held, in point of tax-onomic reality, to be engaged on a feat of hedonistic equilibration in rent, wages, and interest. And that is all there is to it. Indeed, for economic the-ory of this kind, that is all there is to any economic situation. The hedonis-tic magnitudes vary from one situation to another, but, except for varia-tions in the arithmetical details of the hedonistic balance, all situations are, in point of economic theory, substantially alike[7] .

Taking this unfaltering taxonomy on its own recognisances, let us follow the trail somewhat more into the arithmetical details, as it leads along the narrow ridge of rational calculation, above the tree-tops, on the levels of clear sunlight and moonshine. For the purpose in hand - to bring out the character of this current economic science as a working theory of current facts, and more particularly "as applied to modern problems of industry and public policy" (title-page) - the sequence to be observed in question-ing the several sections into which the theoretical structure falls is not es-sential. The structure of classical theory is familiar to all students, and - Mr. Clark's redaction offers no serious departure from the conventional lines. Such divergence from conventional lines as may occur is a matter of details, commonly of improvements in detail; and the revisions of detail do not stand in such an organic relation to one another, nor do they sup-port and strengthen one another in such a manner, as to suggest anything like a revolutionary trend or a breaking away from the conventional lines.

So as regards Mr. Clark's doctrine of Capital. It does not differ substan-tially from the doctrines which are gaining currency at the hands of such writers as Mr. Fisher or Mr. Fetter; although there are certain formal dis-tinctions peculiar to Mr. Clark's exposition of the "Capital Concept." But these peculiarities are peculiarities of the method of arriving at the con-cept rather than peculiarities substantial to the concept itself. The main discussion of the nature of capital is contained in chapter ii. (Varieties of Economic Goods). The conception of capital here set forth is of funda-mental consequence to the system, partly because of the important place assigned capital in this system of theory, partly because of the importance which the conception of capital must have in any theory that is to deal with problems of the current (capitalistic) situation. Several classes of cap-ital-goods are enumerated, but it appears that in Mr. Clark's apprehension - at variance with Mr. Fisher's view - persons are not to be included among the items of capital. It is also clear from the run of the argument, though

---

[7] "The capital-goods have to be taken unit by unit if their value for productive pur-poses is to be rightly gauged. A part of a supply of potatoes is traceable to the hoes that dig them. ... We endeavor simply to ascertain how badly the loss of one hoe would affect us or how much good the restoration of it would do us. This truth, like the foregoing ones, has a universal application in economics; for primitive men as well as civilized ones must estimate the specific productivity of the tools that they use," etc, Page 43.

not explicitly stated, that only material, tangible, mechanically definable articles of wealth go to make up capital.

In current usage, in the business community, "capital" is a pecuniary concept, of course, and is not definable in mechanical terms; but Mr. Clark, true to the hedonistic taxonomy, sticks by the test of mechanical demarcation and draws the lines of his category on physical grounds; whereby it happens that any pecuniary conception of capital is out of the question. Intangible assets, or immaterial wealth, have no place in the theory; and Mr. Clark is exceptionally subtle and consistent in avoiding such modern notions. One gets the impression that such a notion as intangible assets is conceived to be too chimerical to merit attention, even by way of protest or refutation. Here, as elsewhere in Mr. Clark's writings, much is made of the doctrine that the two facts of "capital" and "capital-goods" are conceptually distinct, though substantially identical. The two terms cover virtually the same facts as would be covered by the terms "pecuniary capital" and "industrial equipment." They are for all ordinary purposes coincident with Mr. Fisher's terms, "capital value" and "capital," although Mr. Clark might enter a technical protest against identifying his categories with those employed by Mr. Fisher[8].

Capital is this permanent fund of productive goods, the identity of whose component elements is forever changing. Capital-goods are the shifting component parts of this permanent aggregate" (p. 29). Mr. Clark admits (pp. 29-33) that capital is colloquially spoken and thought of in terms of value, but he insists that in point of substantial fact the working concept of capital is (should be) that of "a fund of productive goods," considered as an "abiding entity." The phrase itself, "a fund of productive goods," is a curiously confusing mixture of pecuniary and mechanical terms, though the pecuniary expression, "a fund," is probably to be taken in this connection as a permissible metaphor. This conception of capital, as a physically "abiding entity" constituted by the succession of productive goods that make up the industrial equipment, breaks down in Mr. Clark's own use of it when he comes (pp. 37-38) to speak of the mobility of capital; that is to say, so soon as he makes use of it.

A single illustration of this will have to suffice, though there are several points in his argument where the frailty of the conception is patent enough. "The transfer of capital from one industry to another is a dynamic phenomenon which is later to be considered. What is here important is the fact that it is in the main accomplished without entailing transfers of capital-goods. An instrument wears itself out in one industry, and instead of being succeeded by a like instrument in the same industry, it is succeeded by one of a different kind which is used in a different branch of

---

[8] Cf. a criticism of Mr. Fisher's conception in the Political Science Quarterly for February, 1908.

production" (p. 38), - illustrated on the preceding page by a shifting of investment from a whaling-ship to a cotton-mill.

In all this it is plain that the "transfer of capital" contemplated is a shifting of investment, and that it is, as indeed Mr. Clark indicates, not a matter of the mechanical shifting of physical bodies from one industry to the other. To speak of a transfer of "capital" which does not involve a transfer of "capital-goods is a contradiction of the main position, that capital is made up of "capital-goods." The continuum in which the "abiding entity" of capital resides is a continuity of ownership, not a physical fact. The continuity, in fact, is of an immaterial nature, a matter of legal rights, of contract, of purchase and sale. just why this patent state of the case is overlooked, as it somewhat elaborately is, is not easily seen.

But it is plain that, if the concept of capital were elaborated from observation of current business practice, it would be found that "capital" is a pecuniary fact, not a mechanical one; that it is an outcome of a valuation, depending immediately on the state of mind of the valuers; and that the specific marks of capital, by which it is distinguishable from other facts, are of an immaterial character. This would, of course, lead, directly, to the admission of intangible assets; and this, in turn, would upset the law of the "natural" remuneration of labor and capital to which Mr. Clark's argument looks forward from the start. It would also bring in the "unnatural" phenomena of monopoly as a normal outgrowth of business enterprise.

There is a further logical discrepancy avoided by resorting to the alleged facts of primitive industry, when there was no capital, for the elements out of which to construct a capital concept, instead of going to the current business situation. In a hedonistic-utilitarian scheme of economic doctrine, such as Mr. Clark's, only physically productive agencies can be admitted as efficient factors in production or as legitimate claimants to a share in distribution. Hence capital, one of the prime factors in production and the central claimant in the current scheme of distribution, must be defined in physical terms and delimited by mechanical distinctions. This is necessary for reasons which appear in the succeeding chapter, on The Measure of Consumers' Wealth. On the same page (38), and elsewhere, it is remarked that "business disasters" destroy capital in part. The destruction in question is a matter of values; that is to say, a lowering of valuation, not in any appreciable degree a destruction of material goods. Taken as a physical aggregate, capital does not appreciably decrease through business disasters, but, taken as a fact of ownership and counted in standard units of value, it decreases; there is a destruction of values and a shifting of ownership, a loss of ownership perhaps; but these are pecuniary phenomena, of an immaterial character, and so do not directly affect the material aggregate of the industrial equipment. Similarly, the discussion (pp. 301-314) of how changes of method, as, e.g., labor-saving devices, "liberate capital," and at times "destroy" capital, is intelligible only on the admission that "capital" here is a matter of values owned by investors and is not employed as a synonym for industrial appliances.

The appliances in question are neither liberated nor destroyed in the changes contemplated. And it will not do to say that the aggregate of "productive goods" suffers a diminution by a substitution of devices which increases its aggregate productiveness, as is implied, e.g., by the passage on page 307,[9] if Mr. Clark's definition of capital is strictly adhered to. This very singular passage (pp. 306-311, under the captions, Hardships entailed on Capitalists by Progress, and the Offset for Capital destroyed by Changes of Method) implies that the aggregate of appliances of production is decreased by a change which increases the aggregate of these articles that respect (productivity) by virtue of which they are counted in the aggregate. The argument will hold good if "productive goods" are rated by bulk, weight, number, or some such irrelevant test, instead of by their productivity or by their consequent capitalised value. On such a showing it should be proper to say that the polishing of plowshares before they are sent out from the factory diminishes the amount of capital embodied in plowshares by as much as the weight or bulk of the waste material removed from the shares in polishing them. Several things may be said of the facts discussed in this passage.

There is, presumably, a decrease, in bulk, weight, or number, of the appliances that make up the industrial equipment at the time when such a technological change as is contemplated takes place. This change, presumably, increases the productive efficiency of the equipment as a whole, and so may be said without hesitation to increase the equipment as a factor of production, while it may decrease it, considered as a mechanical magnitude. The owners of the obsolete or obsolescent appliances presumably suffer a diminution of their capital, whether they discard the obsolete appliances or not. The owners of the new appliances, or rather those who own and are able to capitalise the new technological expedients, presumably gain a corresponding advantage, which may take the form of an increase of the effective capitalisation of their outfit, as would then be shown by an increased market value of their plant.

The largest theoretical outcome of the supposed changes, for an economist not bound by Mr. Clark's conception of capital, should be the generalisation that industrial capital - capital considered as a productive agent - is substantially a capitalisation of technological expedients, and that a given capital invested in industrial equipment is measured by the portion of technological expedients whose usufruct the investment appropriates. It would accordingly appear that the substantial core of all capital is im-

---

[9] "The machine itself is often a hopeless specialist. It can do one minute thing and that only, and when a new and better device appears for doing that one thing, the machine has to go, and not to some new employment, but to the junk heap. There is thus taking place a considerable waste of capital in consequence of mechanical and other progress." "Indeed, a quick throwing away of instruments which have barely begun to do their work is often the secret of the success of an enterprising manager, but it entails a destruction of capital."

material wealth, and that the material objects which are formally the subject of the capitalist's ownership are, by comparison, a transient and adventitious matter. But if such a view were accepted, even with extreme reservations, Mr. Clark's scheme of the "natural" distribution of incomes between capital and labor would "go up in the air," as the colloquial phrase has it. It would be extremely difficult to determine what share of the value of the joint product of capital and labor should, under a rule of "natural" equity, go to the capitalist as an equitable return for his monopolisation of a given portion of the intangible assets of the community at large[10] .

The returns actually accruing to him under competitive conditions would be a measure of the differential advantage held by him by virtue of his having become legally seized of the material contrivances by which the technological achievements Of the community are put into effect. Yet, if in this way capital were apprehended as "an historical category," as Rodbertus would say, there is at least the comfort in it all that it should leave a free field for Mr. Clark's measures of repression as applied to the discretionary management of capital by the makers of trusts. And yet, again, this comforting reflection is coupled with the ugly accompaniment that by the same move the field would be left equally free of moral obstructions to the extreme proposals of the socialists. A safe and sane course for the quietist in these premises should apparently be to discard the equivocal doctrines of the passage (pp. 306-311) from which this train of questions arises, and hold fast to the received dogma, however unworkable, that "capital" is a congeries of physical objects with no ramifications or complications of an immaterial kind, and to avoid all recourse to the concept of value, or price, in discussing matters of modern business.

The center of interest and of theoretical force and validity in Mr. Clark's work is his law of "natural" distribution. Upon this law hangs very much of the rest, if not substantially the whole structure of theory. To this law of distribution the earlier portions of the theoretical development look forward, and this the succeeding portions of the treatise take as their point of departure. The law of "natural" distribution says that any productive agent "naturally" gets what it produces. Under ideally free competitive conditions - such as prevail in the "static" state, and to which the current situation approximates - each unit of each productive factor unavoidably gets the amount of wealth which it creates, - its "virtual product," as it is sometimes expressed. This law rests, for its theoretical validity, on the doctrine of "final productivity," set forth in full in the Distribution of Wealth, and

---

[10] The position of the laborer and his wages, in this light, would not be substantially different from that of the capitalist and his interest. Labor is no more possible, as a fact of industry, without the community's accumulated technological knowledge than is the use of "productive goods."

more concisely in the Essentials[11] one of those universal principles which govern economic life in all its stages of evolution[12].

In combination with a given amount of capital, it is held, each succeeding unit of added labor adds a less than proportionate increment to the product. The total product created by the labor so engaged is at the same time the distributive share received by such labor as wages; and it equals the increment of product added by the "final" unit of labor, multiplied by the number of such units engaged. The law of "natural" interest is the same as this law of wages, with a change of terms. The product of each unit of labor or capital being measured by the product of the "final" unit, each gets the amount of its own product. In all of this the argument runs in terms of value; but it is Mr. Clark's view, backed by an elaborate exposition of the grounds of his contention,[13] that the use of these terms of value is merely a matter of convenience for the argument, and that the conclusions so reached - the equality so established between productivity and remuneration - may be converted to terms of goods, or "effective utility," without abating their validity. Without recourse to some such common denominator as value the outcome of the argument would, as Mr. Clark indicates, be something resembling the Ricardian law of differential rent instead of a law drawn in homogeneous terms of "final productivity"; and the law of "natural" distribution would then, at the best, fall short of a general formula. But the recourse to terms of value does not, as Mr. Clark recognises, dispose of the question without more ado.

It smooths the way for the argument, but, unaided, it leaves it nugatory. According to Hudibras, "The value of a thing Is just as much as it will bring," and the later refinements on the theory of value have not set aside this dictum of the ancient authority. It answers no pertinent question of equity to say that the wages paid for labor are as much as it will bring. And Mr. Clark's chapter (xxiv.) on "The Unit for Measuring Industrial Agents and their Products" is designed to show how this tautological statement in terms of market value converts itself, under competitive conditions, into a competent formula of distributive justice. It does not conduce to intelligibility to say that the wages of labor are just and fair because they are all that is paid to labor as wages. What further value Mr. Clark's extended discussion of this matter may have will lie in his exposition of how competition converts the proposition that the value of a thing is just as much as it will bring "into the proposition that" the market rate of wages (or interest) gives to labor (or capital) the full product of labor (or capital)."In following up the theory at this critical point, it is necessary to resort to the fuller statement of the Distribution of Wealth,[14] the point being not so adequate-

---

[11] Cf. Distribution of Wealth, chaps. xii, xiii, vii, viii; Essentials, chaps. v-x.

[12] Essentials, p. 158.

[13] Distribution, chap. xxiv.

[14] Chap. xxiv.

ly covered in the Essentials. Consistently hedonistic, Mr. Clark recognises that his law of natural justice must be reduced to elementary hedonistic terms, if it is to make good its claim to stand as a fundamental principle of theory. In hedonistic theory, production of course means the production of utilities, and utility is of course utility to the consumer[15].

A product is such by virtue of and to the amount of the utility which it has for a consumer. This utility of the goods is measured, as value, by the sacrifice (disutility) which the consumer is willing to undergo in order to get the utility which the consumption of the goods yields him. The unit and measure of productive labor is in the last analysis also a unit of disutility; but it is disutility to the productive laborer, not to the consumer. The balance which establishes itself under competitive conditions is a compound balance, being a balance between the utility of the goods to the consumer and the disutility (cost) which he is willing to undergo for it, on the one hand, and, on the other hand, a balance between the disutility of the unit of labor and the utility for which the laborer is willing to undergo this disutility. It is evident, and admitted, that there can be no balance, and no commensurability, between the laborer's disutility (pain) in producing the goods and the consumer's utility (pleasure) in consuming them, inasmuch as these two hedonistic phenomena lie each within the consciousness of a distinct person. There is, in fact, no continuity of nervous tissue over the interval between consumer and producer, and a direct comparison, equilibrium, equality, or discrepancy in respect of pleasure and pain can, of course, not be sought except within each self-balanced individual complex of nervous tissue[16].

The wages of labor (i.e., the utility of the goods received by the laborer) is not equal to the disutility undergone by him, except in the sense that he is competitively willing to accept it; nor are these wages equal to the utility got by the consumer of the goods, except in the sense that he is competitively willing to pay them. This point is covered by the current diagrammatic arguments of marginal-utility theory as to the determination of competitive prices. But, while the wages are not equal to or directly comparable with the disutility of the productive labor engaged, they are, in Mr. Clark's view, equal to the "productive efficiency" of that labor.[17].

Efficiency in a worker is, in reality, power to draw out labor on the part of society. It is capacity to offer that for which society will work in return." By

---

[15] Essentials, p. 40.

[16] Among modern economic hedonists, including Mr. Clark, there stands over from the better days of the order of nature a presumption, disavowed, but often decisive, that the sensational response to the like mechanical impact of the stimulating body is the same in different individuals. But, while this presumption stands ever in the background, and helps to many important conclusions, as in the case under discussion, few modern hedonists would question the statement in the text.

[17] Distribution. p. 394.

the mediation of market price, under competitive conditions, it is held, the laborer gets, in his wages, a valid claim on the labor of other men (society) as large as they are competitively willing to allow him for the services for which he is paid his wages. The equitable balance between work and pay contemplated by the "natural" law is a balance between wages and "efficiency," as above defined; that is to say, between the wages of labor and the capacity of labor to get wages. So far, the whole matter might evidently have been left as Bastiat left it. It amounts to saying that the laborer gets what he is willing to accept and the consumers give what they are willing to pay. And this is true, of course, whether competition prevails or not.

What makes this arrangement just and right under competitive conditions, in Mr. Clark's view, lies in his further doctrine that under such conditions of unobstructed competition the prices of goods, and therefore the wages of labor, are determined, within the scope of the given market, by a quasi-consensus of all the parties in interest. There is of course no formal consensus, but what there is of the kind is implied in the fact that bargains are made, and this is taken as an appraisement by society" at large. The (quasi-) consensus of buyers is held to embody the righteous (quasi-) appraisement of society in the premises, and the resulting rate of wages is therefore a (quasi-) just return to the laborer[18].

Each man accordingly is paid an amount that equals the total product that he personally creates[19].

If competitive conditions are in any degree disturbed, the equitable balance of prices and wages is disturbed by that much. All this holds true for the interest of capital, with a change of terms. The equity and binding force of this finding is evidently bound up with that common-sense presumption on which it rests; namely, that it is right and good that all men should get what they can without force or fraud and without disturbing existing property relations. It springs from this presumption, and, whether in point of equity or of expediency, it rises no higher than its source. It does not touch questions of equity beyond this, nor does it touch questions of the expediency or probable advent of any contemplated change in the existing conventions as to rights of ownership and initiative.

It affords a basis for those who believe in the old order -without which belief this whole structure of opinions collapses - to argue questions of wages and profits in a manner convincing to themselves, and to confirm in the faith those who already believe in the old order. But it is not easy to see that some hundreds of pages of apparatus should be required to find one's way back to these time-worn commonplaces of Manchester. In ef-

---

[18] In Mr. Clark's discussion, elsewhere, the "quasi"-character of the productive share of the laborer is indicated by saying that it is the product "imputed" or "imputable" to him.

[19] Essentials, p. 92. Et si sensus deficit, ad firmandum cor sincerum sola fides sufficit.

fect, this law of "natural" distribution says that whatever men acquire without force or fraud under competitive conditions is their equitable due, no more and no less, assuming that the competitive system, with its underlying institution of ownership, is equitable and "natural."

In point of economic theory the law appears on examination to be of slight consequence, but it merits further attention for the gravity of its purport. It is offered as a definitive law of equitable distribution comprised in a system of hedonistic economics which is in the main a theory of distributive acquisition only. It is worthwhile to compare the law with its setting, with a view to seeing how its broad declarations of economic justice shows up in contrast with the elements out of which it is constructed and among which it lies. Among the notable chapters of the Essentials is one (vi.) on Value and its Relation to Different Incomes, which is not only a very substantial section of Mr. Clark's economic theory, but at the same time a type of the achievements of the latter-day hedonistic school. Certain features of this chapter alone can be taken up here. The rest may be equally worthy the student's attention, but it is the intention here not to go into the general substance of the theory of marginal utility and value, to which the chapter is devoted, but to confine attention to such elements of it as bear somewhat directly on the question of equitable distribution already spoken of. Among these latter is the doctrine of the "consumer's surplus,"- virtually the same as what is spoken of by other writers as "consumer's rent[20] .

Consumer's surplus" is the surplus of utility (pleasure) derived by the consumer of goods above the (pain) cost of the goods to him. This is held to be a very generally prevalent phenomenon. Indeed, it is held to be all but universally present in the field of consumption. It might, in fact, be effectively argued that even Mr. Clark's admitted exception[21] is very doubtfully to be allowed, on his own showing. Correlated with this element of utility on the consumer's side is a similar volume of disutility on the producer's side, which may be called "producer's abatement," or "producer's rent": it is the amount of disutility by which the disutility-cost of a given article to any given producer (laborer) falls short of (or conceivably exceeds) the disutility incurred by the marginal producer. Marginal buyers or consumers and marginal sellers or producers are relatively few : the great body on both sides come in for something in the way of a surplus "of utility or disutility. All this bears on the law of "natural" wages and interest as follows, taking that law of just remuneration at Mr. Clark's rating of it. The law works out through the mediation of price. Price is determined, competitively, by marginal producers or sellers and marginal consumers or purchasers: the latter alone on the one side get the precise price-equivalent of the disutility incurred by them, and the latter alone on

---

[20] See pp. 102-113; also p, 172, note.
[21] "The cheapest and poorest grades of articles." Page 113

the other side pay the full price-equivalent of the utilities derived by them from the goods purchased.[22] .

Hence the competitive price - covering competitive wages and interest - does not reflect the consensus of all parties concerned as to the "effective utility" of the goods, on the one hand, or as to their effective (disutility) cost, on the other hand. It reflects instead, if anything of this kind, the valuations which the marginal unfortunates on each side concede tinder stress of competition; and it leaves on each side of the bargain relation an uncovered "surplus," which marks the (variable) interval by which price fails to cover "effective utility." The excess utility - and the conceivable excess cost - does not appear in the market transactions that mediate between consumer and producer[23] .

In the balance, therefore, which establishes itself in terms of value between the social utility of the product and the remuneration of the producer's "efficiency," the margin of utility represented by the aggregate "consumer's surplus" and like elements is not accounted for. It follows, when the argument is in this way reduced to its hedonistic elements, that no man "is paid an amount that equals the amount of the total product that he personally creates." Supposing the marginal-utility (final-utility) theories of objective value to be true, there is no consensus, actual or constructive, as to the "effective utility" of the goods produced: there is no "social" decision in the case beyond what may be implied in the readiness of buyers to profit as much as may be by the necessities of the marginal buyer and seller. It appears that there is warrant, within these premises, for the formula: Remuneration >< than Product. Only by an infinitesimal chance would it bold true in any given case that, hedonistically, Remuneration = Product; and, if it should ever happen to be true, there would be no finding it out. The (hedonistic) discrepancy which so appears between remuneration and product affects both wages and interest in the same manner, but there is some (hedonistic) ground in Mr. Clark's doctrines for holding that the discrepancy does not strike both in the same degree.

There is indeed no warrant for holding that there is anything like an equable distribution of this discrepancy among the several industries or the several industrial concerns; but there appears to be some warrant, on Mr. Clark's argument, for thinking that the discrepancy is perhaps slighter in those branches of industry which produce the prime necessaries of life[24] .

This point of doctrine throws also a faint (metaphysical) light on a, possibly generic, discrepancy between the remuneration of capitalists and

[22] See p. 113.

[23] The disappearance, and the method of disappearance, of such elements of differential utility and disutility occupies a very important place in all marginal-utility ("final-utility") theories of market value, or "objective value."

[24] Only the simplest and cheapest things that are sold in the market at all bring just what they are worth to the buyers," Page 113.

that of laborers: the latter are, relatively, more addicted to consuming the necessaries of life, and it may be that they thereby gain less in the way of a consumer's surplus. All the analysis and reasoning here set forth has an air of undue tenuity; but in extenuation of this fault it should be noted that this reasoning is made up of such matter as goes to make up the theory under review, and the fault, therefore, is not to be charged to the critic. The manner of argument required to meet this theory of the "natural law of final productivity" on its own ground is itself a sufficiently tedious proof of the futility of the whole matter in dispute. Yet it seems necessary to beg further indulgence for more of the same kind. As a needed excuse, it may be added that what immediately follows bears on Mr. Clark's application of the law of "natural distribution" to modern problems of industry and public policy, in the matter of curbing monopolies. Accepting, again, Mr. Clark's general postulates - the postulates of current hedonistic economics - and applying the fundamental concepts, instead of their corollaries, to his scheme of final productivity, it can be shown to fail on grounds even more tenuous and hedonistically more fundamental than those already passed in review.

In all final-utility (marginal-utility) theory it is of the essence of the scheme of things that successive increments of a "good" have progressively less than proportionate utility. In fact, the coefficient of decrease of utility is greater than the coefficient of increase of the stock of goods. The solitary "first loaf" is exorbitantly useful. As more loaves are successively added to the stock, the utility of each grows small by degrees and incontinently less, until, in the end, the state of the "marginal" or "final" loaf is, in respect of utility, shameful to relate. So, with a change of phrase, it fares with successive increments of a given productive factor - labor or capital - in Mr. Clark's scheme of final productivity. And so, of course, it also fares with the utility of successive increments of product created by successively adding unit after unit to the complement of a given productive factor engaged in the case. If we attend to this matter of final productivity in consistently hedonistic terms, a curious result appears. A larger complement of the productive agent, counted by weight and tale, will, it is commonly held, create a larger output of goods, counted by weight and tale [25]but these are not hedonistic terms and should not be allowed to cloud the argument. In the hedonistic scheme the magnitude of goods, in all the dimensions to be taken account of, is measured in terms of utility, which is a different matter from weight and tale. It is by virtue of their utility that

---

[25] it is, e.g., open to serious question whether Mr. Clark's curves of final productivity (pp. 139, 148), showing a declining output per unit in response to an increase of one of the complementary agents of production, will fit the common run of industry in case the output be counted by weight and tale. In many cases they will, no doubt; in many other cases they will not. But this is no criticism of the curves in question, since they do not, or at least should not, purport to represent the product in such terms, but in terms of utility.

they are "goods," not by virtue of their physical dimensions, number and the like; and utility is a matter of the production of pleasure and the prevention of pain. Hedonistically speaking, the amount of the goods, the magnitude of the output, is the quantity of utility derivable from their consumption; and the utility per unit decreases faster than the number of units increase.[26].

It follows that in the typical or undifferentiated case an increase of the number of units beyond a certain critical point entails a decrease of the "total effective utility" of the supply[27].

This critical point seems ordinarily to be very near the point of departure of the curve of declining utility, perhaps it frequently coincides with the latter. On the curve of declining final utility, at any point whose tangent cuts the axis of ordinates at an angle of less than 45 degrees, an increase of the number of units entails a decrease of the "total effective utility of the supply, [28]so that a gain in physical productivity is a loss as counted in "total effective utility." Hedonistically, therefore, the productivity in such a case diminishes, not only relatively to the (physical) magnitude of the productive agents, but absolutely. This critical point, of maximum "total effective utility," is, if the practice of shrewd business men is at all significant, commonly somewhat short of the point of maximum physical productivity, at least in modern industry and in a modern community. The "total effective utility" may commonly be increased by decreasing the output of goods. The "total effective utility" of wages may often be increased by decreasing the amount (value) of the wages per man, particularly if such a decrease is accompanied by a rise in the price of articles to be bought with the wages.

Hedonistically speaking, it is evident that the point of maximum net productivity is the point at which a perfectly shrewd business manage-

---

[26] To resort to an approximation after the manner of Malthus, if the supply of goods be supposed to increase by arithmetical progression, their final utility may be said concomitantly to decrease by geometrical progression.

[27] Cf. Essentials, chap. iii, especially pp. 40-41.

[28] The current marginal-utility diagrams are not of much use in this connection, because the angle of the tangent with the axis of ordinates, at any point, is largely a matter of the draftsman's taste. The abscissa and the ordinate do not measure commensurable units. The units on the abscissa are units of frequency, while those on the ordinate are units of amplitude; and the greater or less segment of line allowed per unit on either axis is a matter of independently arbitrary choice. Yet the proposition in the text remains true,- as true as hedonistic propositions commonly are. The magnitude of the angle of the tangent with the axis of ordinates decides whether the total (hedonistic) productivity at a given point in the curve increases or decreases with a (mechanical) increase of the productive agent,- no student at all familiar with marginal-utility arguments will question that patent fact. But the angle of the tangent depends on the fancy of the draftsman,- no one possessed of the elemental mathematical notions will question that equally patent fact.

ment of a perfect monopoly would limit the supply; and the point of maximum (hedonistic) remuneration (wages and interest) is the point which such a management would fix on in dealing with a wholly free, perfectly competitive supply of labor and capital. Such a monopolistic state of things, it is true, would not answer to Mr. Clark's ideal. Each man would not be "paid an amount that equals the amount of the total product that he personally creates," but he would commonly be paid an amount that (hedonistically, in point of "effective utility ") exceeds what he personally creates, because of the high final utility of what he receives. This is easily proven. Under the monopolistic conditions supposed, the laborers would, it is safe to assume, not be fully employed all the time; that is to say, they would be willing to work some more in order to get some more articles of consumption; that is to say, the articles of consumption which their wages offer them have so high a utility as to afford them a consumer's surplus, - the articles are worth more than they Cost[29] .

Q.E.D. The initiated may fairly doubt the soundness of the chain of argument by which these heterodox theoretical results are derived from Mr. Clark's hedonistic postulates, more particularly since the adepts of the school, including Mr. Clark, are not accustomed to draw conclusions to this effect from these premises. Yet the argument proceeds according to the rules of marginal-utility permutations. In view of this scarcely avoidable doubt, it may be permitted, even at the risk of some tedium, to show how the facts of every-day life bear out this unexpected turn of the law of natural distribution, as briefly traced above. The principle involved is well and widely accepted. The familiar practical maxim of "charging what the traffic will bear" rests on a principle of this kind, and affords one of the readiest practical illustrations of the working of the hedonistic calculus. The principle involved is that a larger aggregate return (value) may be had by raising the return per unit to such a point as to somewhat curtail the demand.

In practice it is recognised, in other words, that there is a critical point at which the value obtainable per unit, multiplied by the number of units that will be taken off at that price, will give the largest net aggregate result (in value to the seller) obtainable under the given conditions. A calculus involving the same principle is, of course, the guiding consideration in all monopolistic buying and selling; but a moment's reflection will show that it is, in fact, the ruling principle in all commercial transactions and, indeed, in all business. The maxim of "charging what the traffic will bear" is only a special formulation of the generic principle of business enterprise. Business initiative, the function of the entrepreneur (business man) is comprehended under this principle taken in its most general sense[30] .

---

[29] A similar line of argument has been followed up by Mr. Clark for capital and interest, in a different connection. See Essentials, pp. 340-345, 356.

[30] Cf. Essentials, pp. 83-90, 118-120.

In business the buyer, it is held by the theorists, bids up to the point of greatest obtainable advantage to himself under the conditions prevailing, and the seller similarly bids down to the point of greatest obtainable net aggregate gain. For the trader (business man, entrepreneur) doing business in the open (competitive) market or for the business concern with a partial or limited monopoly, the critical point above referred to is, of course, reached at a lower point on the curve of price than would be the case under a perfect and unlimited monopoly, such as was supposed above; but the principle of charging what the traffic will bear remains intact, although the traffic will not bear the same in the one case as in the other.

Now, in the theories based on marginal (or "final") utility, value is an expression or measure of "effective utility" - or whatever equivalent term may be preferred. In operating on values, therefore, under the rule of charging what the traffic will bear, the sellers of a monopolised supply, e.g., must operate through the valuations of the buyers; that is to say, they must influence the final utility of the goods or services to such effect that the total effective utility" of the limited supply to the consumers will be greater than would be the "total effective utility" of a larger supply, which is the point in question. The emphasis falls still more strongly on this illustration of the hedonistic calculus, if it is called to mind that in the common run of such limitations of supply by a monopolistic business management the management would be able to increase the supply at a progressively declining cost beyond the critical point by virtue of the well-known principle of increasing returns from industry. It is also to be added that, since the monopolistic business gets its enhanced return from the margin by which the "total effective utility" of the limited supply exceeds that of a supply not so limited, and since there is to be deducted from this margin the costs of monopolistic management in addition to other costs, therefore the enhancement of the "total effective utility" of the goods to the consumer in the case must be appreciably larger than the resulting net gains to the monopoly.

By a bold metaphor - a metaphor sufficiently bold to take it out of the region of legitimate figures of speech - the gains that come to enterprising business concerns by such monopolistic enhancement of the "total effective utility" of their products are spoken of as "robbery," It extortion," "plunder"; but the theoretical complexion of the case should not be overlooked by the hedonistic theorist in the heat of outraged sentiment. The monopolist is only pushing the principle of all business enterprise (free competition) to its logical conclusion; and, in point of hedonistic theory, such monopolistic gains are to be accounted the "natural" remuneration of the monopolist for his "productive" service to the community in enhancing their enjoyment per unit of consumable goods to such point as to swell their net aggregate enjoyment to a maximum.

This intricate web of hedonistic calculations might be pursued further, with the result of showing that, while the consumers of the monopolised supply of goods are gainers by virtue of the enhanced "total effective utility" of the goods, the monopolists who bring about this result do so in great

part at their own cost, counting cost in terms of a reduction of "total effective utility." By injudiciously increasing their own share of goods, they lower the marginal and effective utility of their wealth to such a point as,
probably, to entail a considerable (hedonistic) privation in the shrinkage
of their enjoyment per unit but it is not the custom of economists, nor
does Mr. Clark depart from this custom, to dwell on the hardships of the
monopolists.

This much may be added, however, that this hedonistically consistent
exposition of the "natural law of final productivity" shows it to be It one of
those universal principles which govern economic life in all its stages of
evolution," even when that evolution enters the phase of monopolistic
business enterprise, - granting always the sufficiency of the hedonistic
postulates from which the law is derived. Further, the considerations re-
viewed above go to show that, on two counts, Mr. Clark's crusade against
monopoly in the later portion of his treatise is out of touch with the larger
theoretical speculations of the earlier portions: (a) it runs counter to the
hedonistic law of "natural" distribution; and (b) the monopolistic business
against which Mr. Clark speaks is but the higher and more perfect development of that competitive business enterprise which he wishes to rein-
state, - competitive business, so called, being incipiently monopolistic
enterprise

Apart from this theoretical hearing, the measures which Mr. Clark advocates for the repression of monopoly, under the head of applications "to
modern problems of industry and public policy," may be good economic
policy or they may not, - they are the expression of a sound common
sense, an unvitiated solicitude for the welfare of mankind, and a wide information as to the facts of the situation. The merits of this policy of repression, as such, cannot be discussed here. On the other hand, the relation of this policy to the theoretical groundwork of the treatise needs also
not be discussed here, inasmuch as it has substantially no relation to the
theory. In this later portion of the volume

Mr. Clark does not lean on doctrines of "final utility," "final productivity," or, indeed, on hedonistic economics at large. He speaks eloquently for
the material and cultural interests of the community, and the references to
his law of "natural distribution" might be cut bodily out of the discussion
without lessening the cogency of his appeal or exposing any weakness in
his position. Indeed, it is by no means certain that such an excision would
not strengthen his appeal to men's sense of justice by eliminating irrelevant matter. Certain points in this later portion of the volume, however,
where the argument is at variance with specific articles of theory professed
by Mr. Clark, may be taken up, mainly to elucidate the weakness of his
theoretical position at the points in question. He recognises with more
than the current degree of freedom that the growth and practicability of
monopolies under modern conditions is chiefly due to the negotiability of

securities representing capital, coupled with the joint-stock character of modern business concerns[31].

These features of the modern (capitalistic) business situation enable a sufficiently few men to control a section of the community sufficiently large to make an effective monopoly. The most effective known form of organisation for purposes of monopoly, according to Mr. Clark, is that of the holding company, and the ordinary corporation follows it closely in effectiveness in this respect. The monopolistic control is effected by means of the vendible securities covering the capital engaged. To meet the specifications of Mr. Clark's theory of capital, these vendible securities - as e.g., the securities (common stock) of a holding company - should be simply the formal evidence of the ownership of certain productive goods and the like. Yet, by his own showing, the ownership of a share of productive goods proportionate to the face value, or the market value, of the securities is by no means the chief consequence of such an issue of securities[32].

One of the consequences, and for the purposes of Mr. Clark's argument the gravest consequence, of the employment of such securities, is the dissociation of ownership from the control of the industrial equipment, whereby the owners of certain securities, which stand in certain immaterial, technical relations to certain other securities, are enabled arbitrarily to control the use of the industrial equipment covered by the latter. These are facts of the modern organisation of capital, affecting the productivity of the industrial equipment and its serviceability both to its owners and to the community. They are facts, though not physically tangible objects; and they have an effect on the serviceability of industry no less decisive than the effect which any group of physically tangible objects of equal market value have. They are, moreover, facts which are bought and sold in the purchase and sale of these securities, as, e.g., the common stock of a holding company.

They have a value, and therefore they have a "total effective utility." In short, these facts are intangible assets, which are the most consequential element in modern capital, but which have no existence in the theory of capital by which Mr. Clark aims to deal with "modern problems of industry." Yet, when he comes to deal with these problems, it is, of necessity, these intangible assets that immediately engage his attention. These intangible assets are an outgrowth of the freedom of contract under the conditions imposed by the machine industry; yet Mr. Clark proposes to suppress this category of intangible assets without prejudice to freedom of contract or to the machine industry, apparently without having taken thought of the lesson which he rehearses (pp. 390-390 from the introduction of the holding company, with its "sinister perfection," to take the

---

[31] Cf. chap. xxii, especially pp. 378-392.
[32] Cf. p. 391.

place of the (less efficient) "trust" when the latter was dealt with somewhat as it is now proposed to deal with the holding company. One is
tempted to remark that a more naive apprehension of the facts of modern
capital would have afforded a more competent realisation of the problems
of monopoly. It appears from what has just been said of Mr. Clark's "natural" distribution and of his dealing with the problems of modern industry
that the logic of hedonism is of no avail for the theory of business affairs.
Yet it is held, perhaps justly, that the hedonistic interpretation may be of
great avail in analysing the industrial functions of the community, in their
broad, generic character, even if it should not serve so well for the intricate
details of the modern business situation. It may be at least a serviceable
hypothesis for the outlines of economic theory, for the first approxima-
tions to the "economic laws" sought by taxonomists. To be serviceable for
this purpose, the hypothesis need perhaps not be true to fact, at least not
in the final details of the community's life or without material qualification[33] but it must at least have that ghost of actuality that is implied in
consistency with its own corollaries and ramifications. As has been suggested in an earlier paragraph, it is characteristic of hedonistic economics
that the large and central element in its theoretical structure is the doctrine of distribution. Consumption being taken for granted as a quantitative matter supply, - essentially a matter of an insatiable appetite, - economics becomes a theory of acquisition; production is, theoretically, a
process of acquisition, and distribution a process of distributive acquisition. The theory of production is drawn in terms of the gains to be acquired by production; and under competitive conditions this means necessarily the acquisition of a distributive share of what is available.

The rest of what the facts of productive industry include, as, e.g., the
facts of workmanship or the "state of the industrial arts," gets but a scant
and perfunctory attention. Those matters are not of the theoretical essence of the scheme. Mr. Clark's general theory of production does not
differ substantially from that commonly professed by the marginal-utility
school. It is a theory of competitive acquisition. An inquiry into the principles of his doctrine, therefore, as they appear, e.g., in the early chapters
of the Essentials, is, in effect, an inquiry into the competence of the main
theorems of modern hedonistic economics."All men seek to get as much
net service from material wealth as they can." "Some of the benefit received is neutralised by the sacrifice incurred; but there is a net surplus of
gains not thus canceled by sacrifices, and the generic motive which may
properly be called economic is the desire to make this surplus large[34] .

It is of the essence of the scheme that the acquisitive activities of mankind afford a net balance of pleasure. It is out of this net balance, presumably, that "the consumer's surpluses" arise, or it is in this that they merge.

---

[33] Cf. Essentials, p. 39.
[34] Essentials, p. 39.

This optimistic conviction is a matter of presumption, of course; but it is universally held to be true by hedonistic economists, particularly by those who cultivate the doctrines of marginal utility. It is not questioned and not proven. It seems to be a surviving remnant of the eighteenth-century faith in a benevolent Order of Nature; that is to say, it is a rationalistic metaphysical postulate. It may be true or not, as matter of fact; but it is a postulate of the school, and its optimistic bias runs like a red thread through all the web of argument that envelops the "normal" competitive system. A surplus of gain is normal to the theoretical scheme. The next great theorem of this theory of acquisition is at cross-purposes with this one. Men get useful goods only at the cost of producing them, and production is irksome, painful, as has been recounted above. They go on producing utilities until, at the margin, the last increment of utility in the product is balanced by the concomitant increment of disutility in the way of irksome productive effort, - labor or abstinence.

At the margin, pleasure-gain is balanced by pain-cost. But the "effective utility" of the total product is measured by that of the final unit; the effective utility of the whole is given by the number of units of product multiplied by the effective utility of the final unit; while the effective disutility (pain-cost) of the whole is similarly measured by the pain-cost of the final unit. The "total effective utility" of the producer's product equals the "total effective disutility" of his pains of acquisition. Hence there is no net surplus of utility in the outcome. The corrective objection is ready to hand,[35] that, while the balance of utility and disutility holds at the margin, it does not hold for the earlier units of the product, these earlier units having a larger utility and a lower cost, and so leaving a large net surplus of utility, which gradually declines as the margin is approached. But this attempted correction evades the hedonistic test. It shifts the ground from the calculus to the objects which provoke the calculation. Utility is a psychological matter, a matter of pleasurable appreciation, just as disutility, conversely, is a matter of painful appreciation. The individual who is held to count the costs and the gain in this hedonistic calculus is, by supposition, a highly reasonable person. He counts the cost to him as an individual against the gain to him as an individual. He looks before and after, and sizes the whole thing up in a reasonable course of conduct. The "absolute utility" would exceed the "effective utility" only on the supposition that the "producer" is an unreflecting sensory apparatus, such as the beasts of the field are supposed to be, devoid of that gift of appraisement and calculation which is the hypothetical hedonist's only human trait.

There might on such a supposition - if the producer were an intelligent sensitive organism simply - emerge an excess of total pleasure over total pain, but there could then be no talk of utility or of disutility, since these terms imply intelligent reflection, and they are employed because they do

---

[35] Cf. Essentials, chap. iii, especially pp. 51-56.

so. The hedonistic producer looks to his own cost and gain, as an intelligent pleasure-seeker whose consciousness compasses the contrasted elements as wholes. He does not contrast the balance of pain and pleasure in the morning with the balance of pain and pleasure in the afternoon, and say that there is so much to the good because he was not so tired in the morning. Indeed, by hypothesis, the pleasure to be derived from the consumption of the product is a future, or expected, pleasure, and can be said to be present, at the point of time at which a given unit of pain-cost is incurred, only in anticipation; and it cannot be said that the anticipated pleasure attaching to a unit of product which emerges from the effort of the producer during the relatively painless first hour's work exceeds the anticipated pleasure attaching to a similar unit emerging from the second hour's work.

Mr. Clark has, in effect, explained this matter in substantially the same way in another connection (e.g., p. 42), where he shows that the magnitude on which the question of utility and cost hinges is the "total effective utility," and that the "total absolute utility" is a matter not of what hedonistically is, in respect of utility as an outcome of production, but of what might have been under different circumstances. An equally unprofitable result may be reached from the same point of departure along a different line of argument. Granting that increments of product should be measured, in respect of utility, by comparison with the disutility of the concomitant increment of cost, then the diagrammatic arguments commonly employed are inadequate, in that the diagrams are necessarily drawn in two dimensions only, - length and breadth: whereas they should be drawn in three dimensions, so as to take account of the intensity of application as well as of its duration[36] .

Apparently, the exigencies of graphic representation, fortified by the presumption that there always emerges a surplus of utility, have led marginal-utility theorists, in effect, to overlook this matter of intensity of application. When this element is brought in with the same freedom as the other two dimensions engaged, the argument will, in hedonistic consistency, run somewhat as follows,- the run of the facts being what it may. The producer, setting out on this irksome business, and beginning with the production of the exorbitantly useful initial unit of product, will, by hedonistic necessity, apply himself to the task with a correspondingly extravagant intensity, the irksomeness (disutility) of which necessarily rises to such a

---

[36] This difficulty is recognized by the current marginal-utility arguments, and an allowance for intensity is made or presumed. But the allowance admitted is invariably insufficient. It might be said to be insufficient by hypothesis, since it is by hypothesis too small to offset the factor which it is admitted to modify.

pitch as to leave no excess of utility in this initial unit of product above the concomitant disutility of the initial unit of productive effort[37] .

As the utility of subsequent units of product progressively declines, so will the producer's intensity of irksome application concomitantly decline, maintaining a nice balance between utility and disutility throughout. There is, therefore, no excess of "absolute utility" above "effective utility" at any point on the curve, and no excess of "total absolute utility" above "total effective utility" of the product as a whole, nor above the "total absolute disutility" or the "total effective disutility" of the pain-cost. A transient evasion of this outcome may perhaps be sought by saying that the producer will act wisely, as a good hedonist should, and save his energies during the earlier moments of the productive period in order to get the best aggregate result from his day's labor, instead of spending himself in ill-advised excesses at the outset.

Such seems to be the fact of the matter, so far as the facts wear a hedonistic complexion; but this correction simply throws the argument back on the previous position and concedes the force of what was there claimed. It amounts to saying that, instead of appreciating each successive unit of product in isolated contrast with its concomitant unit of irksome productive effort, the producer, being human, wisely looks forward to his total product and rates it by contrast with his total pain-cost. Whereupon, as before, no net surplus of utility emerges, under the rule which says that irksome production of utilities goes on until utility and disutility balance. But this revision of "final productivity" has further consequences for the optimistic doctrines of hedonism. Evidently, by a somewhat similar line of argument the "consumer's surplus" will be made to disappear, even as this that may be called the "producer's surplus" has disappeared.

Production being acquisition, and the consumer's cost being cost of acquisition, the argument above should apply to the consumer's case without abatement. On considering this matter in terms of the hedonistically responsive individual concerned, with a view to determining whether there is, in his calculus of utilities and costs, any margin of uncovered utilities left over after be has incurred all the disutilities that are worth while to him, - instead of proceeding on a comparison between the pleasure-giving capacity of a given article and the market price of the article, all such alleged differential advantages within the scope of a single sensory] are seen to be nothing better than an illusory diffractive effect due to a faulty instrument. But the trouble does not end here. The equality: pain-cost = pleasure-gain, is not a competent formula. It should be: pain-cost in-

---

[37] The limit to which the intensity rises is a margin of the same kind as that which limits the duration. This supposition, that the intensity of application necessarily rises to such a pitch that its disutility overtakes and offsets the utility of the product, may be objected to as a bit of puerile absurdity; but it is a long time since puerility or absurdity has been a bar to any supposition in arguments on marginal utility.

curred = pleasure-gain anticipated. And between these two formulas lies the old adage, "there's many a slip 'twixt the cup and the lip." In an appreciable proportion of ventures, endeavors, and enterprises, men's expectations of pleasure-gain are in some degree disappointed, - through miscalculation, through disserviceable secondary effects of their productive efforts, by "the act of God," by fire, flood, and pestilence." In the nature of things these discrepancies fall out on the side of loss more frequently than on that of gain.

After all allowance has been made for what may be called serviceable errors, there remains a margin of disserviceable error, so that pain-cost > eventual pleasure-gain = anticipated pleasure-gain - n. Hence, in general, pain-cost > pleasure-gain. Hence it appears that, in the nature of things, men's pains of production are underpaid by that much; although it may, of course, be held that the nature of things at this point is not "natural" or "normal". To this it may be objected that the risk is discounted. Insurance is a practical discounting of risk; but insurance is resorted to only to cover risk that is appreciated by the person exposed to it, and it is such risks as are not appreciated by those who incur them that are chiefly in question here. And it may be added that insurance has hitherto not availed to equalise and distribute the chances of success and failure. Business gains - enterpreneur's gains, the rewards of initiative and enterprise - come out of this uncovered margin of adventure, and the losses of initiative and enterprise are to be set down to the same account.

In some measure this element of initiative and enterprise enters into all economic endeavor. And it is not unusual for economists to remark that the volume of unsuccessful or only partly successful enterprise is very large. There are some lines of enterprise that are, as one might say, extra hazardous, in which the average falls out habitually on the wrong side of the account. Typical of this class is the production of the precious metals, particularly as conducted under that regime of free competition for which Mr. Clark speaks. It has been the opinion, quite advisedly, of such economists of the classic age of competition as J. S. Mill and Cairnes, e.g., that the world's supply of the precious metals has been got at an average or total cost exceeding their value by several fold. The producers, under free competition at least, are over-sanguine of results. But, in strict consistency, the hedonistic theory of human conduct does not allow men to be guided in their calculation of cost and gain, when they have to do with the precious metals, by different norms from those which rule their conduct in the general quest of gain. ,

The visible difference in this respect between the production of the precious metals and production generally should be due to the larger proportions and greater notoriety of the risks in this field rather than to a difference in the manner of response to the stimulus of expected gain. The canons of hedonistic calculus permit none but a quantitative difference in the response. What happens in the production of the precious metals is typical of what happens in a measure and more obscurely throughout the field of productive effort. Instead of a surplus of utility of product above the disutility of acquisition, therefore, there emerges an average or aggregate net hedonistic deficit. On a consistent marginal-utility theory, all production is a losing game. The fact that Nature keeps the bank, it appears, does not take the hedonistic game of production out of the general category known of old to that class of sanguine hedonistic calculators whose day-dreams are filled with safe and sane schemes for breaking the bank. "Hope springs eternal in the human breast." Men are congenitally over-sanguine, it appears; and the production of utilities is, mathematically speaking, a function of the pig-headed optimism of mankind. It turns out that the laws of (human) nature malevolently grind out vexation for men instead of benevolently furthering the greatest happiness of the greatest number. The sooner the whole traffic ceases, the better, - the smaller will be the net balance of pain. The great hedonistic Law of Nature turns out to be simply the curse of Adam, backed by the even more sinister curse of Eve.

The remark was made in an earlier paragraph that Mr. Clark's theories have substantially no relation to his practical proposals. This broad declaration requires an equally broad qualification. While the positions reached in his theoretical development count for nothing in making or fortifying the positions taken on "problems of modern industry and public policy," the two phases of the discussion - the theoretical and the pragmatic - are the outgrowth of the same range of preconceptions and run back to the same metaphysical ground. The present canvass of items in the doctrinal system has already far overpassed reasonable limits, and it is out of the question here to pursue the exfoliation of ideas through Mr. Clark's discussion of public questions, even in the fragmentary fashion in which scattered items of the theoretical portion of his treatise have been passed in review. Put a broad and rudely drawn characterisation may yet be permissible. This latter portion of the volume has the general complexion of a Bill of Rights. This is said, of course, with no intention of imputing a fault. It implies that the scope and method of the discussion is governed by the preconception that there is one right and beautiful definitive scheme of economic life, "to which the whole creation tends."

Whenever and in so far as current phenomena depart or diverge from this definitive "natural" scheme or from the straight and narrow path that leads to its consummation, there is a grievance to be remedied by putting the wheels back into the rut. The future, such as it ought to be the only normally possible, natural future scheme of life, - is known by the light of this preconception; and men have an indefeasible right to the installation and maintenance of those specific economic relations, expedients, institutions, which this "natural" scheme comprises, and to no others. The consummation is presumed to dominate the course of things which is presumed to lead up to the consummation. The measures of redress whereby the economic Order of Nature is to renew its youth are simple, direct, and short-sighted, as becomes the proposals of pre-Darwinian hedonism, which is not troubled about the exuberant uncertainties of cumulative change. No doubt presents itself but that the community's code of right and equity in economic matters will remain unchanged under changing conditions of economic life.

Index

www.ingramcontent.com/pod-product-compliance
Lightning Source LLC
Chambersburg PA
CBHW061156220326
41599CB00025B/4499